American Myth and the Legacy of Vietnam

AMERICAN MYTH AND THE LEGACY OF VIETNAM

John Hellmann

New York   Columbia University Press

Library of Congress Cataloging in Publication Data
Hellmann, John, 1948–
American myth and the legacy of Vietnam.
Bibliography, p.
Includes index.
1. Vietnamese Conflict, 1961–1975—United States.
2. Vietnamese Conflict, 1961–1975—Influence.
3. National characteristics, American. 4. Vietnamese
Conflict, 1961–1975—Literature and the conflict.
5. Vietnamese Conflict, 1961–1975—Motion pictures and
the conflict. I. Title.
DS558.H44 1986   959.704′33′73   85–10986
ISBN 0–231–05878–0
ISBN 0–231–05879–9 (pbk.)
p 10 9 8 7 6 5 4 3
c 10 9 8 7 6 5 4 3 2

Columbia University Press
New York   Oxford

Printed in the United States of America

*Casebound editions of Columbia University Press books are Smyth-sewn
and printed on permanent and durable acid-free paper*

∞

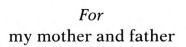

For
my mother and father

Contents

Preface   ix

Acknowledgments   xiii

PART I   ENTERING A SYMBOLIC LANDSCAPE

CHAPTER ONE   "An Angry Dream": The Cold War, Southeast Asia, and the American Mythic Landscape   *3*

CHAPTER TWO   The Return of the Frontier Hero: National Purpose and the Legend of the Green Berets   *41*

CHAPTER THREE   The Antiwar Movement and the Frontier   *71*

PART II   THE JOURNEY BACK

CHAPTER FOUR   Good Sons: The Soldiers' Antimyth   *99*

CHAPTER FIVE   The Hero Seeks a Way Out   *139*

CHAPTER SIX   Epic Return   *171*

CHAPTER SEVEN   Toward New Myth   *205*

Epilogue   *221*

Notes   *225*

Index   *235*

Preface

THIS BOOK first traces the relation of America's mythic heritage to its experience in Vietnam. It then explores the legacy of Vietnam, the awful place it has come to occupy in American myth. By myth I mean the stories containing a people's image of themselves in history. Extreme simplifications, myths may always be debunked as falsifications of reality. But simplification is their strength, since only by ignoring the great mass of infinite data can we identify essential order. A people cannot coherently function without myth. The narrative structures of myths articulate salient patterns that we see in our past and hold as our present value and purpose. A myth is our explanation of history that can also serve as a compelling idea for our future.

Since these patterns originate from ideals and aspirations as much as from actual experience, they form stories that usually transcend logic and facts. Myths enable a nation to cohere by reconciling, in the ambiguous relations of narrative, conflicts that its people cannot solve in the sharply delineated realm of analytical thought. Myths may often distort or conceal, but these stories are nevertheless always true in the sense that they express deeply held beliefs.

Myth can thus have a powerful role in compelling a people to defy rational limits and change facts. If severely divergent from external realities, which may include the force of another myth driving another people's behavior, a myth can be disastrous, causing a nation to veer off into unreality, even collective madness; alternatively, if it expresses actual strengths, myth can energize and elevate a people, compelling them toward achievements that a detached contemporary would not have predicted. A historian may later analyze the extraordinary results as inevitable because of economic, technological, or social factors that were simply not perceptible at the time.

Vietnam is an experience that has severely called into question American myth. Americans entered Vietnam with certain expectations that a story, a distinctly American story, would unfold. When the story of America in Vietnam turned into something unexpected, the true nature of the larger story of America itself became the subject of intense cultural dispute. On the deepest level, the legacy of Vietnam is the disruption of our story, of our explanation of the past and vision of the future.

To understand the relation of the American story to our perception of Vietnam, and of the ensuing experience to the American story, we may look at the many separate stories Americans have set in Southeast Asia. In this book I explore a wide range of tales spanning more than a quarter century, including best sellers, popular articles, memoirs, serious novels, and films. Diverse as they are, these texts, because they are all American narratives in some way related to Vietnam, show us an intersection of that subject—whether as naïve dream, bitter nightmare, or complex reflection—with American cultural values and assumptions. Through these narratives we can detect the relation of American myth to the Vietnam experience.

These texts do not simply "reflect" the consciousness of their authors and audience. Narrative is a duplicitous form of communication, and I have therefore sought to uncover the deep psychological, even unconscious, messages underlying the surface ones. The empirical relation of literary and even popular texts to the people at large is murky, indirect, and partial. Nevertheless, the materials presented here should be sufficiently abundant to demonstrate that their shared themes and motifs must have emerged from forces alive in the culture. This book thus analyzes a wide assemblage of texts to reveal the key elements and patterns of a deeper story in which they converge. In that story we may find the shaping legacy of Vietnam. And in that legacy America's political and cultural leaders will have to find their symbols if they are eventually to persuade the nation that Vietnam, like the Civil War and the Great Depression, is part of an intelligible past from which the nation must proceed improved.

John Hellmann

Acknowledgments

WHEN THIS STUDY was still only an idea, I received a grant from the National Endowment for the Humanities that enabled me to spend a summer in concentrated study of the war in Vietnam and its legacy. Some time later, I began writing the book with the support of a year's fellowship from the American Council of Learned Societies. I was able to complete the final chapter during a quarter in which the Ohio State University had awarded me a Special Research Assignment. I thank each of these organizations for their support.

Material from this manuscript was presented to meetings of the Modern Language Association and the Organization of American Historians, and I benefited greatly from their members' responses. A shortened version of chapter 1 originally appeared as an essay in *Peace and Change,* and an article providing the basis for chapter 6 was first published in *American Quarterly.* I thank the editors of both journals for giving me early opportunities to present some of my findings. I am also grateful to Zoetrope Studios, Lucasfilm, and Universal Studios for allowing me to reproduce film stills.

Throughout this project, Robert D. Schulzinger has generously taken time from his own work to listen to my ideas and criticize my drafts. Without his encouraging and yet frank responses, this book would have been considerably less, and he has my special thanks. James Machor, Wayne Kvam, and Anthony Libby also read the entire manuscript, and William Wells and William Angel read parts of it. Each made valuable suggestions. Morris Beja, chair of the English Department of Ohio State, and James S. Biddle, dean and director of the campus at Lima, were very helpful in enabling me to pursue this project amid favorable conditions. I greatly appreciate their confidence and aid.

Betty Milum and other staff of the Ohio State Library system aided my research in a pleasant and efficient manner. Judy Von Blon expertly typed the manuscript at its every stage of preparation; her skill, dedication, and good humor have made my task much easier.

The late Bernard Gronert, executive editor of Columbia University Press, was excited about this book when it was still only half completed. Kate Wittenberg, the current editor, has since provided the same enthusiasm and help. Leslie Bialler improved the manuscript with his fine copyediting.

During my long preoccupation with this subject, many Americans have shared with me their experiences during the Vietnam era along with their subsequent feelings and views. I thank them all, and I would like to mention specifically veterans Merrill Kaufman and John Cirafici. As always, my wife Marilyn added many valuable perspectives.

The people I have acknowledged above should not necessarily be perceived as agreeing with statements of fact or analysis in this manuscript, for which I am of course responsible.

PART I

Entering a Symbolic Landscape

CHAPTER ONE

"An Angry Dream"
The Cold War, Southeast Asia, and the American Mythic Landscape

In 1958, in the midst of the Cold War, Americans contemplated a bestselling novel that gave a disturbing new twist to a question first posed by an immigrant colonial farmer and asked again by each. succeeding generation. Just before the American Revolution, Hector St. Jean de Crèvecoeur had surveyed his surroundings on the western frontier of New York and made an inquiry he later included in his popular *Letters from an American Farmer* (1782): "What then is the American, this new man?" In *The Ugly American*, published nearly two centuries later, authors William Lederer and Eugene Burdick viewed the frontiers of the Free World extending from Berlin to Saigon. Both former naval officers, Lederer had just retired after serving eight years as special assistant to the Pacific commander-in-chief, while Burdick was a professor of political science at Berkeley. They now in effect asked, What does an American look like? The provocative title summed up their answer. According to *The Ugly American*, Crèvecoeur's "new man" now appeared "fat," "ostentatious," "stupid," and "loud."

Lederer and Burdick's book presented a situation which, in the words of a character in the opening episode, was "like the fable of the rich man who was an idiot."[1] The majority of Americans serving in Southeast Asia were depicted as spending their time in bureaucratic meetings

and elegant cocktail parties within the diplomatic enclaves of the cities, while out in the villages purposeful
communists were quietly winning the common people.
The result, the authors warned in their "Factual Epilogue,"
was that "our free life well may be lost in a succession of
bits and fragments" (p. 271). Influential far beyond its very
large readership, *The Ugly American* helped to create the
atmosphere in which President John F. Kennedy would call
for a national physical-fitness program, declare America's
willingness to "bear any burden," found the Peace Corps,
build up the American Special Forces, and emphasize new
tactics of counterinsurgency to combat communist
"people's war" in South Vietnam.

From the rapid buildup of "advisers" under Kennedy to
the "Vietnamization" of the Nixon years, American leadership would most consistently define the war in Vietnam as
a test of American "will," in effect a symbolic war in which
the true terrain was the American character and the ultimate stakes world history; during that war, the question of
American identity and purpose would provoke an internal
struggle without precedent in the one hundred years since
the Civil War; and by its end, defeat and disillusion would
for the first time be a significant part of the national experience. Focusing on *The Ugly American* as a significant cultural document, we can begin a look back at how the
small, distant, and peripheral country of Vietnam came to
hold its current place in the American mythic landscape.

I

In showing America its reflection in Asia, the authors of
The Ugly American were working within a familiar pattern
of American thinking about the national identity. Americans have perceived themselves as having a world destiny
intertwined with the fate of Asia. Until the appearance of
The Ugly American the mainstream culture had echoed

Crèvecoeur's assertion that the American, having left behind the "ancient prejudices and manners" of Europe for the "immense territory" of the New World, could be identified as a member of the best society in the world. In contrast to Europe, America had "no aristocratical families, no courts, no kings, no bishops," but instead a "people of cultivators" living in a "pleasing uniformity of decent competence" and "animated with the spirit of an industry which is unfettered and unrestrained, because each person works for himself." Along with his view of the special significance of America's landscape, great numbers of later Americans had also shared Crèvecoeur's confidence that "Americans are the western pilgrims, who are carrying along with them that great mass of arts, sciences, vigour, and industry which began long since in the east; they will finish the great circle."[2]

With his reference to "western pilgrims" finishing "the great circle," Crèvecoeur was alluding to the belief, widely held in England and America in the second half of the eighteenth century, that civilization had progressed in a "westward course of empire." This concept held that civilized progress had developed in a westward pattern through the successive empires of the Far East, the Near East, Egypt and Persia, Greece, Rome, the Italian city states, Spain, France, and England. Each of these civilizations was seen as having added some important element to mankind's progress before giving way to its successor. From this perspective the new country of America, positioned between Europe and the Orient, appeared destined to expand westward to the Pacific before completing in Asia the progress that had begun there thousands of years earlier.[3]

The concept of America's special destiny also grew out of apocalyptic ideas of history that had developed among English-speaking Protestants during the period America was being settled. In these theological conceptions, history was seen as progressing toward world salvation in a course parallel with that taken by individual souls. This view suggested that the New World, seemingly held secret by Providence until the appointed moment of the Reformation, had a special role to play in God's redemptive plan. The Puritans conceived of their "errand into the wilderness" as the journey of a Chosen People to found a "shining city on a hill" destined to be an exemplary "beacon to the world." Notions of America as the "redeemer nation" thus came to pervade the culture even before the proclamation of universally applicable political, social, and economic ideals in the Declaration of Independence. America was the leader of the Forces of Light and its enemies necessarily the Forces of Darkness, agents of Satan, a role first assigned to the monarchies of Europe and the native inhabitants of the western forests.

This conception also suggested that America was to be exempt from the cyclical decline and fall of previous civilizations and instead would take its progress forth to establish a world millennium. The concept of America as world savior, later making itself felt in the ideology of Manifest Destiny, in the impulses behind missionary and reform movements, and in the rhetoric of crusades to "make the world safe for democracy," is already apparent in writings during the formative years of the republic. In the early idyll *Greenfield Hill*, for instance, poet Timothy Dwight, grandson of Jonathan Edwards and President of Yale, envisions the new nation spreading grace to the rest of the world:

> Yet there, even there, Columbia's bliss shall spring,
> Rous'd from dull sleep, astonish'd Europe sing,
> O'er Asia burst the renovating morn,
> And startled Afric in a day be born;
> As, from the tomb, when great MESSIAH rose,
> Heaven bloom'd with joy, and Earth forgot her woes,
> His saint, thro' nature, truth and virtue spread,
> And light, and life, the SACRED SPIRIT shed.[4]

America will redeem the world, and part of that process will be its new civilization's "renovating" of the world's oldest.

During the first years of the republic, when Britain excluded its former colony from trade with the Commonwealth, the enterprising but militarily weak nation was drawn west in the direction of Asia as it sought open fields for its energies. Both the American West and the lands of East Asia offered commercial opportunities relatively free from entanglement with European powers. In its pursuit of present trade and future greatness, America naturally turned to its "virgin" wilderness and beyond it to the fabled riches of the Orient. The exploration of the West was itself bound up with American interest in Asia, as the idea of finding a "passage to India," exciting once again the popular imagination when the Lewis and Clark expedition reached the Pacific, kept alive the dream associated with America since Columbus stumbled upon the continent in search of a westward route to India. By 1845, when Asa Whitney proposed building a railroad from the Pacific to Lake Michigan, Americans' interest in the West as a route to the riches of Asia had transposed itself into an interest in Asia as a huge market for the potential riches of the West. From that time the "teeming" populations of Asia, especially China, would periodically fascinate Americans as potential consumers of America's natural bounty.

Charged with such romantic, religious, and commercial expectations, and yet unseen by all but a few Americans, the American West and beyond it China and Japan became symbolic landscapes, separate yet connected, possessing a moral geography in which Americans perceived themselves achieving their identity and working out their special destiny. The West, alternatively imagined as a desert or garden, became in the American mind the setting of its central myth, presented first in the legend of Daniel Boone and the Leatherstocking novels (1823–41) of James Fenimore Cooper, and subsequently embodied in countless essays, personal narratives, speeches, folk tales, dime novels, and later movies and television shows. The prototypical myth features stalwart frontiersmen, entering the vast wilderness alone or in small bands, who draw on the virtues of nature while battling its savage denizens in order to make way for settlements of yeoman farmers. In this frontier, most famously defined by historian Frederick Jackson Turner as the "meeting point between savagery and civilization,"[5] Americans have beheld their self-image of limitless possibility, mastery over nature, democratic equality, self-reliant individualism, and special communal mission.

During the nineteenth century, political and cultural spokesmen favoring the westward thrust into the frontier exulted that it was drawing America away from the stifling influence of Europe toward its ultimate destiny in Asia. During the four decades before the Civil War, Senator and Congressman Thomas Hart Benton delivered countless speeches, wrote editorials, delegated expeditions, and introduced legislation that made him the foremost advocate of westward expansion. In these efforts he emphasized that greater contact with Asia should be a central goal, arguing in part that trade with the Orient would help Americans develop their unique national character. In 1825, Benton expressed the full historical significance he saw in greater American contact with Asia in his famous Senate speech on the Oregon question:

Upon the people of Eastern Asia, the establishment of a civilized power upon the opposite coast of America, could not fail to produce great and wonderful benefits. Science, liberal principles in government, and the true religion, might cast their lights across the intervening sea. The valley of Columbia might become the granary of China and Japan, and an outlet to their imprisoned and exuberant population. The inhabitants of the oldest and the newest, the most despotic and the freest Governments, would become the neighbors, and, peradventure, the friends of each other. They have the same enemies, and, by consequence, should stand together as friends.[6]

To other Americans contact between the world's oldest and newest civilizations suggested the culmination of America's frontier character as the most modern society and yet the one in communion with uncivilized nature. In a number of poems Walt Whitman advocated rejection of the example of Europe while celebrating American expansion in the Pacific. In "Pioneers! O Pioneers!" he declares in 1865 that "all the past we leave behind":

> Have the elder races halted?
> Do they droop and end their lesson, wearied over there
> beyond the seas?
> We take up the task eternal, and the burden and the lesson,
> Pioneers! O pioneers!

Whitman emphasizes the rewards of the frontier experience in contrast to the decadent luxuries of Europe and the city:

> Do the feasters gluttonous feast?
> Do the corpulent sleepers sleep? have they lock'd and bolted
> doors?
> Still be ours the diet hard, and the blanket on the ground,
> Pioneers! O pioneers![7]

Drawing on the same pervasive cultural ideas as did Benton, Whitman in 1871 prophesies in "Passage to India" the culmination of American westward progress in the regaining of civilized man's lost harmony with nature. Portraying America's "purpose vast" being fulfilled in "the rondure of the world at last accomplish'd," he asserts that the work of voyagers and engineers has been "not for trade or transportation only," but for the millennial achievement of "God's purpose from the first":

> O soul, repressless, I with thee and thou with me,
> Thy circumnavigation of the world begin,
> Of man, the voyage of his mind's return,
> To reason's early paradise
> Back, back to wisdom's birth, to innocent intuitions,
> Again with fair creation.

Whitman portrays this climactic union of American progress with Asian origins, of conscious searching with unconscious instinct, in a vision of the modern American nation
as a Younger Brother who "melts in fondness" in the arms
of the Asian "Elder Brother found."[8] Springing from
shared cultural impulses, Whitman's poetic vision, like
Benton's political one, articulates aspects of the mystical
and millennial significance East Asia early held in American myth.

The decisive conclusion of America's struggle over its
identity in the Civil War had brought a renewal of the
national sense of mission. Emerson saw the South as having turned away from American ideals, and the war as
deciding "whether we shall be the new nation, the guide
and lawgiver of all nations."[9] Lincoln, drawing on such
widely current ideas, offered on the recent battlefield at
Gettysburg his vision of the terrible losses being endured
so that the nation could have "a new birth of freedom" and
its principles not "perish from the earth." This energizing
sense of national purpose found expression both in the
rapid settlement of the West, where desperate plains Indians provided newspapers with a unifying enemy, and in
accelerated industrialization. America's progress was perfectly symbolized in the building of the Union Pacific railroad that in 1869 at last provided a "highway to the
Pacific." The vigorous purposefulness also eventually manifested itself in the reform movements of the Progressive
era.

Beyond their borders many Americans looked across the
Pacific to China, where they saw, in addition to a vast potential market for their industrial and agricultural goods,
a challenge for their cultural and religious ideals. Both
customers and conversions were disappointingly few, but
during subsequent decades reports from the missionaries
became the single most important source of American images and attitudes about Asia. Telling of American evange-
lism and good works among an ignorant people, these

reports presented a dark landscape into which small bands of Americans carried light. This view of China as a special beneficiary of American virtue was strengthened after 1900 by the second Open Door note, which the American public perceived as having saved the territorial integrity of China from the designs of the imperialistic powers of Europe and Japan. While the note had little military or diplomatic force, and was primarily a political device satisfying domestic opinion while serving American economic and missionary interests, Americans came to see themselves as China's special friend, the benefactor and protector of a childlike people.

Through the twentieth century this moralistic view of America's relation to China alternated with fear of the "yellow peril." Nevertheless, the "Asian Lobby" or "Asia Firsters," Americans whose lives had been touched by the missionary involvement with China, fostered a continuing American interest in Asia through such influential figures as writer Pearl Buck and editor Henry Luce. While Americans' cultural and commercial exectations in China had yet to be fulfilled, their special interest gained added dimensions during the years China withstood Japanese attacks. Buck published *The Good Earth*, the bestselling novel of 1931. Followed in 1937 by a similarly successful film version, it portrayed the Chinese as noble peasants close to the eternal verities of the land. Appearing coincidentally with the American sympathy evoked by Japanese aggression, *The Good Earth* spawned many similar books and movies. During the same period the government of Chiang Kai-shek, a convert to Christianity, was touted by the Asian Lobby as a potential democratic government.

In 1943, Madame Chiang, wife of China's Nationalist leader, made a trip to the United States in quest of greater aid in the war against Japan. Educated at Wellesley and a Methodist, she appeared a "charming" and "lovely" reflection of American righteousness in China. Madame Chiang became a great celebrity. In a speech enthusiastically received by the House of Representatives, she called on her audience to carry on "the pioneer work of your ancestors, beyond the frontiers of physical and geographical limitations," in order to "help bring about the liberation of man's spirit in every part of the world."[10] By the end of the war in 1945, war news and propaganda had created for Americans an emotion-charged image of China as a weak but gallant ally against imperial Japan. And such feature films as *China Girl* (1942) and *Flying Tigers* (1942) had presented China as a frontier-like landscape where American heroes found adventure and mission.

As a consequence of the historical assumptions and expectations America had projected upon China, the triumph of Mao Tse-tung's communist forces in 1949 caused a trauma in the United States that would distort its domestic politics and policy in Asia through the Vietnam era. The world had seemed on the threshold of Luce's "American Century," and now the special beneficiaries of American mission had turned instead to the Soviet Union, whose revolutionary communist ideals made it appear a kind of Antichrist. The idea that China had done this willingly was a denial of the American conception of history, a massive shock followed by America's unaccustomed experience of a stalemated "limited war" as it faced a formidable Red China in Korea. One result was a refusal to recognize the communist leadership as China's legitimate government, a refusal based on an insistence that the Chinese communists were actually Soviet agents who had conquered China for a foreign power. Another was the "China witch-hunt" of the McCarthy period when the Wisconsin Senator enjoyed the support of those already searching for the traitors responsible for the "loss" of China.

Both responses expressed the panic in a nation that had previously enjoyed a measure of geographical isolation from great-power rivalries and the decisive resolution of its great controversies; this good fortune had seemingly confirmed the nation's special role in the cosmic struggle between the forces of Darkness and Light that its heritage suggested lay beneath historical disputes. Now fully entangled in the world, Americans were psychologically threatened by the prospect of a reevaluation of the complex historical developments that had brought their expulsion from China. Among the consequences were a hardening of Cold War ideology, a purging from the State Department of Asian specialists, and a warning to future administrations of the hazards of "losing" an Asian nation.

While still assimilating events in China and Korea, Americans found themselves involved with another Asian conflict. In Indochina, the French *mission civilisatrice* was being brought to an end by the communist-led Viet Minh nationalists. Recalling the unsuccessful appeasement of Hitler at Munich, Americans had stood in Korea against the aggression of a communist ally of China and found themselves fighting China itself; Indochina appeared simply a southern flank of the larger Asian struggle. The United States provided the French with considerable economic and military support until their defeat at Dien Bien Phu in 1954. Perceiving itself free of the "taint" of colonialism, the United States subsequently pursued a policy of "nation-building" in the southern half of Vietnam, encouraging the anticommunist nationalist Ngo Dinh Diem to frustrate unification under the Viet Minh.

In his memoir *Deliver Us from Evil* (1956), Dr. Tom Dooley provided many Americans with their first vivid image of Southeast Asia since such World War II films as *Objective Burma* (1945). Filled with detailed accounts of horrifying communist atrocities, Dooley's memoir told the story of American medical relief for refugees, mainly Catholic, going south from Haiphong in the aftermath of Geneva. Dooley, a young naval doctor assigned to this responsibility because he knew French, came to Indochina with virtually no previous knowledge of the area but strong Christian and anticommunist principles. In *Deliver Us from Evil* he presented his readers a landscape that evoked the early American wilderness and precommunist China. Fleeing "the demons of Communism stalking outside, and now holding the upper half of the country in their strangling grip,"[11] innocent natives were saved from savagery by the kindness of a small number of American naval personnel. In its imagery, Dooley's Indochina collapsed the familiar settings for Indian fighting and missionary work.

In the same year the prestigious British author Graham Greene published his novel *The Quiet American*, which portrayed the "earnest" and "involved," but also "ignorant" and "silly" efforts of a young American agent named Alden Pyle during the French war with the Viet Minh. The British narrator, a cynical but experienced correspondent who is happiest in his Saigon quarters watching his Vietnamese mistress prepare his opium pipe, characterizes Pyle as a symbol of "youth and hope and seriousness," determined "to do good, not to any individual person but to a country, a continent, a world."[12] Pyle's efforts to create a noncommunist "Third Force," which have their factual basis in the covert operations of the legendary Colonel Edward G. Lansdale,[13] result in bloody disaster, and the British narrator judges him a murderous innocent living his culture's apocalyptic abstractions: "When he saw a dead body he couldn't even see the wounds. A Red menace, a soldier of democracy."[14]

Despite the obvious differences between their activities, Dooley's self-portrait and Greene's Pyle both share the characteristic traits of the American hero: innocence, a desire to "do good," a conception of the world as a battleground between forces of Light and Darkness, a hastily acquired knowledge of a savage landscape and enemy, a belief in the special virtue of Americans in contrast to the colonial past of the Europeans, and an absolute faith in American righteousness and "mission." Greene's jaundiced view of both the American character and America's postwar role in Asia was castigated by American reviewers.

Nathan A. Scott in *Christian Century* called it "gross nonsense," James Ramsey Ullman in the *New York Herald Tribune Book Review* suspected "elaborate leg-pulling," and A. J. Liebling in the *New Yorker* dismissed it as an "exercise in national projection" by a member of the British Empire history had passed by.[15] Dooley, by contrast, became a national hero elevated to "ten-most-admired" lists. The different reactions of Americans to Dooley and Pyle were thus responses to the separate judgments the books made of the American self-concept. When they thought about Indochina, Americans generally saw themselves entering yet another frontier, once again "western pilgrims" on a mission of protection and progress.

II

Published two years after *Deliver Us from Evil* and *The Quiet American*, *The Ugly American* added its title to the American language. Lederer and Burdick told Americans that they were failing in their world mission miserably, and precisely because most of their representatives lacked the qualities of Dooley and Pyle. An immediate popular success, *The Ugly American* stands beside *Uncle Tom's Cabin* (1852) and *The Jungle* (1906) as a work of fiction catalyzing American political debate. Serialized in the *Saturday Evening Post* in fall of 1958, it was offered as an October Book-of-the-Month Club selection. The book went through twenty printings from July through November, stayed on bestseller lists for seventy-eight weeks, and was made into a Hollywood movie in 1962 before eventually selling over four million copies to become one of the most popular books in the nation's history.[16]

Set in Southeast Asia, *The Ugly American* aggravated the tremors still felt from the loss of China. In addition, it appeared in the midst of the anxiety about American prestige and vitality that followed the Russians' 1957 launching of the first space satellite Sputnik. *The Ugly American* thus found a ready audience for its accusations of American failure. In the *New York Times Book Review, San Francisco Chronicle,* and *Chicago Sunday Tribune,* for instance, reviewers enthusiastically praised the book, with each adding his personal observations of American ignorance and misbehavior overseas.[17] An anonymous reviewer in *Catholic World,* noting like many others that the title echoed that of *The Quiet American,* said that it shows "we are beginning to ask ourselves, seriously and objectively, the questions to which Mr. Greene gave an ugly bias." The book also found an audience for its criticisms among youth, as evidenced by Margaret C. Scoggin's review in *Horn Book,* which declared that "older teen-agers themselves have called it to my attention," and that "thoughtful seniors will certainly see from examples how the United States can best be served or most disastrously represented in South Asia."[18]

More restrained and ambivalent, reviews in magazines of news and opinion reflected various positions within the basic ideological consensus that characterized American debate during the Cold War. *Time, Saturday Review,* and the *Nation,* for instance, all disapproved of the vivid but simplistic characterizations. The anonymous reviewer in *Time* called the book a "crude series of black-and-white cartoons." While the Luce publication approved of the book's humane and anticommunist impulses, it was uncomfortable with the readiness of many Americans to feel "guilty and inadequate" about their role in underdeveloped nations, and with the impossibility of fulfilling the authors' seeming demand for "a bunch of saints with engineering degrees." In the intellectual *Saturday Review,* in contrast, Delia W. Kuhn felt that the authors "deserved a hearing" because of their Southeast Asian experience, but expressed dismay that the authors could really believe the "nonsense that 'we can save Asia.'" In the liberal *Nation* Robert Hutch hoped the book would win the authors "a number of angry allies," but disapproved of the Cold War's having become the primary motivation for American "decency and generosity."[19]

The controversy raised by *The Ugly American* soon had political effect. President Eisenhower, reportedly because he had read the book, ordered an investigation of the foreign-aid program,[20] and a number of Democratic leaders were quick to use the claims of *The Ugly American* as ammunition for the approaching 1960 elections. Early in 1959, for instance, an advertisement appeared in the Sunday edition of the *New York Times* announcing that four "distinguished Americans," including then-Senator John F. Kennedy, had sent a copy of the book to every United States Senator.[21] Somewhat later Senator Russell Long, during confirmation hearings for the nomination of C. Douglas Dillon for Under Secretary of State, compared the nominee to the "ugly" Americans of the book.[22] The influence of *The Ugly American* was so pervasive that speakers and writers could assume widespread familiarity with its themes. For example, Kennedy's early supporter and future Under Secretary of State, Chester Bowles, asserted that the Democrats' liberal traditions included Jefferson's belief "that the American Revolution was intended for all mankind." After Democrats regained direction of foreign policy, they would appoint "representatives who will spend more time in the villages and less on the diplomatic cocktail circuit."[23]

The impact of the book elicited both scathing rebuttals and reluctant embraces from those involved in American foreign policy. In September Senator William Fulbright, beginning with the recognition that "a book may sometimes create a pattern of thinking or a viewpoint among a people," denounced *The Ugly American* in a lengthy critique delivered on the Senate floor. Citing actual projects in Southeast Asia that contradicted the claims of the book, he said that "in the world of Lederer and Burdick almost everything is reduced to idiot simplicity." Fulbright found its appeal explicable only in its catering to "the parochial-ism, and the frustration of the American people," and he accused it of following the earlier charges of treason in the State Department made during the McCarthy period with similarly "phony" ones of incompetence.[24] In a speech at the University of San Francisco in April in 1960, Vice President Richard Nixon attempted to turn the book to his own favorite themes as he neared nomination as the Republican presidential candidate. Agreeing that the charges about the behavior and insufficient preparation of Americans serving overseas were partially correct, he told his audience that an overlooked lesson of *The Ugly American* was the need to "know the tactics and strategy of world communism" and to "know why we love our country, and what it stands for."[25]

The sales, controversy, and influence of *The Ugly American* may be explained in part by its success within the boundaries of a popular genre: the sensational exposé of a topical subject (it was trumpeted by the publishers in the first paperback edition as a story that "unmasks the blundering hypocrisy of some of our top-level diplomats")[26] presenting suspenseful action in an exotic locale. But these superficial aspects of the book cannot alone explain how a work of cartoon-like fiction, lacking specific documentation and dealing with remote government policies and personnel, could gain such a strong hold on the American imagination. A book acquires such impact by speaking to powerful elements in the psyche of its society. The broad enthusiasm for *The Ugly American*, later to be translated into support for policies of the Kennedy administration, certainly indicates that the book both reflected and stimulated conscious concerns of a large portion of the public. But a work of fiction does not acquire its power from overt political points alone, nor does a text carry only the meaning contained in its explicit arguments.

A deeper look at the text of *The Ugly American* in its different cultural dimensions reveals that its exposé is itself a mask. The attack on Americans in Asia actually condemns certain tendencies in the postwar American character. The true target of *The Ugly American* is suggested as early as the prefatory note, where the authors claim that the events in their stories have actually taken place "in the fifty-nine countries where over two million Americans are stationed" (p. 7). Only a moment's reflection would have been necessary for the reader to realize that those "two million Americans" were predominantly average citizens in temporary military service. The impact of *The Ugly American* resulted from its providing the American public with a purgative ritual of self-criticism and warning.

III

The Ugly American appeared in the wake of such influential analyses of postwar American society as David Riesman's *The Lonely Crowd* (1950), William H. Whyte, Jr.'s *The Organization Man* (1956), and John Kenneth Galbraith's *The Affluent Society* (1958). These books were widely discussed and alluded to in reviews, columns, and articles. They had such impact because they articulated in persuasive detail suspicions voiced through the decade with steadily increasing anxiety. These suspicions had in common a fear that trends in contemporary American society were fundamentally altering the American character. Conservatives usually focused upon "socialistic" tendencies toward conformity and mediocrity within a network of dependence on the large organizations of government, business, and unions now dominating American life. Liberals more typically emphasized the corrupting effects of a cynical, materialistic consumer society. Underlying these critiques was a shared suspicion that Americans were becoming too "soft," immoral, and greedy to survive the Soviets' dedicated pursuit of world communism.

In 1952, for instance, Louis B. Seltzer, the editor of the *Cleveland Press,* asked in an editorial "What is wrong with us?" and provided an answer that would be received with a torrent of approving telephone calls, letters, and personal congratulations on the street:

> We have everything. We abound with all of the things that make us comfortable. We are, on the average, rich beyond the dreams of the kings of old. . . . Yet . . . something is not there that should be—something we once had. . . .
>
> Are we our own worst enemies? Should we fear what is happening among us more than what is happening elsewhere? . . .
>
> No one seems to know what to do to meet it. But everybody worries.

Forty-one publications all over the country would reprint the editorial. At the end of the decade novelist John Steinbeck received a similar response to the publication of his letter to Adlai Stevenson in which he declared that if he wanted to ruin a nation "I would give it too much and I would have it on its knees, miserable, greedy, and sick. . . . [In rich America] a creeping, all pervading, nerve-gas of immorality starts in the nursery and does not stop before it reaches the highest offices, both corporate and governmental." Steinbeck's letter was also reprinted many times and discussed throughout the country. Luxuriating in a landscape of tailfins, lawn sprinklers, and gray flannel suits, thoughtful Americans were uneasily considering what they had lost in their character and what they might be on their way to losing in the world at large.[27]

Lederer and Burdick's novel presented Americans with confirmation of these fears in melodramatic terms charged with American mythic conceptions. Unlike *The Quiet American,* it attacked not the American character but the failure of many contemporary Americans to retain that character. Presenting confirmation of suspected corruption, *The Ugly American* echoed a traditional American message extending back to the New England Puritans. In *The American Jeremiad,* Sacvan Bercovitch has shown that the political-sermon form of the Puritans known as the jeremiad survived in the political rhetoric of the formative years of the republic, and has continued to be a central ritual of American culture. Combining a criticism of contemporary errors and vision of future disaster with an affirmation of the correctness of the traditional character and purpose of the American "errand," the American jeremiad has enabled speakers and writers to exert a power at once conservative and progressive, demanding of each generation that they return to the way of the fathers and rededicate themselves to the special mission of the culture.[28]

In *The Ugly American* the authors explicitly make this ritualistic call in the epilogue. After finishing their claims for the book's factual basis, the authors begin the ritual with the traditional cry of doom:

The picture as we saw it, then, is of an Asia where we stand relatively mute, locked in the cities, misunderstanding the temper and the needs of the Asians. We saw America spending vast sums where Russia spends far less and achieves far more. The result has been called "an uneasy balance," but actually it is nothing of the sort. We have been losing—not only in Asia, but everywhere.

If the only price we are willing to pay is the dollar price, then we might as well pull out before we're thrown out. If we are not prepared to pay the human price, we had better retreat to our shores, build Fortress America, learn to live without international trade and communications, and accept the mediocrity, the low standard of living, and the loom of world Communism which would accompany such a move. (pp. 283–84)

The authors follow this grim assessment with assurance that the future nevertheless remains conditional, since the responsibility for this imminent catastrophe lies in the present attitude of American society:

Actually, the state in which we find ourselves is far from hopeless. We have the material, and above all the human resources, to change our methods and to win. It is not the fault of the government or its leaders or any political party that we have acted as we have. It is the temper of the whole nation. (p. 284)

They follow this denunciation of the present "temper of the whole nation" with an explanation that the problem lies in a deviation from the past mythos of the nation: "We have so lost sight of our own past that we are trying to sell guns and money alone, instead of remembering that it was the quest for the dignity of freedom that was responsible for our own way of life" (pp. 284–85). Finally, they reassure readers that success is preordained if they will simply return to American principles:

All over Asia we have found that the basic American ethic is revered and honored and imitated when possible. We must, while helping Asia toward self-sufficiency, show by example that America is still the America of freedom and hope and knowledge and law. If we succeed, we cannot lose the struggle. (p. 285)

The fictional text of *The Ugly American* is a narrative version of this jeremiad: its structure of parabolic tales induces anxiety by showing imminent communist victory in Asia, places the blame upon the lapse of the majority of Americans serving there, and offers visions of the completed errand through small but exemplary successes won by a few virtuous Americans. The story then ends with an apocalyptic challenge to the reader in the form of the Secretary of State's rejection of the heroic few on the grounds that not enough Americans would be willing to make the sacrifices necessary for such policies. The characters of this drama symbolize the concepts intrinsic to the jeremiad from Puritan times to the nineteenth century: the Asian villagers are the American Indians or the Chinese, living in a *terra profana,* to be converted to the Forces of Light; the Soviet agents the clever and ruthless Forces of Darkness; the Viet Minh guerrillas the "savage" Indians manipulated by the Dark Forces; the British and French colonial officials the "dead hand of the European past"; the "ugly" Americans the Chosen who have fallen away from the errand; and the few "non-ugly" Americans, as Lederer and Burdick referred to them in a subsequent *Life* article,[29] the traditional heroes of American mythic history.

The resulting allegory is played out upon an Indochina as much imagined as observed, an Indochina overlayed with the mythic landscapes represented in the American mind by the frontiers of the American West and nineteenth-century China. Set in the invented nation of Sarkhan and such actual nations as Vietnam, Burma, and Cambodia, *The Ugly American* imposes upon an exotic but generalized Southeast Asian topography and demography the "moral geography" characterizing American thought since the colonial period. The dominating features of the resulting symbolic landscape are the classic images of city and country, embodying the stark opposition between civilization and wilderness, Europe and America, technology and nature, the conscious and unconscious, that such critics of classic American literature as D. H. Lawrence and Leslie Fiedler have identified as obsessions of the American psyche. The power of the book lies in its presentation of the struggle in Indochina, and by extension the global Cold War, in images holding mythic resonance.

In their prefatory note Lederer and Burdick protest that "what we have written is not just an angry dream, but rather the rendering of fact into fiction" (p. 7). But, however strong the basis of *The Ugly American* in actuality, its fictional power is precisely that of dream, the collective dream of authors and readers in a text based in shared myth. The vivid but formulaic prose, the alternately sentimental and horrific plot, and the sharply drawn but stereotypical characters call easily upon cultural memory. We can compare *The Ugly American* in this aspect to such myth-laden children's tales as Parson Weems' fable of George Washington and the Cherry Tree, which presented generations of American schoolchildren with a symbolic resolution of the psychological conflict of a culture both revolutionary and conservative in its origins. Though it functions as a jeremiad as opposed to the celebration of Weems' fable, *The Ugly American* possesses a similar power and method in its symbolic, and ultimately uncritical, presentation of American cultural conflict.

In the symbolic landscape of *The Ugly American*, the success of the external struggle with Soviet agents and their "savage" Asian army of Viet Minh depends upon the outcome of an internal struggle taking place within the American psyche and the American society. The crucial conflict in *The Ugly American* is thus between two types of Americans. The "ugly" Americans, far from being simply incompetent diplomats, represent the "temper of the whole nation" that is in error. They present grotesque reflections of those contemporary Americans who have fallen away from American virtue and mission. In the moral geography of American myth found in the novel, the journey of the ugly Americans west to Asia is ironically a spiritual flight east back to Europe. The targets of the exposé in *The Ugly American*—narrow careerists in the diplomatic service, pleasure-seeking staff members, and "big" foreign-aid projects conferring wealth and status on the native elite without actually helping the people—are the means by which the book indirectly points its accusing finger at the loss of the frontier virtues in postwar society.

In its attacks on American policies and personnel in Asia, *The Ugly American* shows its American readers a mirror of their own "ugliness." Lederer and Burdick depict Americans in Washington being recruited to service overseas with assurances that they will "be living with a gang of clean-cut Americans" on "the high American standard," for even "in Saigon they stock American ice cream, bread, cake, and, well, anything you want" (p. 80). A friendly Asian leader observes that "something happens to most Americans when they go abroad. . . . Many of them, against their own judgment, feel that they must live up to their commissaries and big cars and cocktail parties" (p. 108). Readers in 1958 and later could recognize in these images the pervasive conformity, affluence, and status-seeking characterizing their postwar society.

In carrying out its jeremiad, *The Ugly American* shows that "most Americans when they go abroad" forsake their heroic ancestors' journey into a frontier, instead seeking the comforts and securities associated with Europe. Refusing to go out into the countryside, the "ugly" Americans huddle within the diplomatic enclaves of the cities, mixing only with the European-educated among the native populace and respectfully deferring to the policies of the British and French. Indeed, they are depicted as revelling in the colonial lifestyle and attitudes of European aristocrats. In the chapter "The Girl Who Got Recruited," for instance, 28-year-old Marie MacIntosh writes back to her former roommates in Washington of her new job as secretary at the embassy in Sarkhan:

> And there are built-in servants! Honest. We have three servants to look after us. It's a family of them, father, mother, and a fourteen year old girl. They do the cooking, cleaning, laundering—everything. Oh, how they baby us! When they wake me in the morning, they bring a glass of orange juice and a cup of tea. This is real living.
>
> The Americans here are very friendly. They all give parties and plenty of them; there's at least one cocktail party or dinner every night. It's easy to do, of course, because everyone has help. All I have to do is check with my housemates to see if it's okay, and then call the servant. "Ehibun," I say, "we're having ten for dinner next Tuesday. Can you handle it?"
>
> "Yes, mum," she says, and that's all there is to it. And what a dinner for ten it turns out to be! Just like in the movies. (pp. 84–85)

Such a deviation from the "pleasing uniformity of decent competence" in American society celebrated by Crèvecoeur is matched by the aristocratic remoteness of foreign-service bureaucrats. In the moral scheme of *The Ugly American*, bureaucracy, the pervasive new force in government and business transforming American society after the New Deal and the war, is simply a modern form of aristocracy. This perception is implicit in the bitter judgment of the title character, an ~engineer whose physical ugliness contrasts with the spiritual virtue of his unaffected character and thus ironically underscores the point of the title. Viewing a group of American, French, and Vietnamese officials, he collapses European aristocracy and American bureaucracy into the single moral opprobrium of "princes of bureaucracy" (p. 205).

The use of Europe to represent the moral direction of contemporary American society is most elaborately developed in the chapter "How to Buy an American Junior Grade." A young American husbandry expert, who has found happiness in his sucessful work with villagers in Cambodia, is determined to return to Washington to denounce American and French officials. The French, however, offer him an opulent tour of the Far East financed by themselves and climaxing in France, where this "junior-grade" American is seduced by the arts, cuisine, wines, gifts, and bikinied ladies of the country Americans since Jefferson have feared as a corrupter of their youth. In the portrayal of a contemporary American society abandoning its self-reliant individualism and democratic equality for bureaucratic conformity and hedonistic affluence, *The Ugly American* condemns a generation of Americans who are in effect turning their backs on the frontier for the ease of Europe. This is the "temper of the whole nation" the authors decry in the epilogue.

In opposition to the trends of contemporary American society, *The Ugly American* presents the traditional answer of the jeremiad: the example of the fathers. In contrast to the typical American in Asia, *The Ugly American* presents a small number of Americans acting quite differently and with great effect. Six of these Americans are the successive centers of episodes exemplifying how America can fulfill its mission in Asia. These characters, in the words of the friendly Asian leader referred to earlier, are "unaffected" Americans "in their natural state" (p. 108), a phrase carrying special resonance for Americans from their frontier heritage. Indeed, these "natural" Americans, though in contemporary garb and partly based on actual contemporary Americans,[30] have walked into the novel's Indochina straight out of the American mythos.

In their acquired skills, they serve in roles esteemed in the postwar society: a former OSS agent who has become the successful manager of his family's powdered-milk business, an Irish-Catholic priest with credentials as an intellectual and administrator, an army major decorated in World War II and Korea, an Air Force colonel who serves as an "adviser" to Asian leaders, an engineer who has made a small personal fortune, and the engineer's well-to-do wife. But, as they are portrayed, each of these modern characters, all professionals with the exception of the housewife, turns out to be a duplicate of a heroic figure from American myth, history, or folklore: the yeoman farmer and minute man, the missionary, the Indian fighter, the "ringtailed roarer," the smalltown inventor, and the pioneer wife. And they embody as a group the traits of self-reliance, democratic idealism, homespun practicality, adaptability, ingenuity, humor, and generosity making up the national character associated with its frontier ethic. These characters bring the remembered virtues of the American mythical-historical past to the service of modern goals and ideals. Self-fulfilled, they find their continuing satisfaction in serving their society and, what is seen in *The Ugly American* as the same thing, the world.

These characters are oblivious to the temptations of current American affluence and conformity, and hostile toward the cupidity and rigidity of what the engineer calls "these damned French" (p. 212). John Colvin, for instance, the independent businessman who served in the Sarkhan jungle during World War II as an OSS agent, returns to Sarkhan because of a feeling of "personal responsibility" (p. 21) when he hears of communist turmoil. His motivations are selfless, for as soon as his business efforts have enabled the people to improve their economy, he intends "to sell out his shares and leave" (p. 22). And Emma Atkins, reacting to her engineer-husband's giving up his $150,000-a-year income to go to Indochina, is "pleased to move into a smaller house where she could manage things with her own hands, and where she wouldn't need servants" (p. 214).

Motivated by a practical idealism, these "unaffected" Americans display the traits that Americans have held as the special virtues of their heritage. Father John Finian happily leaves "comfortable New England" for the Burmese jungle because he is sure "a special task awaited him in Asia" (p. 44) to save the natives from the communist "face of the devil, altered slyly and shrewdly, but still the devil's face, put on earth to test again the morality of men" (p. 47). Calling to memory Roger Williams by his teaching the American religious ideal of toleration, he represents the righteous certitude of the redeemer nation carrying forth American principles. Major "Tex" Wolchek, who comes to Vietnam from Texas to serve as an observer with the French army, teaches his French compatriot to adapt the Maoist tactics of the Viet Minh guerrillas in order to defeat them on their own terrain. Rejecting European warfare, Wolchek is a reincarnation of the American frontiersman who learned the skills of the Indian to defeat the Indian, an adaptation of great mythic significance to Americans in defining their superiority to Europe.

The Air Force "adviser" Colonel Edwin B. Hillandale is shown to have helped the Philippine leader Ramon Magsaysay defeat the communist-led Huk rebellion. He does so by convincing workers that he is "just folks" when he plays his harmonica, shows his empty pockets, jokes good naturedly, and joins them in boisterous eating and drinking. While shocking American diplomats, he gains the trust of Sarkhanese leaders when he tells revealing fortunes during palmistry performances at diplomatic dinners. A Georgian, Hillandale displays the ungenteel behavior and wit that Southerners have immortalized in their tall tales of such frontier tricksters as Davy Crockett. Homer Atkins, a Pennsylvanian, who is a practical, quaintly irascible inventor, turns out to be a double for Benjamin Franklin. Like Franklin, the engineer is a self-made man disdaining patents and ostentation.

These characters inevitably conflict with the Europeans and "ugly" Americans, for as embodiments of American mythic history they represent the rejection of the past—Europe and the city—for the future, the frontier, and the countryside. Atkins unhappily contemplates a meeting of French, American, and French-educated Vietnamese bureaucrats: "They sat in their freshly pressed clothes, ran their clean fingers over their smooth cheeks, smiled knowingly at one another, and asked engineers like Atkins silly questions" (p. 205). As he opposes the plans of the officials for huge TVA-like programs, he notices that "he still had the smell of the jungle about him; the other men, Vietnamese, French, or American, all smelled of aftershave lotion" (p. 206). The rowdy Colonel Hillandale uses his skills at palmistry, which are aided by covert intelligence work, to persuade the Sarkhanese prime minister to move his troops north to meet a possible communist attack; when his efforts are frustrated by the petty concerns of the careerist diplomat George Swift, he punches him in the eye.

The conflict climaxes when Major "Tex" Wolchek, the pragmatic Ambassador Gilbert MacWhite, and the "redeemed" Foreign Legion officer Major Monet confront the French high command. MacWhite, who has witnessed Wolchek's success, informs the French admirals and generals (as well as an associated American major general) that "you ignored [Mao's] every lesson for fighting on this type of terrain" (p. 139); Monet, citing his unconventional victory over the Viet Minh, tells them "it contradicts everything that I was taught at St. Cyr and everything that this American general was taught at West Point" (p. 140). But despite what MacWhite calls the evidence of "your own eyes and ears" (p. 140), the American general joins the French command in adhering to traditional theory. The ugly American has come to value theory and tradition over first-hand experience, which in American myth is a preference for Europe over the western frontier, for the shadow of the past over the possibility of the future. Such episodes told the American reader of the late 1950s that only by returning to the heritage of the frontier "fathers" could America succeed in Asia, and by implication, in the world.

IV

What did *The Ugly American* tell its readers that America would achieve with the return to American values and the completion of its errand in Asia? The answer again lies in the function of Indochina as a symbolic landscape embodying the opposed mythic values of city and country. The authors portray the aspiration of the underdeveloped world to come into the modern age as the desire, familiar to Americans, to leave the country for the city. The Europeans and the "ugly" or "affected" Americans represent that city in its exploitative, self-indulgent relation to the country; Soviet-directed communism is depicted as offering the country the attraction of complete, machine-like imposition of the progress of the city. Within these terms, the "natural" Americans, representing the true values of progress, seek to achieve what Leo Marx called in *The Machine in the Garden* (1964) the "middle landscape."[31] Here is the millennial vision for which Americans are summoned to apocalyptic struggle in Asia and the rest of the world.

In the opening chapter of *The Ugly American* Lederer and Burdick depict a particularly horrifying example of the ugly American in the person of "Lucky" Louis Sears, Gilbert MacWhite's predecessor as Ambassador to Sarkhan. John Colvin, warned by Sears "about free-wheeling here in the hills" (pp. 31–32), lies in a Sarkhanese hospital terribly beaten by a mob of Sarkhanese women. He is in fact, however, a victim of the impulses exemplified by "Lucky" Louis Sears and the Soviet ambassador, "Lucky" Louis Krupitzyn. The shared given name and nickname of the two ambassadors suggest their underlying ironic tie.

While Sears is an incompetent political appointee and Krupitzyn a dedicated professional, each represents a distorting relation of civilization to nature, the extremes of self-indulgent exploitation and ruthless repression.

The false revolutionary ideal presented by the Russian Louis and the false image of the United States presented by the American Louis have led Colvin's former Sarkhanese friend Deong, now a communist, to dupe the people into believing Colvin is planning a diabolical scheme to rape their daughters. Through a flashback we learn that Colvin first came to Sarkhan in 1943 as an OSS agent, where he survived only because the rural youth Deong provided knowledge of the landscape. Their original meeting is portrayed as the white American's immersion in nature, which, while presented in a clichéd scene lifted from B-westerns, is described in particulars echoing famous baptisms in classic American literature. Deong saves Colvin from encircling Japanese when he leads him to a ditch, takes some hollow reeds, and pushes him beneath the water. After Colvin is saved by the stock breathe-through-the-reeds trick, he sits up, "muddy water dripping from his face and body," to see Deong "grinning at him" (p. 18). This rebirth into a harmonious relation with nature and a dark "natural" man, a dream Fiedler showed in *Love and Death in the American Novel* (1960) running through classic American literature, is followed by an eight-month period in which Deong and Colvin "roam" over Sarkhan. During this time Colvin comes to love the "small, delicate people, their skins a lovely shade of brown, all of their motions graceful and restrained" (p. 20). He also finds that he represents the progress these more natural people desire, learning that "Deong was a country boy and he came from a simple family, but he wanted to live in a city and to find out about bigger and more exciting things" (p. 19). Yet their fraternal relation is achieved through their common opposition to invading machines. During this period, they "blew up twelve Japanese munitions trains, demolished six military bridges, and put time bombs on the hulls of eight armed Japanese river patrol boats" (p. 18).

The effects of American interaction with Asia are thus portrayed in classic terms of American culture going back to Benton and Whitman. Colvin finds in Asia the "innocent intuitions" Whitman saw residing in a primitive state of original nature and ancient civilization, while Deong acquires from contact with an American the aspiration to progress. In 1952, however, after reading of communist turmoil in Sarkhan, Colvin returns to find himself betrayed by a transformed Deong. Disillusioned with the "clerks" America sends to "buy" the Sarkhanese, the Asian brother has become a communist pressing a pistol into Colvin's ribs. Though Colvin insists that "we've still got the power and the will," Deong remains convinced that "America had its chance and it missed" (p. 24). America's historical errand into Asia has unleashed a dynamic that America's subsequent lapse from its completion has allowed to turn evil.

Colvin's scheme for helping the Sarkhanese is never given a chance, but that scheme as well as the successful work of Homer Atkins provides images in *The Ugly American* of the progress America should properly bring to Asia. That progress is a vision of Asia turned into a "middle landscape" standing ideally between primitive nature and artificial civilization, a balance of free instinct and ordered design. In effect, it is a projection of American fantasy, a painting of Indochina with a lovely future that is really a wished-for American past. In both episodes the central element is a machine which will bring out the possibilities of the Asian garden without turning it into a European-like city.

Colvin's plan is to use his powdered-milk machine to lead the Sarkhanese into making use of the rainy hillsides which are not suitable for their farming, but which he has determined would provide excellent grazing for a certain breed of cattle developed in Texas. Figuring that "if the people of Sarkhan could be taught to use milk and its by-products, there was no reason why the cattle would not prosper on land that was otherwise useless," he has also already calculated how the Sarkhanese could use all the products of the cattle: "The butter could be reduced to *ghee* and sold to India, the leather could be tanned and made into finished goods by the artisans of Sarkhan, the entrails could be used in the native medicines preferred by non-Christians" (p. 22). Colvin's vision of the complete economy of the cow, with its respectfully frugal use of nature, resembles nothing so much as the buffalo economy of the plains Indian. Only now, instead of the destruction of the buffalo in the service of the railroad, the white man will provide the animal that will make possible the bountiful garden. With this remarkable expiation of the historical guilt incurred with the march westward of American progress, Colvin seeks to use a machine of that progress to bring the Sarkhanese "up" to a pastoral version of the "vanished" plains Indians' hunting economy.

The successful work of Homer Atkins in late chapters of the book provides a climactic substitute for Colvin's "loss of the vision he had of himself and the people of Sarkhan, and their friendship" (p. 28). Atkins improves the agriculture of a Sarkhanese village and enables it to start a "thriving, although tiny, industrial complex" (p. 269) through his invention of a water pump that makes use of a part of a simple bicycle, the rudimentary technology already part of their economy. In addition, he makes this invention with the help of a young Sarkhanese who is his symbolic dark younger brother:

Jeepo looked like a craftsman. His fingernails were as dirty as Atkins', and his hands were also covered with dozens of little scars. Jeepo looked back steadily at Atkins without humility or apology, and Atkins felt that in the mechanic's world of bolts and nuts, pistons and leathers, and good black grease he and Jeepo would understand one another.

And Jeepo was ugly. He was ugly in a rowdy, bruised, carefree way that pleased Atkins. The two men smiled at one another. (p. 220)

With their invention, Homer and Jeepo become business partners who enlist the rest of the village as salesmen and workers. As a result, the machine, instead of disrupting the village, actually improves it. This communal achievement culminates when they learn that their small capitalistic venture has found ready customers in other villages:

> There was a deep sigh from the crowd and everyone turned and looked at Jeepo and Atkins. These two squat, ugly, grease-splattered men stared at one another for a moment, and then let out shouts of joy. Jeepo hugged Atkins. Atkins hugged Jeepo, and then Jeepo hugged Mrs. Atkins. Then everyone in the village hugged everyone else. For several hours an improvised party involved the entire village. (p. 230)

The chapter ends with Atkins and Jeepo engrossed in an argument over how they can improve the pump, while Homer's wife Emma lays out "a huge breakfast in front of the two men" (p. 321). The self-made American has brought the noisy harmony of smalltown American independence and progress to Asia. And in doing so this white American builder, benign successor to the frontier hunter and farmer, wipes out the stain of racist hierarchy still on the American landscape a century after the abolition of slavery, while retaining the inherently superior relation of older brother to younger. Like Colvin's plan, Atkins' achievement is a painless expiation of American sins against nature and "natural" men.

These millennial visions of progress brought to Asia and the love received in return are clearly as sentimental and nostalgic as Norman Rockwell's depictions of American life on the covers of the magazine in which *The Ugly American* was serialized. Those *Saturday Evening Post* covers attest that America had been able to hold onto the ideal of the "middle landscape" of Jefferson's agrarian ideal and Franklin's small-businessman virtues long after the reality of technological progress had transformed America into a largely industrial landscape, dominated by the ills of the city supposedly left behind in Europe. It should not be wondered at, then, that *The Ugly American* could so blithely impose these visions upon a Southeast Asian landscape barely known to most Americans.

In addition, this fantasy conveyed to Americans messages containing appealing unspoken messages: "small" technology would best bring the Indochinese people the tangible progress for which they would return love and imitation, but as a result these Asian masses would also offer no foreseeable disruption of the postwar industrial preeminence of America;[32] at the same time, this vision of the American role in Indochina offered Americans a field upon which they could engage in their errand of progress while virtually arresting that progress, thus creating the ideal middle landscape envisioned by their forefathers and still dominating their political and social rhetoric. Here America could contemplate the achievement of perfect balance which its opposed ideal of progress constantly disturbed at home. And here America could find the grateful Asian ally foreseen by Benton and the Asian brother longed for by Whitman.

The Ugly American offered its readers an Indochina representing a frontier where Americans could return to the remembered virtues of their heritage and at the same time free themselves from the burden of their past. There they could once again leave the corruptions of the city to find progress and virtue in the rigors and basic values of nature; on this frontier, however, they would protect the dark man rather than destroy or enslave him, and improve rather than destroy his natural landscape. It was a vision of redemption, openly for the world but secretly for the American as well.

V

As a political slogan, the New Frontier echoed the compelling themes of *The Ugly American*. Kennedy's campaign for the presidency and subsequent programs and policies answered the anxieties of the country about the national purpose and character, which by 1960 had burst into a major debate carried on by political and cultural spokesmen. Kennedy asserted that America was not America when it stood still, chose the path of ease, shrank from crisis, thought in the clichés of the past, failed to exert leadership, and sacrificed individual action to bureaucratic caution and rigidity. But Kennedy also avoided radical new concepts and distrusted passionate actions. Instead, he extolled pragmatism in pursuit of idealism, vigor tempered by restraint, the unconventional in the service of the traditional; the classic balanced structures of his Inaugural Address embodied his vision of the continuing vitality of the American middle way.

The New Frontier proclaimed that the western frontier, officially closed in 1890 by the Superintendent of the Census to mark for Turner the ominous end of the first era of American history,[33] could remain in its metaphorical dimensions an open landscape of challenge and possibility. In this symbolic frontier America could regenerate its traditional virtues while serving future progress. Here the individual American could flee the city yet spread the dominion of that city, take forth progress yet bring back natural virtue, and thus resolve in a middle landscape the conflict between contemporary American society and traditional American character and purpose in the same way it had been resolved in American mythic experience since Cooper's Leatherstocking Tales. The Peace Corps, the Alliance for Progress, the domestic emphasis on physical fitness, the "get-the-country-moving-again" economic policies, the support for black civil rights, the space program, the "can-do" cabinet team—every aspect of the New Frontier evoked the ideal found in *The Ugly American*, the ideal central to the American mythic heritage: that America could preserve the rewards of grace only by a disregard for them in pursuit of its errand.

On the Cold War battleground of the underdeveloped world, Lederer and Burdick's warning that America was in danger of losing its power and integrity in "bits and fragments" seemed confirmed by Soviet Premier Khrushchev's speech, two weeks before Kennedy's inaugural, in support of "wars of national liberation." The response of the Kennedy administration was an emphasis on developing tactics of "counterinsurgency," a theory of warfare identical in its primary points to the ideas for fighting communism in Asia presented in *The Ugly American*. The primary role in this warfare was given to the Special Forces, the "Green Berets" who became a leading symbol of the New Frontier. Kennedy dramatically increased their number and forced the army to return to them the distinctive headgear it had removed. Originally organized in the early 1950s as guerrilla experts to be left behind the advancing armies of a Soviet invasion of western Europe, they were transformed into elite counterguerrilla specialists fulfilling the call of *The Ugly American* for "a small force of well-trained, well-chosen, hard-working, and dedicated professionals" (p. 284). As the authors had demanded in the epilogue, they were "willing to risk their comforts and . . . their health" to operate alone or in small bands in remote areas, and they studied their countries of assignment well enough that they spoke "the language of the land" and ideally were "more expert in its problems than are the natives" (p. 284). Like Father Finian, they went armed with a strong sense of mission; like Colonel Hillandale, they would serve as trusted "advisers" to native leaders; like Major "Tex" Wolchek, they had learned the tactics of the enemy and would use them in combination with American technical ingenuity to defeat the enemy; like John Colvin, they would adapt to the land and seek the love of its people; like Homer Atkins and his wife Emma, they would improve the lives of the people in the villages with small "civic action" projects. Above all, the Green Berets symbolized the rededication to the American errand, the reassertion of the virtues and imperatives of America's frontier mythos, that lay at the heart of both *The Ugly American* and the New Frontier.

In Paris in spring of 1961, President de Gaulle of France warned the visiting President Kennedy to avoid increased involvement in Vietnam: "For you, I told him, intervention in this region will be an entanglement without end. From the moment that nations have awakened, no foreign authority, whatever its means, has any chance of imposing itself on them. You are going to see this."[34] De Gaulle had been responsible for the French effort to hold onto Indochina, and thus spoke from bitter experience. But colonialism and failure were precisely the consequences of European decadence from which America believed that, with small and temporary exceptions, it had always turned away to answer the call of its errand and win the inevitable victory. A few weeks earlier, with no announcement, Kennedy had ordered a detachment of 400 Green Berets to the jungles of South Vietnam. They were real men going into a real country, but they were also symbolic heroes entering a symbolic landscape—a landscape of American memory redrawn in *The Ugly American.*

With headband, streaked face, prominent knife, and background of thick foliage, the protagonist of *The Deer Hunter* evokes the frontier hero who becomes like an Indian to fight Indians. (Photograph courtesy of Museum of Modern Art, copyright © 1978 by Universal Pictures, a Division of Universal City Studios, Inc. Courtesy of MCA Publishing, a Division of MCA, Inc.)

CHAPTER TWO

The Return of the Frontier Hero
National Purpose
and the Legend of the Green Berets

DURING THE FIRST TWO YEARS of the New Frontier, the periodical press widely publicized the Special Forces. A series of adulatory articles suggested that the Kennedy administration was answering the call of *The Ugly American*.[1] In the November 1961 issue of *Esquire*, for instance, George J. W. Goodman reported that "there is every possibility of a positive use of Special Forces in underdeveloped areas, in the manner of the 'Colonel Hillandale' of *The Ugly American*, who had such a great personal influence on Asian people by offering medical aid to their children." A March 1962 article on the Green Berets in *Time* quoted Secretary of Defense Robert McNamara's declaration that communist guerrillas would be met in Southeast Asia "not with massive forces and nuclear weapons, but 'with companies and squads and individual soldiers.'" And the following June a feature by Will Sparks in *Commonweal*, describing the work of these "advisers" in South Vietnam, similarly echoed *The Ugly American:*

All too often in Asia, the pattern of Western military aid has taken the form of high-level briefings for ministers and generals and training in military schools abroad for sons of upper-class families destined for commissions in the local Army, Navy, or Air Force—while, in the meantime, Communist agents infiltrate native villages, seek out the disaffected and, through a combination of persuasion and threats, recruit followers among a population inured by long habit to the insufficiencies of food and shelter which are the guerrilla's lot. In Vietnam, U.S. Special Forces are proving to be one of the first effective answers to such tactics.[2]

The celebration of the Special Forces signified more than assurance of America's preparedness to meet the threat of "wars of national liberation." Like *The Ugly American* itself, these articles symbolically addressed deeper concerns about American society and destiny, anxieties that had grown since the initial controversy surrounding the book's publication. When Premier Khrushchev visited the United States in September 1959, cultural and political spokesmen had perceived an elemental challenge. Americans had already been startled by his declaration that the Soviet Union, in the inevitable progress of history toward world communism, would "bury" America. Despite the passing hope of the conciliatory "spirit of Camp David," the enduring response to Khrushchev's visit was a bursting forth of the desire to renew the American mission that had long been boiling beneath the placid surface of the 1950s.

During the Soviet Premier's stay, Walter Lippmann worried aloud that America had lost the sense of "great purpose and of high destiny" necessary to compete with the Soviet Union: "The public mood is defensive, to hold on and to conserve, not to push forward and to create. We talk about ourselves these days as if we were a completed society, one which has achieved its purposes and has no further great business to transact." Several weeks later George Kennan expressed similar sentiments:

If you ask me . . . whether a country in the state this country is in today: with no highly developed sense of national purpose, with the overwhelming accent of life on personal comfort and amusement . . . with an educational system where quality has been extensively sacrificed to quantity, and with insufficient social discipline even to keep its major industries functioning without grievous interruptions—if you ask me whether such a country has, over the long run, good chances of competing with a purposeful, serious, and disciplined society such as that of the Soviet Union, I must say that the answer is "no."[3]

Quoted again and again in the ensuing months, these doubts were taken up by Republicans and Democrats, in editorial series in *Life* and the *New York Times*, and in symposia and articles in periodicals ranging from *Time* to the *New Republic.* In February 1960 Eisenhower created a President's Commission on National Goals, and numerous national organizations placed the subject on their agendas. Widely publicized in the press, the concern over the "national purpose" figured prominently in the presidential politics of the year.

These speeches and essays, filling the press through 1960 and the first months of 1961, conveyed a remarkably consistent message. They repeatedly reminded Americans that the traditional purpose of the United States was the preservation and extension of liberty, that world communism now presented the greatest threat in history to that mission, and that the present generation must therefore renew the determined advance of freedom. Unhappy references were made either to the complacency of postwar consumerism and corporate conformity or to the defensive psychology of a foreign policy of containment and massive retaliation. Liberals envisioned renewed domestic reform that would make America a more attractive model for emerging nations, while conservatives urged a more relentless anticommunism; they agreed that a strong president must recapture the initiative in the Cold War by identifying specific goals and then leading the people toward their achievement. Like *The Ugly American,* which foreshadowed it, this "debate" was actually an exhortation echoing the periodic calls for rededication to the American errand extending back through Lincoln's Civil War addresses to seventeenth-century Puritan sermons.

Perfectly matching its mood, Kennedy campaigned as a young war hero and Pulitzer Prize-winning man of letters promising to lead Americans back out of the materialism and mediocrity of the 1950s. Entering a New Frontier, they could regenerate their past virtues in pursuit of their renewed mission. After his inaugural announcement that a new generation was taking up the "torch" of the fathers, the new President coupled his attempts to regain the Cold War offensive with efforts to reinvigorate American society. Programs such as the Council on Physical Fitness and the Peace Corps had important symbolic value, offering Americans participation in a ritualistic return to the hardiness, self-sacrifice, and purposefulness of the true American character.

In an address to Peace Corps trainees in August 1962, for instance, Kennedy wished aloud that "all Americans could hear that litany of countries that you're going to, your willingness to do it," and told them "the White House belongs to all the people, but I think it particularly belongs to you."[4] And a month earlier *Sports Illustrated* published an article by the President on "The Vigor We Need." Acknowledging the "paradox" that America's national vigor had created the economic and technological progress now "draining that vigor," he asserted that the physical-fitness program was furthering American democracy by liberating the individual to "realize fully the potential value of his capabilities and the pursuit of his individual goals." He also linked the men who "subdued a continent and wrested a civilization from the wilderness" to a "new group of vigorous young Americans" who were protecting freedom "today, in our time, in the jungles of Asia and on the borders of Europe."[5] The Peace Corpsman and the soldier were symbolic links to the nation's frontier heritage.

I

The Green Beret, an elite combination of the Peace Corpsman and the soldier, became the quintessential symbol of this renewal. Kennedy's well-publicized interest in the Special Forces made them extensions of the commander-in-chief, just as the Hunters of Kentucky and the Rough Riders had once magnified the respective images of Andrew Jackson and Theodore Roosevelt. In lieu of the aristocratic European powers defeated by Jackson and Roosevelt, the press at first depicted Kennedy and his charges battling symbolically with the bureaucratic hierarchies dominating postwar American life. During Kennedy's first year in office portraits of the Special Forces emphasized his leadership of their vigorous individualism against stifling institutions. In March 1961, for instance, *Newsweek* began its report with a description of how the Regular Army, an emasculating "mother hen" uncomfortable with a "duckling in her brood," had downgraded the Special Forces in the 1950s when it "stripped them first of their jaunty green berets, then gradually eased them back into the regular tables of organization, made them the stepchildren of the nuclear age." The article climaxed with the Special Forces' "new champion" decisively vanquishing the powerful Pentagon: "From now on, President Kennedy told the Joint Chiefs of Staff, the Special Forces would no longer languish in the shade of the atomic missile, and they would, in fact, take on a whole series of new duties." In *Esquire* Goodman similarly portrayed the "constant battle" Kennedy was waging with a Regular Army determined to make the "wacky, individualistic" Special Forces shine their buckles and keep the base lawns tidy rather than to let them hone their wilderness skills and devise innovative new tactics.[6] In such articles Kennedy's support for the Special Forces against the Pentagon represented his freeing of America's frontier character from the urban, conformist, and European-like influences of postwar institutions.

By 1962 this image of a resurgent American character had crystallized into a portrayal of the Green Beret as a contemporary reincarnation of the western hero. The Green Beret personified the combined virtues of civilization and savagery without any of their respective limitations. Articles depicted this hero striding forward from the walled city of containment and massive retaliation into the thrilling woods of America's mission; Southeast Asia was now presented as the frontier where a resurgent American character was once again on the move. A major five-page feature by Kennedy-favorite Joseph Kraft in a 1962 issue of the *Saturday Evening Post,* typical in its overall thrust and specific details, was a particularly lavish and well-crafted portrait.

"Hot Weapon in the Cold War" opened with a large photograph, placed just below the title and subheading, showing a pontoon raft of Special Forces paddling straight at the reader. With their capped heads, fierce gazes, bristling rifle barrels, and camouflage of branches and leaves, they looked like a canoe full of Roger's Rangers emerging from the forest streams of the American past. This iconography was juxtaposed with the subheading "At President Kennedy's urging, the Army is beefing up its Special Forces, the politico-military experts who are trained to combat Red guerrillas around the globe." The combination created a fused image of sophisticated contemporary professional and rough Indian fighter. According to Kraft's subsequent text, the Green Berets were counterinsurgency specialists, the "Harvard Ph.D.'s of warfare," who studied the works of Mao Tse-tung and Che Guevara as the most up-to-date and influential texts in their field. At the same time, their adaptation of such enemy doctrine placed them squarely in the American tradition of skill in irregular fighting "from the French and Indian wars through Marion in the Revolution, Mosby's Rangers in the Civil War and Merrill's Marauders in World War II."[7]

Kraft wrote the article in a rigidly journalistic tone that included a cautionary note concerning the difficulties facing white men in Asia; nevertheless, his resonant imagery presented the Green Beret as a rebirth of America's central mythic hero. Kraft filled out his characterization with a cataloguing of Green Beret skills that suggested an extraordinary command of both primitive and technological strengths. He emphasized that both the individual Green Beret and the standard operational unit, an "A" team of twelve men "cross-trained" in each other's specialities, were self-reliant, able to survive and complete their mission even if separated in the wilderness. A full-page photograph showed a bereted soldier, against a background of thick forest, leaping across a stream as a caption described the "grueling conditioning" endured by each Special Forces soldier; the facing page displayed photographs of a Green Beret leaping from an airplane and of others wearing earphones in indoor booths during foreign-language training. The text reported that each Green Beret had "a detailed knowledge of weapons ranging from the bow and arrow to the howitzer," and was capable of acquiring "by helicopter, boat, bicycle or even mule" mobility greater "than the guerrilla's." The principle was identical with that represented by the wearer of buckskin skilled with both Indian knife and Winchester rifle.

What indeed distinguished the Green Beret from earlier versions of the western hero was the sheer ease with which he encompassed savagery and civilization. The western hero was not only self-reliant but self-restrained, a chaste "saint with a gun"; similarly, the Green Beret was a man skilled in "hand-to-hand combat" whose "courtesy, deportment and other such traits must be excellent." But the Green Beret took the paradox of the genteel killer, the death-dealing innocent, far beyond the previous incarnations of the western hero, for he spent much of his time engaged in the missionary work of the Peace Corpsman: "Like most American exports they bear a distinct trademark. With the use of force they combine the doing of good works, the bringing of medical care and all the other arts of progress." As a single hero representing the ideal answer of the New Frontier to the calls for renewal, the Green Beret of the periodical press occupied in a single timeless moment the whole of American myth. Hunter at the wooded edge of civilization, builder and teacher in the pastoral landscapes behind, the Green Beret subsumed the separate heroes of *The Ugly American,* who were themselves projections of the successive geographical and historical phases of the original American frontier. This new western hero, to a greater degree than his previous incarnations, carried within him both America's return to the frontier and its advance to the millennium.

He also enjoyed a less troublesome relation to his society. The frontiersman of Cooper's Leatherstocking Tales was a lover of the anarchic freedom of the woods who had to remain on the margins of the society he had led in its wilderness conquest. The cowboy of Owen Wister's *The Virginian* (1902), a descendant of Leatherstocking, avoided the fate of the frontiersman by becoming a foreman and finally a husband, thus accepting a measure of incorporation and finally even domestication as the nineteenth-century frontier gave way to the urban-industrial society of the twentieth century. But the Green Beret suggested that the frontier character could now return in professional form, making possible a balanced harmony with the corporate, genteel society that had overwhelmed him. Indeed, it was emphasized that he would rarely, if at all, use his deadly arts to actually kill; he was primarily a teacher of those arts to native students who could then use them for their own protection. For the New Frontier, the Green Beret symbolized that contemporary Americans could possess the virtues both of the wild and of the domestic.

This significance was encapsulated in the five-paragraph story of a Special Forces operation in Southeast Asia with which Kraft began the *Post* article. The opening imagery echoed a classic scene from westerns: "Into the rugged mountain country of northeast Laos one day last year a military helicopter dropped a Thai interpreter and a small party of American soldiers." As successors to the standard band of frontiersmen accompanied by an Indian scout, they had entered a wilderness that, in the global context of the Cold War, was a meeting point between savagery and civilization: "The captain and his men were in the fluid no man's land between the pro-Western Royal Laotian Army and the Communist Pathet Lao." The description of the subsequent encounter of the Americans with primitive Meo tribesmen resonated pleasantly with American frontier myth. In constrast to the exploitative actions of both the Royal Laotians (similar to European colonials) and the Pathet Lao (communist Forces of Darkness), the Green Berets were shown winning the good will of the suspicious Meos by bringing the arts of civilization while also showing natural virtue:

Medical services—at the rate of 250 treatments daily—were made available. Demolition equipment was handed over for village construction projects. Instead of taking food, the Americans shot their own game, caught their own fish, and paid generously for rice and fruit.

The story concluded with the Special Forces' return from this frontier, leaving behind disciplined, trained companies of Meo allies who had "chased all Pathet Lao bands from the immediate neighborhood" and who were "bringing in daily intelligence reports on Pathet Lao movements in adjoining areas." Their work and example were shown to have remade another frontier into an improved landscape, and yet that progress involved no element of dispossession or occupation.

In this symbolic landscape the middle-American readers of the *Post* could envision the fulfillment of many American dreams. They could vicariously return to instinctual communion with the wilderness, yet take satisfaction in the Green Berets' rational imposition of order upon it. The more conservative could applaud them as anti-communist warriors, while liberals could approve them as model reformers. Indeed, their success with the Meos provided the reader with a completed vision of the stalled domestic agenda of the New Frontier: an easy accomplishment of Medicare, Urban Renewal, and Civil Rights. It was also a marked revision of the destruction civilized "progress" formerly brought to the American continent. Instead of bringing the natives new diseases, wasting their forests, and massacring their hunting game, the whites here re-sketched Manifest Destiny with lovely scenes of philanthropic medicine, building, and hunting. These scenes exemplified Kennedy's declaration a month before the *Post* article appeared that America's mission was not the "oversimplified" Wilsonian imperative "to remake the world in the American image"; instead, America should seek to "speed progress toward a more flexible world order" that would frustrate the communist "idea of a monolithic world."[8] In the Southeast Asia of the *Saturday Evening Post*, a resurgent American hero was once again in the wilderness pursuing the national purpose, a purpose more enlightened, selfless, and daring than ever before.

II

This symbolic message was not a cynical cover but rather an expression of deep cultural impulses, both conscious and unconscious. Kennedy of course confronted Vietnam within the contexts of the domestic political scene and the global struggle with the Soviet Union. He was vulnerable after the Bay of Pigs and the neutralization of Laos to charges of incompetence and timidity. He had returned "shaken and angry," as James Reston perceived him, from his June 1961 meeting in Vienna. Khrushchev "had bullied him and threatened him with war over Berlin" while rebuffing his objections to Soviet-supported "wars of national liberation" with the warning that "ideas cannot be stopped." Khrushchev's aggressive claim for the communist future of the developing world must have made De Gaulle's similar warning in Paris a few days earlier seem merely the voice of a defeated colonial European past. Kennedy is reported to have told Reston that "now we have a problem in making our power credible, and Vietnam looks like the place."[9]

But Kennedy had already sent an initial force of Green Berets to South Vietnam before his meeting with the Soviet Premier. Certainly Vietnam did not "look like the place" because of its greater importance than Germany or Cuba. Rather, it sharply contrasted with Checkpoint Charlie, where American and Soviet tanks silently sat facing each other on the brink of World War III, and the Caribbean island, where further open efforts to overthrow Castro would evoke worldwide denunciations of America's colonial aggression. Vietnam promised instead the qualities of America's remembered frontier triumphs: remoteness from dangerous confrontation with a major European power, a savage enemy who could be righteously hunted down, a wilderness landscape in which the American could renew his virtues where the European had proved only his vices, and the Asian people America historically saw as the appointed beneficiaries of its destiny.

On a mythic Asian plain, the Special Forces could solve the tensions of bureaucratization, affluence, and racism; the frustrations of containment and nuclear stalemate; the desire to demonstrate alignment with post-colonial peoples; and the anxious need to prove the "toughness" of the contemporary American character. This wish-fulfilling vision was later configured tellingly by Adam Yarmolinsky, a young New Frontiersman who came from Harvard to serve as special assistant to the Secretary of Defense. After the fall of Saigon, Yarmolinsky recalled to an interviewer the strong desire in the Kennedy administration to end the "no longer practical" and "morally unacceptable" policy of massive retaliation, as well as to disprove the perception in the developing countries of the United States as an old nation aligned with the status quo. He described "that kind of almost euphoria" early in the Kennedy administration that through counterinsurgency all we were going to have to do was send one of our Green Berets out into the woods to do battle with one of their crack guerrilla fighters and they would have a clean fight, and the best man would win and they would both get together and start curing all the villagers of smallpox.[10]

Kennedy's policy in Vietnam was thus determined by the conflicting mythic imperatives of his New Frontier. Such works as Richard Walton's *Cold War and Counterrevolution* (1972) and Garry Wills' *The Kennedy Imprisonment* (1981) have described how America, far from being dragged into a quagmire, "charged" into Vietnam behind a president eager to prove the techniques of counterinsurgency. Yet Leslie Gelb and Richard Betts' *The Irony of Vietnam* (1979) and Norman Podhoretz's *Why We Were in Vietnam* (1982) have also described how Kennedy tried to fulfill the previous commitments of the Truman and Eisenhower administrations on the "military cheap," avoiding the full measures of regular combat troops and bombing that his military advisers informed him were necessary to achieve victory.[11] He left at his death a "divided legacy" of a greatly expanded commitment of over 16,000 troops that he insisted were in Vietnam only as "advisers."[12] Behind his enthusiasms, anxieties, and restraints in Vietnam lay his ideal vision of the American symbolized by the Green Beret. Kennedy was determined that America prove itself the nation of "our ancient heritage" invoked in his Inaugural Address.

Through the old combination of wilderness skills and progressive arts, the American of the New Frontier would prove his preeminent power and virtue. Succeeding where the French colonial had failed, the Green Beret would be, as so many Americans had believed themselves to be, at once more savage and more truly civilized than the European. America would not fight the war with a vast army or nuclear bombs, nor would it seek any economic rewards for itself; rather it would risk entering the Asian wilderness alone or in small bands, combining the modern ingenuity represented by its helicopters, automatic rifles, and penicillin with an adaptation to the primitive terrain and people. What America would win for itself was a demonstration, to itself and to the world, that it continued to carry the light of the fathers. This desire, with strong if differently expressed appeal to both conservatives and liberals, was the force of the American mythic heritage articulating itself in a specific policy. Robert Kennedy later reported that his brother felt that the United States should stay in Vietnam for "psychological and political reasons 'more than anything else.' "[13] Since that was the case, the Green Beret would perform a symbolic drama of America's remembered past and dreamed future. In the articles of 1961 and 1962, Americans observed a Southeast Asia where a resurgent American character was about to prove American destiny.

III

Still the bestselling novel to be produced by the Vietnam War, Robin Moore's *The Green Berets* (1965) holds a pivotal position in the legend of the Special Forces. The book drew on the fascination with its heroes already created in the periodical press, and it appeared in the same months Lyndon Johnson's introduction of American combat units filled the front pages with Vietnam. *The Green Berets* sold close to 100,000 copies in hardcover during 1965, finishing fifth on the bestseller list. When it appeared in paperback in November, buyers at drugstore racks made it what *80 Years of Best-Sellers* calls "the phenomenon of the year, with 1,200,000 printed in only two months."[14] It reportedly induced so many enlistments of young men hoping to become Green Berets that the Selective Service was able to suspend draft calls during the first four months of 1966.[15] A few years later a Green Beret would nostalgically recall how following the book's publication Americans had sent "cookies and stuff . . . to us in Vietnam."[16]

Such enthusiasm was not shared by the Pentagon or the press. The Pentagon claimed that the book included sixteen security violations while grossly distorting the role of the Special Forces; the publisher was compelled to paste a label over the dust jacket stating "Fiction Stranger Than Fact."[17] The press showed a similar skepticism concerning Moore's claims that *The Green Berets* was a "book of truth" in which the disguises of fiction could more accurately present the facts he learned while serving with the Special Forces in Vietnam during the first six months of 1964.[18] An anonymous reviewer in *Time*, for instance, objected to the impression made on the "ordinary reader" by its "sly commingling of fact and fiction."[19]

Time's worries seemed validated by the liberal reviewers in other publications, who in the middle months of 1965 reviewed not just the book but the new American war now clearly underway in Vietnam. Gordon Harrison in the *New York Times Book Review* felt that "fiction being fiction the reader doesn't know what to believe and ends up believing what in fictional terms comes credibly alive." He concluded that those scenes "make one feel that the crusade against Communism has led us into the ultimate political quicksands in Southeast Asia." In the August issue of *Commonweal* Emil Capouya, repelled by the love of violence he saw in "Mr. Moore, and his ultimate expression, the foreign policy of the United States," argued that either as fact or romance "the most important thing we can learn from the gabble of cheerful idiocy that makes up *The Green Berets* is that the enemy is us." Calling the recent shift to conventional forces unfortunate, Daniel Ford was more sympathetic to the book in the *Nation*, but hoped that the Special Forces had "a more realistic understanding of revolutionary warfare in South Vietnam" than suggested by Moore's simplistic lack of distinction between the Viet Cong and the North Vietnamese.[20]

In its relation to the portrayal of the Special Forces in the periodical press, Moore's book represented an "unofficial" transmutation of an "official" myth. In this the Green

Berets' legend resembled the earliest incarnation of the western myth. The legend of Daniel Boone had also existed in two distinct if overlapping versions separately expressing public ideals and less acknowledged anxieties and desires. Early celebrators of Boone such as John Filson and Daniel Bryan presented him as an Enlightenment hero transforming the Kentucky wilderness into a rich civilization. In his epic *The Adventures of Daniel Boone* (1813) Bryan especially emphasized Boone's dedication to social progress. Early in this paen to Manifest Destiny, in a Miltonic council in heaven, the Spirit of Enterprise rises to urge his fellow angels to select Boone as agent of the divine plan to replace the wilderness stretching from the Alleghenies to the Pacific with "rich fields, Green-waving Meads, and flosculous Gardens." Enterprise explains that Boone is a man of civilized dutifulness and tenderness whom he has trained to survive savage conditions:

> No passion reigns,
> Tyrannic o'er his reason, Patriot love
> With daring majesty his soul inspires,
> And would with equal valor make him brave
> The lurking dangers of the savage wild;
> Or face in open field the frowning front
> Of thundering Battle. Generous, guileless, kind,
> The gripe of sneaking Avarice ne'er compress'd
> His princely heart.

The angels choose this hero because his civilized character may win the Indians to Christian Enlightenment while his wilderness skills may vanquish them if their savage passions are inspired by devilish spirits.[21] The Boone originally popularized by writers such as Bryan is clearly the same hero that in 1962 emerged in the *Saturday Evening Post* and other periodicals; he has simply traded buckskin for beret and moved on from Kentucky to Southeast Asia.

But during the early nineteenth century the popular mind created in its folklore another Boone, an anti-social primitive who moved more deeply into the woods at the first sight of a neighbor's chimney smoke. This misfit was the hero of numerous jokes printed in American newspapers and was picked up by Lord Byron in the eighth canto of *Don Juan*, the lines of which were in turn enthusiastically quoted again and again in American newspapers back across the Atlantic.[22] In flight from civilization, this Boone was a romantic embodiment of primitivist virtue. He scorned what Byron called "the dwarfing city's pale abortions," preferring "the green woods" to the ambitions, vanities, and artificial pressures of society.[23]

In the subsequent American imagination, the conflicting attractions of the progressive and primitive Boones were resolved, if not solved, in such western heroes as Leatherstocking and the Virginian. The fully conceived western hero first appears in Cooper's pages, and is then kept alive by the popular mind in the subsequent protagonists of dime novels, Hollywood movies, and television shows down to the 1960s. He is a reflection of the tension in American culture between the anarchic impulses of its individualistic ethic and the social ideals of its perceived communal mission. From Leatherstocking through the Virginian to the Green Beret, the democratic balance of self-reliance and self-restraint is a combined Enlightenment and Romantic ideal possessing a dark underside of passionate conflicts, longings, and anxieties.

Like the Boone of American folklore and newspapers, Moore's bestselling version of the Green Beret mirrors the fantasies of a significant portion of the populace. These fantasies are implicit but repressed in the "official" Green Beret created in the periodical press. The latter, like Filson's and Bryan's Boone, is a reflection of the acknowledged ideals of his society and is thus significant as an index of the intent of the nation for itself and for the world. But Moore's Green Beret, like the Boone of newspaper folklore and Lord Byron, is a darker image of the unconscious, or at least less willingly acknowledged, longings, tensions, and anxieties submerged just below the public ideals. In the case of Boone, this meant the eruption of primitivist impulses powerfully present in the young American mind, and the embracing of the self-concept of the unique virtue accompanying America's rejection of Europe's decadent civilization. These impulses were also of compelling importance in the Green Beret of Moore's novel. In the case both of Boone and of the Green Beret, the opposition was between a hero exemplifying public ideals and a hero revealing private desires lurking just beneath, even within, those ideals.

The Green Berets, as an amalgam of fiction and its author's experience, takes the Green Beret of the periodical press and makes him a character both more human and more fanciful. Moore, author of a previous book on guerrilla warfare in the Caribbean, and a former advertising and public relations executive, says that he undertook the project after the Kennedys had urged him to write a book celebrating the Special Forces.[24] The love of male prowess he exhibits in the book, so marked that one reviewer suggested it "would make a pychiatrist raise an eyebrow,"[25] was certainly consistent with the "toughness" so self-consciously sought by the Kennedys and emphasized in the original Green Beret image; however, in Moore's psyche these aggressive tendencies, self-righteously freeing themselves from institutional restraints, are also joyously free to operate without the personal restraints of compassion and empathy that were the balancing other half of the New Frontier and its desired image for the Special Forces. *The Green Berets* is animated by an unashamed fascination with violence and an underlying theme of "Germanic" Anglo-Saxon racial superiority leavened only by sentimentality. The popularity of the book reflects these aspects of the American unconscious lurking within western heroes from Cooper's Leatherstocking to the press's Green Beret. The themes of the magazine articles on the Green Beret, regeneration of frontier virtue and renewed pursuit of American mission, become in Moore's Southeast Asia a freewheeling crossing of the institutional, geographical, and moral boundaries of the official mission. Moore's new frontiersmen transcend the conformist materialism of corporate society. They refuse the careerist pressures and institutional traditions of their Regular Army superiors by frustrating communist operations with illegal preventive measures of their own.

This motif begins with the opening tale, "A Green Beret—All the Way." It centers upon the defense of a Strategic Hamlet by a Captain Kornie, a "blue-eyed Nordic giant," who as a Finn and later a member of the German army formerly fought the Russians. Kornie is faced with the devious tactics of the Viet Cong, the betrayals of his South Vietnamese troops, the selfish indifference of the Saigon government, and the "conventional" concern with rules of war and obedience to higher command of a Regular Army colonel on temporary tour with Special Forces. He prevails over them all by ruthlessly ingenious adaptations to the situation. The Regular Army colonel voices the constraints of institutional authority midway through the episode:

"Kornie, you know you can't go off attacking across borders, hiring bandits, acting like"—he sputtered—"like the CIA. We're part of the United States Army." He picked up the green beret on the table beside him. "Do you think this hat gives you some kind of special license to go off on your own, conduct operations that may endanger the peace of the world?" (pp. 49–50)

The episode ends with Kornie's double triumph in defeating the Viet Cong attackers and winning over the Regular Army colonel to his tactics. Like Kennedy in the 1961 *Time* article, Kornie vanquishes the hidebound thinking of the contemporary institutional "father" to reassert the frontier vigor of the true American fathers; here this renewal means a lawless ruthlessness in pursuit of a morality and wisdom superior to institutional and social restraint. The self-reliant western hero is approvingly presented as a self-appointed vigilante.

This motif runs throughout the loosely related episodes of *The Green Berets*. They encompass the cynical duping of a South Vietnamese Cao Dai priest, callous enlistment of a South Vietnamese woman into service as a prostitute-spy, "grim" acceptance of the torture of captured infiltrators, and contemptuous frustration of the prerogatives of the South Vietnamese allies. In context, these actions are at least arguably justified: the Cao Dai priest is a superstitious fool manipulated by the communists; the South Vietnamese woman uses her body to ruin a communist who has had her family brutally executed; the torture of a Viet Cong infiltrator reveals the existence of other enemies within the hamlet and of the planned attack, and the Green Berets do attempt to persuade the South Vietnamese interrogator that there are more effective methods than simple brutality; finally, the South Vietnamese are portrayed as so vicious, corrupt, and incompetent that frustrating their rights as allies is the only way to be true to the American mission. Thus the adaptation of the Green Berets to the savagery of both their enemy and their ally, especially since it is always held finally in check by the purity of the Green Berets' civilized purpose, is presented as self-evidently correct. Based on day-to-day experience of the grim actuality of guerrilla war, *The Green Berets* reveals the "tough-mindedness" advocated by *The Ugly American* and the New Frontier in candid hues unacceptable to the public discourse of the Pentagon and the press.

At the same time, the elements of the book most "fictionally alive," because most freely charged with the author's imaginative projection, reveal the antisocial fantasies lurking on the underside of the ideal of regenerated frontier virtue. *The Green Berets* is competently written in the style of men's adventure literature, and in its lurid prose the hero's sacrifices thinly disguise the gratifying indulgence of primal instincts. The characters whom the western hero traditionally has confronted in his mythic frontier landscape—the European and the savage—have major roles in *The Green Berets*. As in *The Ugly American*, the American heroes move back and forth between the city and the countryside, the worlds of Europe and the wilderness, civilization and nature, the conscious and the unconscious. But the heroes' relations to the characters associated with those opposed principles are here starkly primal.

The city is once again the world of complacency, artifice, and corruption. It is most generally characterized by the Vietnamese officer class, who are depicted as stupid brutes marked by their relentless pursuit of "face," sadism, and greed; and by their troops, who are cowardly and vicious young men exemplified by one unit of juvenile delinquents "volunteered" from the jails of Saigon. Revealingly, however, the most personal confrontation with the world of the city occurs in an episode centering on a Frenchman.

In "Coup de Grace," a Green Beret ensnares a handsome French plantation owner he knows is secretly a leader of Viet Cong guerrillas. The Green Beret, a former Hitler Youth who emigrated with his parents to the United States, supposedly sets out to destroy the Frenchman because he murdered a wounded American in cold blood. In a French country club in Saigon, however, the Green Beret makes an outburst revealing the larger dimension of the Frenchman's significance:

"Just because the damned frogs couldn't win their own war over here, and got kicked out of their richest colony, they can't stand to see us win now.

"The French have the funny notion they can do business with the Communists. If these people"—he waved, taking in the whole anachronistic group of French colonials—"and France, can persuade the United States to sit down at the bargaining table and neutralize South Vietnam, they think the Commies will let them keep their rich properties instead of having to sell control of them to the Vietnamese according to the agreements signed in Geneva after they were licked at Dien Bien Phu."
(pp. 143–44)

After summing up this characterization of De Gaulle's Vietnam policy with an assertion that the "French are a mean, money-grabbing, spiteful" lot, the Green Beret manages to meet the French plantation owner, named Huyot, who quickly reveals himself as a representative of the Europe obsessed with its loss of power and status to America:

We could have won our war here instead of losing it in 1954. But our generals and colonels were all conventional soldiers, unsuited to this war in Vietnam. Our St. Cyr War Academy leaders refused to accept this war as different from what they were taught. They knew little of guerrilla tactics and had no concept of how the jungle fighter thinks. (p. 146)

An "anachronistic" colonial European turned renegade, "cowboy"—as Huyot is known by the Americans in his guerrilla identity—is a perfect enemy for the Green Beret, an antitype of the latter's frontier character.

But in their meeting at the Saigon country club, where the Green Beret tricks the Frenchman into a subsequent jungle ambush, a more personal, and thus deeply psychological, dimension to the American's hatred acquires concrete projection. The handsome, wealthy Frenchman is accompanied by a "pretty, suntanned blonde" who is his fiancée. The ensuing scene is characterized by the stock terms of American male-literature fantasies, in which the sensual French women prefer the natural appeal of American men to that of their own "refined" men. The Green Beret gives "a long moment of unabashed admiration of the girl, whose tennis shorts and halter top showed her off to striking advantage" (p. 145), and finds that she returns the intent: "The girl looked up at Scharne, her eyes wide, smiling at his frank appraisal of her face and figure. 'We will be most—how you say?—disappointed, if you do not join us.'" Despite her obvious "natural" attraction to the American Green Beret, she belongs to the Frenchman, who jokes that "she loves the country and the properties so much I sometimes wonder if it is me or the estates she is marrying" (p. 147). The "large diamond shimmering on the appropriate finger" and her plaintive questions about whether she will be able to continue to enjoy Vietnam's "varied scenery and climate" make her a representation of the decadent prize of European colonialism.

When Scharne outwits Huyot in the countryside, he kills him in a feat of marksmanship, which in American popular culture has signified the frontier American's superiority to the European. With "astonishing accuracy," the Green Beret uses an M–79 grenade launcher to bring down the French renegade with a perfectly placed shot at 300 yards. As the triumphant American frontiersman stands over the dying European, the narrator's description makes it clear that Huyot has suffered a fate befitting his, and France's, sin, the betrayal of the white race: "Other rangers gathered to look at the formidable cowboy, barely identifiable as a Caucasian now except perhaps for his great size" (p. 163). The Green Beret's thoughts then turn to Huyot's fiancée: "I hope his girl has good friends out here. Maybe you could figure some way to break the news to her" (p. 163). This concern surely must be recognized as a mask—for the Green Beret, the author, and the reader. It thinly disguises the pleasure of utterly dispossessing the Frenchman of his inherited handsomeness, wealth, and manners.

Moore portrays the Montagnards as symbolic opposites to the Vietnamese and French, a savage contrast to urban civilization. Living in small villages deep in the mountainous jungle areas of Indochina, these primitive tribespeople are portrayed as premoral creatures of instinct and feeling. Generous, accepting, and loyal, they are also given to riotous ceremonies and undisciplined blood lust. Considerable emphasis is placed on their victimization at the hands of the South Vietnamese, who despise them as "moi" (savage), and they are portrayed as essentially innocent. The Americans must protect them from the communists as well as from the Royal Laotians and South Vietnamese. But what this means is that the Montagnards embody natural drives that the Green Berets must use, restrain, and indulge in a controlled manner for larger ends. In other words, presented as projections of the wilderness in which the Green Beret moves, they are also projections of his own chaotic nature, his instinctual drives for gratification.

This significance is fully elaborated in the centrally placed tale "Home to Nanette." A lone Green Beret—in a virtual sequel to the *Saturday Evening Post* story—returns to the Meo tribesmen in Laos whom his "A" team had earlier trained. Now that the 1962 neutralization of Laos has been supposedly established by the United States and the Soviet Union, Major Arklin is assigned to the CIA to prepare clandestinely for the inevitable communist violations. Arklin, a solitary figure among savages in the "neutral" jungle of Laos, is thus the perfect Green Beret in the perfect New Frontier setting: a man who, amid the political constraints of the Cold War, is able to confront communist evil with the directness of an Indian fighter in the dark and bloody forests of eighteenth-century Kentucky. More than any other Green Beret in the book, Arklin fits the official portrayal of the periodical press. He is motivated purely by his sense of mission, living unofficially with the Meos under CIA auspices despite a sincere preference to be back in the United States living peacefully on a military base with his family, wearing a starched Regular Army uniform, and advancing to colonel up the regular career ladder. At the same time, he genuinely likes the natives and dutifully adapts to their ways while trying to improve their behavior and protect them.

These self-sacrificing acts of an agent of progress become, however, a necessary indulgence in the primitive strikingly different from the actions of the Green Berets in the *Saturday Evening Post*. To fulfill his mission, this American professional first accepts that he must adapt to his savage circumstances: he *must* strip his uniform off to wear a loincloth, he *must* take part in ceremonies of riotous drinking and animal sacrifices, he *must* organize games of violent skill, he *must* allow the chief's bare-bosomed daughter to share his hut, he *must* lead a bloody ambush of invading communists. Possessing the character, motivations, and goals of Bryan's hero of advancing civilization, he is required to make the primitivist Boone's retreat into nature. Arklin later finds that he *must* revolt against the conformist pressures of an institution of his society. Backed by his crossbow-wielding followers, he faces down the Regular Army colonel who, outraged by his savage appearance, his Meo girl, and his independent operations, demands that Arklin step into the returning helicopter or face the ruin of his career. The Green Beret indulges in primitive impulse and revolts against institutional authority, yet like the western hero is actually restrained by his own higher sense of natural law that is at one with his true civilized duty. He is the autonomous American character self-governed by his internalized balance of the savage and the civilized.

Yet his triumph is actually the superficial and self-congratulating self-deception offered readers by escapist literature. The pressures on Arklin are really opportunities for the reader to enjoy guiltlessly instinctual fantasies of gratification and anarchy. Even the Green Beret's subsequent fulfillment of his mission provides readers yet another vicarious dream, the enjoyment of complete mastery over an enemy, who appear here as Chinese officers found personally directing the communist subversion. He trusses them, injects them with an enervating drug, and has them thrown into a CIA helicopter. In the end he abandons the Meo girl, learns that the CIA has maneuvered the Regular Army superior into the "bowels of the Pentagon" (p. 221), and receives his promotion to colonel. In the middle 1960s "Home to Nanette" provided the deepest American fantasy of an escape from society into nature, from the constraints of the conscious mind into the indulgence of the unconscious, within the self-satisfying guise of a pursuit of the righteous American purpose.

Moore's novel ends with a vivid tale of a covert Green Beret operation in North Vietnam that extends the dream of counterinsurgency into the realm of apocalyptic fantasy. While acknowledging the necessity of accepting the constraints of limited conflict in a Cold War of nuclear stalemate, it provides a satisfying vision of taking righteous American wrath into the territory of the communist enemy. The aim of the mission is, as the title of the story says, to "Hit'em Where They Live." Secretly operating as guerrillas in North Vietnam, Green Berets create havoc that they envision will lead the communist rulers to negotiate an end to the war:

"The theory is," said Buckingham, "that Hanoi will be so shaken when it sees what we're doing it will start wanting to negotiate. Uncle Ho doesn't want the Chinese to come down to North Vietnam any more than we do. The Viets had the Chinks for two thousand five hundred years and hated every day of it." (p. 318)

One should not wonder that this argument seems to cancel out the entire rationale of the American effort in South Vietnam, even more so in Moore's book where the South Vietnamese appear hardly worthy of saving from anything. Like the rest of *The Green Berets*, this episode works on the level of the irrational, offering Southeast Asia as an alluring landscape of primitive satisfactions, a dark frontier where the psyche may contemplate eternally having a communist to kill and a native woman to lose oneself in. The climactic story thus appropriately ends with a Green Beret telling another to spend the night with a Meo girl:

"It's a new kind of war we fight today, yes? No such thing as win or lose. Just which side has the muscle to make the other side agree when the bargaining starts."

DePorta winked at Smith. "What are you waiting for? Get onto that sleeping platform while you have a chance. Before you know it we'll be on the move." (pp. 337–38)

That final phrase of *The Green Berets* (other than the brief essay by the author that follows as epilogue) expresses a dark unconscious desire lurking on the underside of the response to candidate Kennedy's call five years earlier to "get the country moving again." That rhetoric articulated idealistic imperatives and anxious concerns everywhere present in the public quest of 1960 for a renewed pursuit of the national purpose. In 1965, as Johnson led America into a full-scale war that would cast to the side the theories of counterinsurgency, *The Green Berets* spoke to a part of the American mind only weakly repressed by its conscious ideals and purposes. In contrast to the liberal ideals of *The Ugly American*, we can see in Moore's bestselling tale a darker reflection of the desire to return to the frontier in Southeast Asia.

IV

Earlier, in the fall of 1963, continued communist successes and the televised self-immolations of protesting Buddhist monks had for Americans already transformed Vietnam into a spectral landscape. In the weeks before his assassination, desperately attempting to salvage his policy, Kennedy had supported a generals' coup against the unpopular and ineffective Diem government. From the perspective of subsequent events, Kennedy's experiment in counterinsurgency appears to all but a few remaining enthusiasts to have been doomed from the beginning. Despite Kennedy's urgings, the larger American military presence was never willing or able to adjust to unorthodox methods of warfare. The Saigon government, whether the Diem brothers or the generals, was as unwilling or unable to enact the reforms necessary to gain popular support. The realities of a contemporary American institution and of a remote Asian society proved impervious to the ideal of the Green Beret.

Nevertheless, while his experiment in counterinsurgency makes Kennedy responsible for the greatly expanded commitment to Vietnam that would confront Johnson, the optimistic symbolism of the Green Beret had consistently emphasized the reservation, as Kennedy personally asserted in a September television interview, that America could only help and advise the Vietnamese in "their" war.[26] If he had made an error in raising the stakes for the United States in Vietnam, he had thus prudently kept open a political route of withdrawal. Mike Mansfield, majority leader of the Senate, and Kenneth O'Donnell, Kennedy's assistant, both later reported that Kennedy had expressed to them during 1963 his profound dismay at his previous actions in Vietnam and his determination to extricate American forces after the 1964 election.[27] His aide Arthur Schlesinger Jr. has told us that Kennedy once predicted to him that the introduction of conventional American troops would disastrously make Vietnam into the setting of "a white man's war."[28] Would he have finally accepted failure, as he did at the Bay of Pigs, rather than have the United States perceived in the world as imposing its neocolonial will? Would he have responded to the pressure of deteriorating events, as he did in the civil rights struggle, by daring to shift course and accept a loss of popularity in order to avert a larger disaster? The only historical answer is that such a decision was not to be his to make.

His successor, the reputedly more "realistic" Johnson, would launch a major bombing campaign against North Vietnam that would prove unable to significantly slow infiltration to the South or to damage the morale of the North, but which would provide images of cold technological aggression against an agrarian society. On the ground, he would pursue a strategy of attrition that would not seek out the primary source of the enemy's manpower, North Vietnam, but which would present statistics of dead Vietnamese as the measure of American progress. Johnson would massively infuse American wealth into South Vietnam, visibly transforming the setting of an American war for the principle of "self-determination" into a corrupt and distorted American dependency. He would stake the whole of American prestige against an enemy mobilizing for total war but would insist that American society, rather than sacrifice, could continue to enjoy a domestic policy of "guns and butter." Fearful of providing conservatives in Congress with a pretext for scuttling the domestic programs of his Great Society, he would reject advice to declare war and even refuse to arouse passions by focusing propaganda on the evil of the enemy.[29] The necessary manpower for the undeclared war would in the meantime be obtained through conscription, made at first more palatable to influential elements through the complicated, class-structured deferment system, a calculation that would eventually result in a highly combustible mix of fear, guilt, and moral dismay among the temporarily privileged youth on the college campuses.

Early in his administration, Johnson would dazzle liberals with his ability to pass legislation that had been stalled in Congress under Kennedy. In striking contrast to Kennedy's concern for the image of the United States in developing countries, he would impress conservatives with his decisive use of American power in the Gulf of Tonkin and the Dominican Republic. But Johnson would eventually undercut his power, and the foreign-policy consensus of the American people, through his failure in the symbolic dimension that Kennedy had understood so well. He would give the American people a war that could not have been more carefully planned to reflect back to them stark images of their worst self-suspicions.

In the conventional war Johnson determinedly escalated in Vietnam, the Special Forces were of course relegated to a secondary role. Nevertheless, in a war notable for its dearth of celebratory popular literature, music, films, and propaganda, the Green Beret continued to stride through American consciousness. He appeared in more magazine articles and popular novels; in Barry Sadler's song "The Ballad of the Green Berets" and accompanying album

Ballads of the Green Berets (1966), both of which would sell over a million copies; and in John Wayne's movie *The Green Berets* (1968), which would prove a resounding success at the box office even amid the widespread disillusionment that by then surrounded the war. In the midst of the abstract statistics and fragmentary images of violence pervading the newspapers and television news, this carrier of the aspirations of the New Frontier remained at the center of popular dreams of the war.

Through his creation of the Green Beret as symbolic hero, Kennedy had offered the American psyche a vision of friendship with the Asian native and triumph over the communist adversary; he was apparently confident that he could pull away if the situation failed to respond to his best efforts and intentions. Kennedy could no more have foreseen his assassination in Dallas than most Americans could have foreseen their coming defeat and disillusion in Vietnam.

CHAPTER THREE

The Antiwar Movement and the Frontier

THE EARLY CRITICISM by intellectuals and youth of Johnson's lack of "style" actually registered a far deeper wound left in American consciousness by Kennedy's murder. As American society moved into the 1960s, Kennedy had exerted a symbolic, a deeply psychological and cultural, leadership. Older and far less open to new perspectives, Johnson could not feel, much less connect with, the subterranean force of the huge post-World War II "babyboom" generation that was then moving through adolescence. However adept Johnson seemed at carrying through Kennedy's domestic political program, however decisive he appeared in foreign affairs, Johnson was incapable of carrying on Kennedy's role as cultural model and leader.

As Johnson's escalations and the rising draft calls began changing Americans' image of the Vietnam landscape, the babyboomers, now flooding colleges and universities across the land, were already moving toward a broad cultural revolt against their society. The television and movie culture of the 1950s had surrounded them with heroic portrayals of the Old West and World War II, while their parents had raised them in placid suburbs. As they moved into adolescence at the end of the decade, these pampered beneficiaries of the World War II generation's sacrifices and triumphs had been caught, even more than their parents, between the call of the culture's mythos and the temptations of the affluent, corporate society. "We want you to have what we didn't have," they would be told as they were given transistor radios and sports cars. "You're spoiled," they would be told when they responded to these created wants by wanting more. Through the media and the echoing judgments of their elders, they had heard the worries over the supposed lack of toughness shown by young American prisoners during the Korean War, the condemnations of aimless juvenile delinquents and motorcycle gangs, the general disapproval of the conformity and apathy ascribed to the slightly older "silent generation" of the 1950s. Seeking both larger meaning and freer pleasures, many would eventually look with growing dismay at the "inauthentic" lives committed only to conspicuous consumption that were nevertheless being set out for them.

During the 1960 presidential campaign they had found a model for their conflicting desires in the young man who seemed to be speaking both for them and to them. Conveying an impatient idealism and yet a detached "cool," a desire to serve coupled with a reaching for greatness, a frontier vigor and yet a sophisticated "class" that included his wife's refined tastes in the "finer things" of life, Kennedy resolved within his public image the conflicting aspirations of middleclass youth. Almost brash toward his elders Truman and Eisenhower, the Presidents of contemporary stalemate and ease, Kennedy seemed to be looking back to his true "fathers," the visionary Presidents—the two Roosevelts, Lincoln, Jackson, Jefferson—who had each in turn reinvigorated the American errand. At his inaugural Kennedy asked Americans to "bear the burden of a long twilight struggle" against "tyranny, poverty, disease and war itself." The younger generation especially heard his challenge to them in the words "ask not what your country can do for you; ask what you can do for your country."

During his three years in office, Kennedy pursued this vision with a pragmatic caution that would disappoint many. He was faced with a powerful coalition of Republicans and Southern Democrats in Congress, the limits set by nuclear stalemate, an unprecedented series of foreign-policy crises around the world, and the growing racial conflict that threatened to tear apart the society at home. Kennedy struggled to manage events while trying to avoid getting too far in front of the broad populace he was leading. In the final months of his presidency, reporters were being told that the agenda of the New Frontier would be accomplished with the solid liberal Democratic majority Kennedy would bring with him into his second term. But Kennedy had already catalyzed a youthful desire for change that was itself a political power, as yet only dimly recognized, destined to transform the nation later in the decade. Before Kennedy gave it mainstream political meaning, that emerging force had been foreshadowed only in the alienated sullenness of a James Dean, the anarchic sensuality of an Elvis Presley, the restless adventuring of a Jack Kerouac.

Even if he had avoided a major war in Vietnam, Kennedy could hardly have confined these drives to the channels he had provided by his own example and by such symbols as the Peace Corps, the space program, and the Green Berets. The radical student movement that would subsequently barricade Johnson in the White House was already gestating during Kennedy's years. The "Port Huron Statement," prepared by future antiwar leader Tom Hayden for the 1962 convention of the Students for a Democratic Society (SDS), included a critique of the New Frontier as a "mediating, rationalizing, and managerial" attempt at "adjusting to the revolutions of the new era in order that the old order of private corporate enterprise shall be preserved and rationalized."[1] But as socialist Michael Harrington would implicitly acknowledge four years later in his introduction to Jack Newfield's laudatory book on the New Left, *A Prophetic Minority* (1966), Kennedy had held a unique symbolic relation to the radicals' youthful passion:

Perhaps the first major political figure who benefited from, and even incarnated, the youthful mood of turning from business to service was John F. Kennedy. And it is significant that many of the New Leftists were first provoked into thought and commitment by the late President. They were to become disillusioned with the liberalism of the New Frontier as they turned to a more radical critique of American institutions. Yet the symbolic and catalytic role of Kennedy remains a most important fact in their collective autobiography.[2]

With his mixture of romanticism and pragmatism, Kennedy conceivably could have continued to open up his metaphor of the New Frontier into visions that would have retained for the majority of youth a sense of possibility, idealism, and adventure connected to the culture. Certainly the New Left, never more than a small minority of wealthy, highly privileged college students,[3] could not have found widespread support among their classmates without the symbolism Johnson provided with his policies in Vietnam.

Acutely sensitive to tangible concentrations of political influence, Johnson would from his first decisions to escalate the war refuse advice to call up the reserves, fearing the disruption that such mobilization would cause among middleclass communities. But he apparently never imagined, in striking contrast to Kennedy's presentation of Vietnam as the setting for the nostalgic yet progressive figure wearing the Green Beret, how his new policies in Vietnam would look to an American youth uncomfortable with the affluence, bureaucracy, technology, and racism of their society. The New Left had its sources in the civil rights struggles of the early 1960s and in the Berkeley Free Speech Movement led by Mario Savio in 1964. But it was Johnson's escalations in Vietnam in 1965 that provided radicals with images of blatant technological and bureaucratic violence against an agrarian landscape that they could point to as proof of the less visible brutality pervading Americans' lives.

That April, during the first of the mass demonstrations that would follow with steadily increasing frequency and size, Paul Potter, then president of SDS, would tell a Washington protest march that the "incredible war" in Vietnam was an expression of a "system" that in America itself

disenfranchises people in the South, leaves millions upon millions of people throughout the country impoverished and excluded from the mainstream and promise of American society, that creates faceless and terrible bureaucracies and makes those the place where people spend their lives and do their work, that consistently puts material values before human values—and still persists in calling itself free and still persists in finding itself fit to police the world.[4]

In the rhetoric of the New Left, as in *The Ugly American* and the New Frontier portrayals of the Green Beret, Southeast Asia was a landscape in which Americans could perceive images symbolic of an internal American struggle. That struggle was between a bureaucratic, decadent, technological society and a minority true to the original American dream of democracy, racial brotherhood, authentic personal relations, and harmony with nature and the self. But in the version of this landscape that the New Left was able to create from Johnson's war, Americans who wanted to align themselves with nature against the machine would have no alternative but to reject the American society itself.

Indeed, the New Left was intertwined with the development of a larger Counterculture whose members might or might not involve themselves in political protest but who all repudiated the "system." Foreshadowed by the "rebel without a cause," the "hipster," and the "beatnik" of the 1950s, they discovered their shared alienation in their common escape from university bureaucracies, suburban parents, and corporate fantasies; but it was their flight from forced service in Vietnam that led large numbers to full rejection of the culture. They "dropped out," growing long hair, wearing buckskin and beads and headbands, sharing peyote-like drugs, and often joining in tribe-like communes. They were taking on the guise of the Indian, the natural man who in the popular culture of their childhoods had been presented as the savage or noble Other confronting the white American on the frontier. The "hippies" or "freaks" sought the authenticity, the possibility, the harmony that philosophers such as Herbert Marcuse, drug gurus such as Timothy Leary, and acid-rock groups such as the Jefferson Airplane told them their society, Amerika as it was now often spelled to label it as a Kafkaesque, Nazi-like system, had taken from them. With the close of the decade, Yale professor Charles Reich summed up the meaning of the Vietnam War to the Counterculture in his best-selling and much-discussed *The Greening of America* (1970):

> The war did what almost nothing else could have: it forced a major breach in consciousness. The breaches in consciousness caused by the consumer-worker contradiction or the rigidity-repression syndrome were significant, but they were slow acting and might have taken indefinite time. It might have been years before marijuana and riots catalyzed disillusionment. The war did that with extraordinary rapidity. It rent the fabric of consciousness so drastically as to make repair almost impossible. And it made a gap in belief so large that through it people could begin to question the other myths of the Corporate State.[5]

Following the American impulse to shed past civilized forms for "a new consciousness," the youth of the Counterculture rejected a society that Vietnam had seemingly exposed as being after all only an extension of Europe. America appeared to them to be the latest manifestation of a civilized obsession with control. It laid waste to natural landscapes and enervated the vital nature within its own people.

In addition to the youth of the New Left and the Counterculture, a number of older artists and intellectuals made up the third major element of the radical antiwar move-

ment. Throughout the 1950s, these members of the intellectual elite had chafed at seeing how completely the Cold
War seemed to overturn traditional American values. They
had deplored a peacetime atmosphere of war that sup-
pressed political dissent and enforced cultural conformity;
they had likewise looked distastefully at the bureaucratic
power and consumer obsessions that stifled individual expression and ignored racism at home while culturally and
economically dominating the emerging nations of the
Third World. With these feelings, and with the impatience
many had felt with Kennedy's administration and finally
the frustration, even despair, many more had experienced
with his assassination, Johnson's escalations in Vietnam
became the focus of the long-repressed grievances of intellectuals and artists against their society.

"Teach-ins" by university faculty and boycotts of White
House functions by distinguished writers would be among
the first expressions of opposition to the war. And soon
many of them became involved in antiwar demonstrations
alongside members of the New Left and the Counterculture. Among the most famous were Norman Mailer,
Dwight Macdonald, Robert Lowell, Noam Chomsky, Mary
McCarthy, Paul Goodman, and Susan Sontag. These intellectuals agreed with the New Left and the Counterculture
in seeing the war as an expression of an imperial, racist,
bureaucratic, and technological Establishment that was
ruining the physical and spiritual landscape of America as
surely as it was Vietnam.

Mailer, McCarthy, and Sontag each wrote influential
narratives during the Johnson years that articulate what
Vietnam had come to mean to a growing body of youth and
intellectual opinion. In these works we can see how the
American story, the American idea of its meaning in the
flow of history, was transformed for many Americans by
the landscape they now saw in Vietnam. Perceiving Vietnam as a confrontation between the forces of technology
and nature, each of these writers portrays the war in terms

of the American frontier; however, this landscape reveals the meeting of savagery and civilization to have a different meaning from that of traditional American myth. And it is on that deep cultural level that the antiwar movement has had its most enduring impact on the legacy of Vietnam.

II

In his deeply paradoxical stance—hip yet earnest, ideological yet anarchic, scatalogical yet intellectual— Norman Mailer spoke for and yet critiqued both the "respectable" intellectuals and artists of the older generation and the "crazy" leaders of the younger generation. Winning early fame for his bestselling and highly acclaimed novel of World War II, *The Naked and the Dead* (1948), Mailer had through the 1950s suffered a steadily diminishing reputation as a novelist. In 1959, however, he began with stunning brilliance directly addressing political and cultural issues, and by the mid-1960s was poised to launch the most prestigious and controversial phase of his career. In a series of articles and books, Mailer viewed Vietnam as the expression of a frontier culture that had become a corporation society. Widely read and debated by intellectuals, journalists, academics, and students, these writings provide a dramatized reflection of the Counterculture and New Left's perception of the American involvement as a manifestation of a sick society. As the highly self-conscious probings of an important American artist, they afford as well an older intellectual's ironic and deeply ambiguous analysis of the conflict within the American psyche which Vietnam had come to symbolize.

Mailer's key work in this regard is *Why Are We in Vietnam?* (1967). Originally dismissed by the majority of critics as gratuitously obscene and laughingly simplistic, this brief novel has grown in reputation over the years. Mailer repeated its thesis in his account of the 1967 antiwar demonstration in Washington D.C., *The Armies of the Night: History as a Novel/The Novel as History* (1968), which would be awarded the Pulitzer Prize and National Book Award. But while *The Armies of the Night* was more accessible, *Why Are We in Vietnam?* more complexly stated Mailer's answer to the question posed by its title.

The book is narrated within the mind of a white adolescent who calls himself D. J. (for Dr. Jekyll), but who suggests that he may really be a black genius in Harlem. Sitting at a Dallas dinner party, he recalls a big-game hunt in Alaska two years earlier. The novel abruptly concludes with the narrator's announcement on the last page—the only time the war is mentioned—that the next day he and his friend Tex Hyde are going to Vietnam. The Texas setting evokes the older frontier in its most heroic and troubling form. It enables Mailer to call to mind both the cherished memory of a small band of volunteers standing at the Alamo against faceless forces commanded by the petty European-style Emperor Santa Anna, and the less-happily remembered aggression in the later Mexican War of a bullying United States against a weak neighbor. With D. J.'s reference to "Dallassassians,"[6] the Texas setting also forces to consciousness the violent termination only four years earlier of the New Frontier. In addition, it pervades the novel with the ethos of the Texan who succeeded Kennedy and is directing the war in Vietnam. Finally, it overlays the novel with the continuing American dream of an endless frontier, since Texas has become the center of the space program, with which D. J.'s father is connected through his work as an executive for a plastics corporation.

With the plot of the novel consisting primarily of the recalled hunt in Alaska, America's last territorial frontier, the action drives toward answering the question of the title by addressing what a contemporary frontier means for a society that has given itself over to corporation and machine. The hunting party is controlled by D. J.'s father

Rusty and is guided by a corrupted Natty Bumppo figure named Luke. The ensuing events reveal that the innocent Huck Finn and Tom Sawyer youths—D. J. and Tex—are really an American image of Jekyll and Hyde. Using a helicopter and an array of high-velocity weapons, the hunting party transform their animal prey into pitiful, maddened objects of slaughter. The setting, characters, and plot thus link a clearly perverse activity to the mythic imagery of the American frontier myth and to the disturbing contemporary images of Vietnam.

Though widely dismissed by critics, *Why Are We in Vietnam?* elicited some strongly affirmative responses. In a six-page article entitled "Vietnam and Obscenity," published in *Harper's* in February 1968, John Aldridge explained to readers that Mailer's portrayal of D. J.'s corporate father diagnosed a society suffering a "psychosis." This condition resulted from the contemporary blockage of the creative impulses and sense of imaginative possibility once embodied by the physical frontier.[7] Referring to Mailer's famous 1960 essay on John Kennedy called "The Existential Hero," Aldridge argued that Kennedy had briefly reawakened "the fantasy of heroism," giving the culture a sense of new direction and possibility; the assassination, however, had left a "cancerous emptiness" creating "psychological pressures that have driven us to commit the atrocity of Vietnam." In a 1971 article in *Modern Fiction Studies*, Richard Pearce saw in the novel an even deeper cultural indictment, a "radical critique of frontier values." Mailer was revealing that

the primitivistic cult adapted by the civilized white man—with all its attendant sexual and social sublimations and which is central to the American myth of the frontier—that this primitivistic cult does not stand opposed to society's rapacity, possessiveness, and exploitiveness, but is a singular expression of it.[8]

The myth of America, embodying its deepest values and heroic self-concept, was ugly—the "shattering message" D. J. finds in the entrails of a dying bear.

Such commentators disagreed on Mailer's ultimate message about America's frontier ideal, but they agreed that Vietnam resulted from a sick contemporary American society perversely acting out the lost rituals of its heritage. Late in the novel D. J., after the competitive hunt has climaxed in his suffering a final disillusionment with the father's corrupt values, ventures with his friend Tex into wilderness so deep that technology-equipped hunters have not yet ruined it. At Tex's insistence, they ritualistically strip themselves of their weapons and most of their gear. The two youths subsequently experience a briefly transcendent communion with each other and the surrounding nature, as they lie nude together in a sleeping bag. Not through killing but through freedom from the corruption of "things," they momentarily approach spiritual regeneration, the benign aspect of the frontier myth from Thoreau's persona and Cooper's Natty Bumppo to Kennedy's volunteer in the Peace Corps or Green Berets.

They fulfill the ideal of purifying self-reliance in nature; but when the night passes without the expression of their erotic energies, they become "killer brothers," and in the novel's last sentence we learn that the day after the dinner party from which the hunt is being recalled D. J. and Tex will be "off to see the wizard" in Vietnam. However ambiguous about his ultimate judgment upon the frontier dream, Mailer portrays the America of Johnson and the Pentagon as a landscape in which the frontier myth seems not innocently unique but rather the worst European rapacity. On his maternal side, Tex Hyde traces his descent to the Alamo, and his father is half-Indian and half-German. Thus he truly is D. J.'s Hyde—the revelation of the savage nature underlying American as much as European civilization.

The central motifs of *Why Are We in Vietnam?*—the assault of a corrupt machine society upon a beleagured nature; the alienation from one's own nature; the disillusionment of a youth with a father who is part of the corporate machine; the resulting need to escape from the society, from the father, from things, into uncorrupted nature with a more natural man who is also a fellow youth—these were the elements of American mythology that underlay the ethos of the antiwar movement and that would dominate the literary and cinematic works of the Vietnam era. But what was just as significantly apparent in Mailer's novel was that no amount of alienation and rejection would remove the American rebel from the landscape of his culture's myth. He would simply seek a new position from which to act out the traditional self-concept.

Two of the most revealing works in this regard are Mary McCarthy's *Hanoi* (1968) and Susan Sontag's *Trip to Hanoi* (1968), both highly self-conscious personal accounts of their separate journeys to North Vietnam. McCarthy was known as the *grande dame* of American letters, and the younger Sontag was at the height of her fame as McCarthy's apparent successor. Despite their different generations, both came out of the elite New York culture. Highly influential with the intellectual and academic audience, McCarthy first published articles on her journey in the *New York Review of Books* and Sontag in *Esquire*. Sontag's account was subsequently printed yet again in her widely reviewed collection called *Styles of Radical Will* (1969). In *Why We Were in Vietnam* Podhoretz credits McCarthy and Sontag with having had a major effect in forming the images of the North Vietnamese and the Americans that would increasingly characterize the passions of opponents of the war.[9]

Both McCarthy and Sontag frankly inform their readers from the outset that they went to North Vietnam repelled by their own society and distraught over its actions in Southeast Asia. Sontag, after first explaining that she made her journey out of a "sense of moral dilemma at being a citizen of the American empire,"[10] confesses that before her trip she had idealized Vietnam in the simple terms of the beautiful Other under assault from "what's most ugly in America: the principle of 'will,' the self-righteous taste for violence, the insensate prestige of technological solutions to human problems" (p. 40). Her "helpless peasants being napalmed by swooping diving metal birds" (p. 19) duplicates Mailer's Alaskan hunting scenes. Speaking in similar terms, McCarthy reports her realization that she went to Vietnam because she could not live at ease while her country was engaged in "that brutal, brutish onslaught."[11] While there, she sees her society through North Vietnamese eyes as "not just grotesque, but backward, primitive, pitiably undeveloped, probably because of its quality of infantile dependency." She reports a story, "surely true," told in Hanoi of a shot-down American pilot who tried to buy his way out of captivity with promises of his millionaire-sister's ransom (p. 122). Confronting a captured American pilot, she concludes that his robotlike answers are the result of his formative experiences in an assembly-line American system of education reinforced by military training. In the Vietnam landscapes of both Sontag and McCarthy, America is a technological, brutal, huge, virtually invincible, unnatural, and decadent empire.

McCarthy's and Sontag's portrayals of their country are thus quite close to the portrayal of Americans and Europeans in *The Ugly American*. But where Lederer and Burdick present a small number of American heroes who show the way to regeneration by returning to the frontier virtues, McCarthy and Sontag can imagine turning only to the enemy, the complete Other. This identification is made despite their initial discomfort with the Vietnamese. Reaching across an immense cultural and ideological gulf, McCarthy discovers "an unspoken feeling of conflict with the North Vietnamese value system" (p. 123), and Sontag repeatedly comes back to her perception that "part of me can't help regarding them as children—beautiful, patient, heroic, martyred, stubborn children" (p. 15). Structuring their memoirs as journeys toward understanding the true nobility of the North Vietnamese, they appear to have simply projected the cultural ideal that they so painfully found lacking in their society.

Sontag, for instance, admits that at first the North Vietnamese disappointed her need for a heroic idol: "The first experience of being there absurdly resembled meeting a favorite movie star, one who for years has played a role in one's fantasy life, and finding the actual person so much smaller, less vivid, less erotically charged, and mainly different" (p. 8). By the closing pages of her book, however, she anticipates accusations that she has fallen into the centuries-old pattern of western intellectuals picturing a "pastoral ideal" in a remote land. She concludes that, "In the end I can only avow that, armed with these very self-suspicions, I found, through direct experience, North Vietnam to be a place which, in many respects, *deserves* to be idealized" (p. 72).

What Sontag and McCarthy find is indeed the "pastoral ideal" seemingly usurped in their own land by a technological and decadent society. Sontag, confronted with the face her North Vietnamese hosts show her, replaces her original "fantasy" image with one in which "the delicate build of the Vietnamese and their sheer physical gracefulness can set a gawky, big-boned American on edge." She wonders at how "they appear so singularly and straightforwardly involved with the virtue of courage, and with the ideal of a noble, brave life," when "we live in an age marked by the discrediting of the heroic effort" (pp. 69–70). The almost embarrassed intensity of her conclusion could not more plainly confess the pain of alienation from her own culture that compels her to project the need for an ideal self-concept upon an opposed Other:

It is *not* simple to be able to love calmly, to trust without ambivalence, to hope without self-mockery, to act courageously, to perform arduous tasks with unlimited resources of energy. In this [American] society, a few people are able just faintly to imagine all these as achievable goals—though only in their private life. (p. 77)

While she certainly implies no such connection, one can hear in this pained apology for the idea of heroic patriotism the silent longing of the youth of the 1950s for a call to sacrifice and idealistic mission. Seemingly answered in Kennedy's Inaugural Address, it had been translated under Johnson into a war fought without vivid imagery but with an elaborately class-structured draft-deferment system.

The similar "identity crisis" (p. 123) that McCarthy portrays herself undergoing in North Vietnam turns out, also like Sontag's, to be a shocked sense that Vietnam is the America that no longer exists—except as a place in a few minds—back in the United States. Towards the close of her book, McCarthy confesses that she brought with her to North Vietnam "the confidence of the American who knows himself to be fair-minded, able to see both sides, disinterested, objective, etc. as compared to the single-minded people he is about to visit." Still believing that she possesses these qualities, she now sees them as the "fossil remains of the old America, detached by an ocean from the quarrels of Europe, having no colonial interests compared to the Great Powers, a permanent outsider and hence fitted to judge or bear witness, enjoying a high material standard of living, which ought to exclude any venality or pettiness" (p. 123). McCarthy's early shock upon arriving in North Vietnam has been at discovering a duplication of the Old West:

North Vietnam is still pioneer country, where streams have to be forded; the ethnic minorities, Meos, Muongs, and Thais, in the mountains of the wild west, though they do not wear feathers, recall American Indians. The old-fashioned school desks and the geometry lesson on the blackboard in an evacuated school, the kerosene lamps in the villages, the basins of water filled from a well to use to wash up before meals on an open porch, the one- or two-seater toilets with a cow ruminating outside brought back buried fragments of my personal history. I was aware of a psychic upheaval, a sort of identity crisis, as when a bomb lays bare the medieval foundations of a house thought to be modern. (pp. 15–16)

In North Vietnam, McCarthy finds the American landscape she thought existed only in nostalgic memory as a
mere "fossil" of an ideal.

Ironically, both Sontag and McCarthy see North Vietnam as achieving its pastoral virtues in response to the
pressures of the American aggression. Their enthusiastic
portrayal of the North Vietnamese situation exactly duplicates the preferred self-concept of Americans that animated such early visions of American involvement in
Vietnam as *The Ugly American* and the portrayal of the
Special Forces, only in reverse. For all her disgust with the
American concept of "will," Sontag admiringly asks,
"who—except the Vietnamese themselves—would have
predicted on February 7, 1965, that this small, poor nation
could hold out against the awesome cruelty and thorough-
ness of American military force?" (p. 85). McCarthy, viewing the war as "a cowboys-and-Indians story, in which the
Indians, for once, are repelling the cowboys," assures the
reader that "no normal person, set down in a North Vietnamese rice field beside an antiaircraft unit manned by
excited boys and girls, could help being thrilled" (pp.
89–90). Identifying with North Vietnam against the
United States, Sontag and McCarthy can enjoy the mythically correct American self-concept of a vital individual
role in a small band contending with an overwhelming
force. Like John Colvin with Deong against the Japanese in
The Ugly American, like Major Arklin with the Meos
against the Chinese communist officers in Moore's *The
Green Berets*, Sontag and McCarthy identify themselves
with pastoral heroes against a machine-like urban empire.

Sontag and McCarthy eulogize the North Vietnamese
achievement of rebirth through forced loss of civilized luxuries. Sontag reports that "people have discovered the positive advantages of being stripped of everything: that one
becomes more generous, less attached to 'things'" (p. 60).
McCarthy draws a landscape in which the Vietnamese, in
response to America's attacks, are achieving the American

ideal of a middle landscape in which country and city flow into each other in Edenic harmony:

But in rural North Vietnam, under the stimulus of the U.S. bombing, a vast metamorphosis . . . is taking place, not as a figure of speech, but literally. Mountains, up to now, have not been moved, but deep caverns in them have been transformed into factories. Universities, schools, hospitals, whole towns have been picked up and transferred from their former sites, dispersed by stealth into the fields; streams have changed their courses. City children have turned into peasants. Nomad tribes—horse people—thanks to irrigation projects, have been settled as farmers and equipped with bicycles. Rice has been made to grow on dry land. (p. 48)

Like Lederer and Burdick in *The Ugly American,* McCarthy sketches a utopian vision in Southeast Asia of the American pastoral memory and dream; here, however, the darkskinned Asian—and vicariously the white urban American intellectual—achieves the vision by opposing American will.

Sontag is even more euphoric in describing the uses to which the Vietnamese put downed American bombers:

Each plane that's shot down is methodically taken apart. The tires are cut up to make the rubber sandals that most people wear. Any component of the engine that's still intact is modified to be reused as part of a truck motor. The body of the plane is dismantled, and the metal is melted down to be made into tools, small machine parts, surgical instruments, wire, spokes for bicycle wheels, combs, ashtrays, and of course the famous numbered rings given as presents to visitors. Every last nut, bolt, and screw from the plane is used. The same holds for anything else the Americans drop. In several hamlets we visited, the bell hanging from a tree which summoned people to meetings or sounded the air-raid alert was the casing of an unexploded bomb. Being shown through the infirmary of a Thai hamlet, we saw that the protective canopy of the operating room, relocated, since the bombing, in a rock grotto, was a flare parachute. . . . To observe in some of its day-to-day functioning a society based on the principle of total use is particularly impressive to someone who comes from a society based on maximal waste. (pp. 65–66)

In *The Ugly American*, Lederer and Burdick portray an American introducing a powdered-milk machine into a Southeast Asian nation to persuade the natives to accept a breed of Texas cattle from which they will be able to use every part in a complexly pastoral economy. This vision reverses the historical American relation to the natural landscape and its native inhabitants. In doing so, it expiates the destruction of the native American's buffalo economy by the white American's machine (the railroad). Sontag similarly evokes this guilty American image of a natural way of life doomed by her own culture's civilized progress. She, however, shows the North Vietnamese "Indians" defeating the destructive machine by naturalizing and domesticating it into the equivalent of a buffalo or cow.

In ambivalent historical memory, the American introduces the machine to subdue nature to civilized progress, but in the process incurs the guilt of killing the natural man; in the dream of *The Ugly American*, promising to be fulfilled in the New Frontier mission of the Green Beret, the American introduces the machine to improve nature for the natural man, thus purifying the national mission of the stains of the past; in the alienated vision of Sontag's *Trip to Hanoi*, the American introduces the machine to destroy the natural man, only to have the latter dismantle it, triumphantly transforming its parts into elements of an improved pastoral setting. But Sontag, and her sympathetic readers, are "natural" Americans helping native villagers against the "ugly" visage of an America revealed to be a transplanted European empire. Johnson's policies ignored the crucial urge that had made Vietnam appear an alluring field for American dreams—the romantic desire of Americans to escape their own machines, their own affluence, their own racism, their own alienation. Now that impulse provided the passion compelling the opposition to the war in Vietnam.

III

The 1968 spring Tet offensive had a devastating psychological impact on American opinion. After three years of reporting bland statistics that indicated progress, the media now filled American consciousness with vivid symbols seemingly supporting the claims of the antiwar movement. Newspapers and magazines widely quoted a statement by an American artillery officer that "It was necessary to destroy the city to save the city." *Life* published pictures that showed an American civilian fighting off attacking Vietnamese within the compound of the U.S. embassy in Vietnam. And television newscasts presented a Saigon police chief firing a pistol into the head of a Viet Cong suspect. Such images did not correspond to the roles that the national myth ascribed to the American, his noble native ally, and their mutual enemy the savage or European aggressor.

Subsequent studies have shown that these media images seriously distorted the events of Tet: the Viet Cong took terrible losses in a failed effort at sparking a popular urban uprising; South Vietnamese troops acquitted themselves well; and the North Vietnamese methodically executed and even buried alive targetted South Vietnamese civilians in the city of Hue.[12] However, Johnson had failed to prepare the media and the nation for the possibility of such an attack, and he subsequently proved unable to explain the meaning of the images apparently overturning the previous months' official optimism.[13] Soon prestigious commentators such as CBS anchorman Walter Cronkite, leading politicians such as Robert Kennedy, and even crucial planners of the war such as presidential aide Harry McPherson would openly or quietly abandon faith in the official policy. In the New Hampshire primary on March 12, a surprising 42 percent of voters would choose peace-candidate Eugene McCarthy over the

President, and Kennedy would enter the race four days later. On March 31 Johnson withdrew, and polls soon registered a dramatic shift to majority disillusionment with the war.

Analysts have properly cautioned that this disillusionment with Johnson's policies and with the initial involvement did not for most Americans include an embrace of the antiwar movement's position that the war was an American crime and the desired result American defeat. Many New Hampshire voters for McCarthy in March would turn in November to George Wallace, who demanded ruthless use of military force to achieve victory. Most Americans expressing disillusionment with the war called it a "mistake" and a "mess," and were unwilling to support a policy of accepting defeat.[14] Yet, as Podhoretz argues, such a negative position of only not wanting to lose reflected the influence of the antiwar movement.[15] Most Americans were not willing to give up their mythic heritage and oppose America as the true Force of Darkness; nevertheless, after Tet they were left without a convincing story of the conflict in Vietnam with which to oppose that passionate vision.

In that context, we can perceive in the response to John Wayne's film *The Green Berets* the desolation Vietnam had brought to the American mythic landscape. Wayne, Hollywood's greatest hero of the Old West and World War II, had written the President in December 1965 asking for cooperation in his planned adaptation of Moore's novel into a major motion picture. Presidential-aide Jack Valenti advised Johnson that the hawkish Wayne "would be saying the things we want said"; after Wayne commissioned an acceptable screenplay retaining only token elements of Moore's book, the Pentagon also fully supported the production. *The Green Berets* appeared in the summer of 1968, just after the series of spring shocks culminating in Robert Kennedy's assassination in early June.

Drawing to theaters laughing, cheering crowds and sign-carrying, bomb-threatening protesters, *The Green Berets* immediately became a focus for the intense passions that had come to divide America.[16] Standing aloof from these passions, the national press ridiculed the film without evaluating either its political stance or its entertainment value. Instead, the reviewers in the mainstream news magazines consistently complained that *The Green Berets* ludicrously imposed the world of the Hollywood western and war film—the American mythic landscape—upon the Vietnam setting. The anonymous reviewer in *Time*, for instance, observed that, "Built on the primitive lines of a standard western, *Berets* even has the South Vietnamese talking like movie Sioux: 'We build many camps, clobber many V.C.'" Writing in *Life*, Richard Schickel dismissed Wayne's confusion of the reality of Vietnam with the illusory world of his previous films:

His reference point is not life but movie tradition—that long gray line of barracks' humor, fighting speeches and small-unit bravery, stained by the catsup bottles of a thousand makeup men—the contemplation of which stirs neither the peasants' hearts nor minds, only such nostalgia as one feels for matinees of childhood.

Joseph Morgenstern opened his review in *Newsweek* by mocking the naïveté of the western fan ("In the Alamo section of *The Green Berets*, when the yellowskins are about to overrun the fort and the air cavalry is nowhere in sight . . . "); he then mimicked the portrayal of Vietnam as the apocalyptic battleground of yet another World War against the Forces of Darkness ("Our boys are fighting to prevent 'Communist domination of the world,' and they are the same boys you've been rooting for since *What Price Glory*").[17]

These criticisms were in themselves fair enough. In the first half of the film Wayne's Green Berets protect peaceful Montagnards from Viet Cong who literally "whoop" like marauding Indians; in the second they aid a South Vietnamese nightclub singer in capturing a North Vietnamese colonel, who like a Nazi commander in occupied France indulges his lusts in the refined setting of his chateau headquarters, guarded by heel-clicking soldiers. The reviewers failed to acknowledge, however, that such depictions of Vietnam had only a short time before been quite prevalent. Like *Deliver Us from Evil, The Ugly American,* Moore's original novel, and not least of all the articles on the Special Forces appearing in these same news magazines, Wayne's film was showing Americans their preferred self-image: a small band of rugged yet pure-hearted individualists, on a frontier landscape, aiding pastoral natives against both wild savages emerging from the anarchic forest and robot-like soldiers extending the oppression of their machine-like society.

Time, Life, and *Newsweek* were massive institutions of the press cautiously reflecting mainstream public opinion while subtly shaping it. Answering respectively to the same editors, reviewers of *The Green Berets,* like the news writers, did not adopt the claim of the antiwar movement that the American policy in Vietnam was immoral. The *Time* reviewer, for instance, merely derided the film's "primer-simple" view of the war that "There's them and there's us." Morgenstern in *Newsweek,* for all his sarcastic suggestiveness, made no direct comment on the war whatsoever, and in *Life* Schickel loftily assured "peaceniks" that as war propaganda the film was "its own worst enemy." The reviewers compensated for this political coyness by their strong ridicule of Wayne's use of the genres of the western and war film. While not provoking readers with challenges to the American position in Vietnam, the magazines placated the antiwar passions of other readers by emphasizing that Vietnam was distorted by Wayne's archaic Hollywood formulas.

These reviews thus both reveal the impact of the antiwar movement's story upon public consciousness, and represent a powerful new recounting of it. Without a convincing assertion by the Johnson administration of an opposite interpretation, and with the vivid evidence of Tet, a *Time* or *Newsweek* conceded the movement's less immediate points. If they did not go so far as to portray Americans as villains, they did portray Americans in a "complex" maelstrom affording no clearly "right" position. In terms of myth, of an intelligible, coherent view of one's relation to the world, such "complexity" draws a people down toward psychological chaos.

Despite the ridicule, Americans packed the theaters in sufficient numbers to make the large-budget film a substantial financial success. Audiences apparently welcomed two hours of escape into a Vietnam that resembled Wayne's earlier westerns and war films. For the larger public less ready or willing to reconceive the psychological ground upon which they stood, *The Green Berets* could be enjoyed as the way Vietnam ought to be, if only someone—the government, the protesters, the press, the South Vietnamese— would let it. Afflicted with doubt, Americans were now regarding the American mythic landscape in terms exceedingly close to nostalgic, self-conscious fantasy. Up and down the levels of the culture, the American frontier myth was, to use Paul Tillich's term for such a phenomenon, being "broken."

IV

Johnson had attempted to fight a terrible, long war without the tangible elements of myth—a vivid villain, an identifiable grail, a convincing explanation of how unfolding events fit the larger mythic pattern. Support for not giving up on the war could now be elicited only by appeals to emotional patriotism in pursuit of complex national interests. Succeeding the discredited Johnson to the presidency, Richard Nixon based his appeal to the "silent majority" on this inversion of Kennedy's foreign policy, which had projected the American mythic self-concept of pragmatic pursuit of visionary goals. Insisting on "peace with honor" and on demonstrating that America had not become a "pitiful, helpless giant," Nixon expanded the war while withdrawing from it, mined Haiphong harbor while negotiating *détente* with the Soviet Union and China, and denounced opponents of the war while ending the draft. Meanwhile, the revelation in February 1970 of the American massacre of the women, old men, and children of My Lai, followed by a rush of repressed atrocity stories from reporters and veterans, seemed to confirm the darkest accusations of the antiwar movement. Conservatives and liberals alike, though in opposite regards, would perceive Nixon's maneuvers, guided by his expert in *Realpolitik* Henry Kissinger, as the cynical calculations of a Metternich. Kissinger himself referred to the United States as a "great power," an unsettling self-concept for a people who had regarded themselves as superior to the self-interested and amoral balance-of-power calculations of European states. Although the majority of Americans would support Nixon against the apparent alternative of apology and naïveté offered in 1972 by George McGovern, he presided over a barren mythic landscape.

Few novels were published about Vietnam during these years, and those that were went unnoticed. Documentary films such as Emile de Antonio's *In the Year of the Pig* (1968) and Peter Davis' *Hearts and Minds* (1974), which won the Academy Award, reinforced the imagery and themes presented by Mailer, Sontag, McCarthy, and—after My Lai—the media. The only narrative response to Vietnam during this period to actually form a genre was not set in Vietnam at all, but rather in the primary landscape of American myth. Hollywood, showing no desire to follow up the controversy that accompanied the financial success of *The Green Berets*, found the Old West a safer setting in which to appeal to the passions of the youth audience. The Vietnam western or antiwestern, epitomized by Ralph Nelson's *Soldier Blue* (1970) and Arthur Penn's *Little Big Man* (1971), portrayed the settling of the frontier as a succession of My Lai's. In *Little Big Man*, the orphaned antihero (Dustin Hoffman) attempts to fill a number of roles in the mythic scheme of the Old West—gunfighter, homesteader, traveling medicine man, cavalry scout—but can find true identity and community only with the Cheyenne Indians. With them, he is forced to witness the perversion and destruction of the earth by the invading white man and his unnatural civilization. The Vietnam western was a short-lived genre; antimyth has no substance beyond the myth it is consuming. When it was gone, the classic western, at least the central form in which the Indian plays the role of the Other, was gone with it.

Slightly over a decade earlier, John F. Kennedy had energized Americans with his vision of their heroic possibilities on a New Frontier. He had celebrated the American mythic landscape in a poetic image that called for imaginatively transforming the idea bound up in America's past geographical drive West into a many-leveled pursuit of national adventure and mission. As a metaphor, the New Frontier drew its power to direct a people with conflicting desires as much from its abstractness as from its concreteness. The Green Beret in Southeast Asia was only one of the specific images in which Kennedy projected his vision of the contemporary American reinvigorating the American errand, but a decade after his death Vietnam seemed to have cut Americans off from both their past and future frontiers. Vietnam was now a landscape in the American consciousness that would have to be journeyed through many times over, self-consciously experienced through narrative art as myth and symbol, if Americans were to begin to understand what had happened to their story, and to their idea of themselves.

PART II
The Journey Back

In *Apocalypse Now,* a renegade Green Beret has pursued the mythic American ideal only to become an ugly image of imperialistic rapacity and savage self-indulgence. (Photograph courtesy of Museum of Modern Art. Photograph courtesy Zoetrope Studios. All rights reserved.)

CHAPTER FOUR

Good Sons
The Soldiers' Antimyth

AFTER THE COLLAPSE of South Vietnam in the spring of 1975, President Gerald Ford and Secretary of State Henry Kissinger called on Americans to refrain from recriminations and put Vietnam behind them. The country had passed through a decade of turbulence focusing on the war, culminating in the forced removal of a president as a result of illegal conduct that began as a response to opposition to that war. Now Americans watched televised images of hastily abandoned American technology and of Vietnamese clutching at departing American helicopters. Turning from these final visions of American failure in Vietnam, they searched not for a scapegoat but rather for a figure who would somehow lead them back to the mythic landscape they inhabited before Vietnam. Conservative Republicans, led by Ronald Reagan, mounted a challenge against Ford in the 1976 primaries that focused on Kissinger's foreign policy of *détente*, which they saw as a betrayal of America's moral mission and destined greatness. Reagan's challenge barely failed, but Democrat Jimmy Carter subsequently defeated Ford by campaigning as a pastoral outsider from Plains, Georgia. He promised to save America from a corrupt Washington and an amoral foreign policy and return it to the natural goodness of its people.

Early in his administration Carter lectured Americans on their "inordinate fear of communism," and made the protection of human rights around the world the symbolic center of American foreign policy. But Carter's confession of a former American paranoia, a cleansing *mea culpa* with which he sought to reassert America as a moral force in the world, was not a stance from which Americans could coherently respond to the Iranian revolution and the Soviet invasion of Afghanistan. In the second half of his term Carter quickly reverted to Cold War rhetoric. Americans wanted to feel that they were good, but the majority also wanted to see that goodness confirmed by power. During Carter's years in office America seemed as dismally lacking in the signs of grace as it had during Vietnam itself. As Americans tried to forget Vietnam, they were finding that, like the world itself, the questions posed by their failure would not go away.

When in April 1979 an estimated 70 million television viewers watched that year's Academy Awards ceremony, years of virtual collective amnesia on the war came to their symbolic end. On the stage, John Wayne presented the award for Best Picture to *The Deer Hunter*, while former antiwar activist Jane Fonda accepted the award for Best Actress in *Coming Home*. In a major story entitled "Vietnam Comes Home," Lance Morrow speculated in *Time* that the country was perhaps ready to contemplate the lessons of the war. In attempting to begin such meditation, the *Time* article and similar features in the press usually went beyond discussion of the two films, both of which centered on a young man's traumatized return from Vietnam, to discussion of veterans' recent memoirs and novels.[1]

Two years later, with the return of the hostages from Iran and the inauguration of President Ronald Reagan, Americans sought to restore to themselves their sense of innocence and power; they soon found that they were not going to be able to honor themselves without facing those who had participated in America's failed war. The Vietnam veterans, dismayed by the emotional welcoming of the returned hostages, were at last voicing their pain at years of national rejection. Flesh-and-blood ghosts of abandoned dreams, they had long remained silent but now insisted upon displaying their scars and mutilations, most especially their psychological ones. In a *Time* cover story in July lamenting the treatment given to veterans, Morrow quoted a Yale psychiatrist's assertion that "America is trying to confront Viet Nam through its veterans."[2] Congress, while going along with virtually all of President Reagan's budget cuts, was nevertheless moving to increase veterans' benefits, and plans were underway for a Vietnam memorial in Washington. With *Time* and other publications drawing renewed attention to veterans' memoirs and novels, bookstores throughout the country began setting up prominent displays of Vietnam literature, which now made up a large body of work.

Both veterans and America at large had journeyed from the buoyant optimism of Kennedy's 1960 inaugural through twenty years of revolt, division, fragmentation, and subsequent depression. Yet, however great the moral passion of "hawks and doves," it was the veteran who had most undeniably paid a price for answering Kennedy's call to "ask what you can do for your country." Unlike Wayne and the cheering audiences of *The Green Berets*, he had found in Vietnam a landscape that refused to conform to those of westerns or World War II movies. Unlike Susan Sontag, Mary McCarthy, and their readers in the antiwar movement, he had met the Vietnamese Other as both victim and tormentor. And while in the "Me Decade" of the 1970s others could pursue "self-fulfillment" to distract themselves from the "malaise" Carter's chief pollster found in the country, the Vietnam veteran had languished in a personal despondency inextricably bound up in the national one. Distinguishing the lingering problem from the familiar "combat fatigue" of World War II, psychiatrists labeled the symptoms "post-traumatic stress disorder."

The veterans' literary memoirs and realistic novels have thus provided routes by which to begin retaking the national journey through Vietnam. As the war took on the

features of a humiliating and degrading reflection of ourselves, most Americans were pleased to keep it remote and
unreal, a television show happening to someone else. Once
it was over, the overwhelming desire was to deny it as a
part of American history. But the veterans, because the
war is so tangibly a part of their personal history and thus
so clearly for them a part of their nation's history, have not
been able to forget the distance they traveled, the identity
they lost, or the expectations with which they had set out.
Possessing the credibility of actual experience, their works
have begun remythologizing Vietnam as a territory different in configuration from the simple hawk-dove contrasts
depicted earlier. That landscape is an awful inversion of
American assumptions and values—a nightmare version
of the landscapes of previous American myth.

The more developed veterans' literary accounts connect
the authors' actual experiences to the American myth they
had previously assimilated from popular culture. The
works most praised by reviewers, critics, and feature writers as convincing, insightful depictions of the American
soldier's experience in Vietnam are three memoirs—Ron
Kovic's *Born on the Fourth of July* (1976), Philip Caputo's *A
Rumor of War* (1977), and Tim O'Brien's *If I Die in a Combat
Zone* (1979)—and two novels—William Turner Huggett's
Body Count (1973) and James Webb's *Fields of Fire* (1978).
Whether memoir or realistic novel, each of these works
represents a veteran's actual experience in Vietnam pat-
terned into a narrative by his subsequent recollection and
interpretation of that experience. While these five authors
came to Vietnam from varied backgrounds and served in
different phases of the war, they tell a remarkably similar
story. Underlying their separate works is a common allegory, an ironic antimyth in which an archetypal warrior-
representative of the culture embarks on a quest that dissolves into an utter chaos of dark revelation. In discovering the elements of that quest, we can perceive on an
intense personal level the trauma of Vietnam for American

myth, for the relation of the American self to its past and future history.

I

Early in these memoirs and novels, we find the protagonist unhappily contrasting his present world to that of the American past. Whether his world is rural, urban, or suburban, the youth finds it uncomfortably peaceful and constraining, not affording him the heroic errand in which the ideal American character finds its definition. The most immediate target of his scorn is his father, who appears as a false parent. In *Fields of Fire*, whose author James Webb served as a platoon and company commander while becoming one of the most decorated Marines of the war, this pattern of a perceived conflict between contemporary American society and traditional American mission is given its most obvious form. Marine Lieutenant Robert E. Lee Hodges, Jr. has grown up on a Kentucky farm where his mother, in order to avoid the jealous ire of her husband, thinks it wise not to speak of her actual father, slain in France in World War II. With his true father's memory not allowed in his false father's house, Hodges finds himself drawn to the remnants of his father's heroic military service stored in a trunk in the back of the barn. These talismans gain a further aura from stories his grandmother tells him of his family's long tradition of service in American wars.[3]

Less overtly romantic and symbolic, other works nevertheless share in more subtle terms this motif of revolt against the immediate father (contemporary society) in order to faithfully return to the mission of the true father (the American mythic ideal). In *Body Count* William Turner Huggett, who like Webb served in Vietnam as an infantry combat officer with the Marines, has his protagonist, Chris Hawkins, decide to give up his deferment as a graduate student in psychology at Princeton to enlist as a lieutenant in the Marine Corps. In doing so he defies his father, a member of the corporate establishment working with government officials in Washington. Throughout the novel Hawkins bitterly recalls his father's insistence that he stay in school to train for a career and at the very least not join "animals" like the Marines.[4] Yet another Marine lieutenant, Philip Caputo in his memoir *A Rumor of War*, joins the Corps as "an act of rebellion" against his parents, who plan for him "a respectable job after school, marrying a respectable girl, and then settling down in a respectable suburb."[5] Sometimes the protagonists are not so openly hostile to their fathers, but merely sorry for them. In his memoir *Born on the Fourth of July*, Ron Kovic realizes that he "didn't want to be like my Dad, coming home from the A&P every night." Kovic dreads the prospect of laborious, constraining domesticity wearing him down as it has his father, "a strong man, a good man, but it made him so tired, it took all the energy out of him."[6] Kovic, who would subsequently be paralyzed from the waist down in Vietnam, joins the Marines to escape this fate and instead fulfill his desire "to be a hero" (p. 63).

Revolting against the contemporary world offered by their fathers, these protagonists go to Vietnam to emulate the "true" fathers of their mythic heritage, the nearest of whom is the soldier of World War II, the violent but pure-hearted American GI who saved the world from the brutal imperialism of Japan and Germany. The protagonists do not acknowledge that the youthful heroes of World War II are the parents who have shaped the postwar American society; the two identities apparently seem too separate for the protagonists to easily contemplate that the latter could have followed the former. Unhappily residing in the peaceful and prosperous American landscape for which their fathers had fought, the protagonists long to escape into the global frontiers of challenge and mission portrayed in films of the war. Caputo, Kovic, and Webb all portray their pre-Vietnam protagonists' fascination with John Wayne's *Sands of Iwo Jima* (1949), a film that is perhaps perfect for them because Wayne's Sergeant Stryker dies as soon as he has ensured the triumph of American mission, and thus one need not imagine him as domesticated in American society after the war.[7] Only Tim O'Brien, who served as an enlisted man in the Army, refers in his memoir *If I Die in a Combat Zone* to his father's participation in World War II. When he portrays his father as a soldier of that war, however, he sees an impersonal, godlike figure ("My father came from leaden ships of sea, from the Pacific theater") or a mythic group persona ("We bought dented relics of our fathers' history, rusted canteens and olive-scented, scarred helmet liners"),[8] while the father he knows in his present world is a Little League baseball manager far removed from the main drama of life: "My father coached us, and he is still coaching, still able to tick off the starting line-up of the great Brooklyn Dodgers teams of the 1950's" (p. 21).

Many of the protagonists are portrayed in their youth seeking communion with their mythic fathers through ritualistic play. In relatively open land on the edges of their domestic environment, they imagine themselves in the landscapes where their true fathers performed heroic deeds. O'Brien recalls how, after acquiring the sacred relics of Army surplus, "then we were our fathers, taking on the Japs and Krauts along the shores of Lake Okebena, on the flat fairways of the golf course" (pp. 20–21). Kovic remembers childhood moments of glory in neighborhood woods: "We set ambushes, then led gallant attacks, storming over the top, bayonetting and shooting anyone who got in our way. Then we'd walk out of the woods like the heroes we knew we would become when we were men" (p. 55). Kovic's game places him in the World Wars, while the wooded setting is a remnant of the original American wilderness suggesting the timeless significance of American war as frontier: a savage landscape into which the civilized youth flees domestic order before returning as the savior of that order.

The American frontier landscape is a ghostly presence in the veterans' work, a mythic past by which the protagonists measure their present pitiful world. O'Brien is keenly aware that the "whole desolate prairie" on which he lives is mirrored by the town ("flat, tepid, small, strangled by algae, shut in by middleclass houses, lassoed by a ring of doctors, lawyers, CPA's, dentists, drugstore owners, and proprietors of department stores" [p. 23]). This dubious progress achieved by the European immigrants who took "the plains from the Sioux" overlays a historical landscape full of mythic wonder:

It had been Indian land. Ninety miles from Sioux City, sixty miles from Sioux Falls, eighty miles from Cherokee, forty miles from Spirit Lake and the site of a celebrated massacre. To the north was Pipestone and the annual Hiawatha Pageant. To the west was Luverne and Indian burial mounds. (p. 21)

For O'Brien, who would go to Vietnam despite his private opposition to the war, the landscape originally belonging to the Indians is troubling but deeply haunting. With less ambiguity, the protagonist of Webb's *Fields of Fire* finds as a youth in the Kentucky mountains a "religion" in the tangible presence of the mythic past: "He could cross a field and come up with a handful of arrowheads. He would go to bed and know he slept above Shawnee bones" (p. 33).

Of these authors, Caputo most probingly portrays the psychological conflict which the memory of the mythic American frontier creates in the context of contemporary society. Explaining what prompted him to enlist in Marine ROTC in 1960, he says he made the decision "partly because I got swept up in the patriotic tide of the Kennedy era but mostly because I was sick of the safe, suburban existence I had known most of my life" (p. 4). The two reasons actually express a single impulse, a desire to escape an enervating society for a New Frontier where the protagonist will enter the lost mythic landscape. Caputo vividly recalls his 1950s boyhood in a suburban town which "rose from the prairies" between Chicago and Illinois farmland, where he hated "the dullness of it, the summer barbecues eaten to the lulling drone of power mowers" (pp. 4–5).

Describing nearby farm and pasture areas where he hunted on weekends, Caputo portrays a contemporary American landscape in which the machines of society move with the coming winter to eradicate nature:

I remember the fields as they were in the late fall: the corn stubble brown against the snow, dead husks rasping dryly in the wind; abandoned farm houses waiting for the bulldozers that would tear them down to clear space for a new subdivision; and off on the horizon, a few stripped sycamores silhouetted against a bleak November sky.

Here Caputo appears a descendant of Leatherstocking, a contemporary hunter who in his relation to the land and society suggests the loss of all possibility of the frontier virtues, for as a 1950s youth he is from the beginning trapped in a dilemma as pitiful as Cooper's hunter was as an arrested poacher in his old age in *The Prairie* (1827):

I can still see myself roaming around out there, scaring rabbits from the brambles, the tract houses a few miles behind me, the vast, vacant prairies in front, a restless boy caught between suburban boredom and rural desolation.

The youthful protagonist occasionally escapes from this seeming dead-end of American progress into what remains of original American nature: "The only thing I really liked about my boyhood surroundings were the Cook and DuPage County forest preserves, a belt of virgin woodland through which flowed a muddy stream called Salt Creek." Here he finds fish, small game, and even an occasional deer, but "most of all a hint of the wild past, when moccasined feet trod the forest paths and fur trappers cruised the rivers in bark canoes." Discovering "flint arrowheads in the muddy creek bank," Caputo imaginatively leaves the suburban landscape of his father for the frontier landscape of his cultural fathers: "Looking at them, I would dream of that savage, heroic time and wish I had lived then, before America became a land of salesmen and shopping centers" (p. 5).

The youthful President Kennedy emerges early in the narratives of Caputo, Kovic, and Huggett as a figure affirming that the protagonists should reject their present society for the frontier past properly the future of America as well. Their protagonists hear Kennedy's rhetoric as daring them to go forth from the safe, secure, comfortable world provided by their fathers. They want to follow the example of Kennedy himself, who has rejected the elderly complacency of Eisenhower and returned to the frontier virtues of the activist presidents. Huggett's protagonist Hawkins, depressed by his father's espousing of safe, corporate careerism, draws from his desk at Princeton a passage he keeps because it tells "his story." The maxim is a quote he heard in a speech made by Kennedy beginning, "The credit belongs to the man who is actually in the arena, whose face is marred by dust and sweat and blood" (p. 31). Kovic, after earlier recounting the deep sense of personal loss he felt at Kennedy's assassination, portrays his pride when enlisting that now "we could serve our country like the young president had asked us to do" (p. 74). Early in the veterans' narratives, Vietnam often appears to be the promised New Frontier into which the youth may flee his contemporary society and return to his mythic fathers' pursuit of America's mission.

II

The protagonists of the veterans' novels and literary memoirs go to Vietnam with varying expectations. Caputo and Kovic, both of whom enlisted when America still had only "advisers" in Vietnam, go to Southeast Asia with the early combat units. They confidently anticipate the real-life equivalent of their boyhood journeys into the neighboring woods or forest preserves: a brief, bloody, and heroic reenactment of the mythic history they know from westerns and war films. By contrast, O'Brien, Huggett, and Webb depict protagonists entering the military when the war is being openly opposed by many at home. O'Brien, Hawkins, and Hodges nevertheless go because they share with Caputo and Kovic the felt cultural imperative to answer the call to war in order to live in the American mythic landscape. In *Fields of Fire* Webb characterizes Hodges as going because the "will to face certain loss, unknown dangers, unpredictable fates" (p. 33) has been passed down to him through his heroic American lineage. In Huggett's *Body Count* Hawkins goes to Vietnam admitting to himself that he does not know if the war is just, but phrasing his desire for the tough challenge celebrated by Kennedy as a need to see the war for himself. And O'Brien in *If I Die in a Combat Zone*, convinced that the war is "wrongly conceived and poorly justified" (p. 26), accepts orders to Vietnam because of "family, the home town, friends, history, tradition, fear, confusion, exile: I could not run" (p. 73).

Each of these protagonists, then, goes to Vietnam to enter the landscape of American myth. Because these protagonists vary in background and personality as well as in the circumstances and eras of their Vietnam service, the portrayals of the war vary in significant respects. In all of them, however, Vietnam resonates against the American mythic landscape carried in the consciousness of the protagonists.

In *A Rumor of War, Born on the Fourth of July*, and *If I Die in a Combat Zone*, Vietnam completely inverts the landscapes that American heroes stride across in stories of the American West and World War II, for the special conditions of the war do not allow the protagonists to identify themselves with the ideals of American myth. The American military's dual strategy of attrition (the repeated taking and abandoning of the same territory in pursuit of a high enemy "body count") and pacification (involving intrusion into villages for enemy caches of documents and supplies)[9] is shown placing the American soldier in a setting at once hauntingly familiar and nightmarishly unacceptable. All three books include episodes in which the protagonists uneasily sense that they themselves are the enemy of the population they have ostensibly come to save, successors not to their own mythic forebears but rather to the Europeans against whom those forebears defined themselves.

Caputo, entering the huts of a village to rummage through the belongings of its inhabitants, feels like "one of those bullying Redcoats who use to barge into American homes during our Revolution" (p. 83). Facing the impassive stare of a young mother nursing her baby, he tries to put on the chivalrous character of the American hero: "I smiled stupidly and made a great show of tidying up the mess before we left. See, lady, we're not like the French" (p. 84). Kovic also portrays his efforts in Vietnam to avoid hating the Vietnamese and his desire to make them understand that he is there as a savior. Later, he recounts the traumatic horror of being part of an accidental atrocity that left old men and children dead and mutilated (pp. 207–9). O'Brien, seeking to find some cultural framework or model to guide him, concludes that Hemingway is an inadequate guide for the American soldier in Vietnam because the heroes of his stories of the Great War struggle with mere futility, rather than with a dilemma analogous to that of the "conscripted Nazi" (p. 97).

The American mythic landscape is a place fixed between savagery and civilization, a middle landscape where the hero sheds the unnecessary refinements of the latter without entering into the darkness of the former. Ever-receding, this frontier gains its validation as a setting for the mythic hero because his killing makes way for the progress of the civilization advancing behind him. In the memoirs of the Vietnam War, however, the American hero has somehow entered a nightmarish wilderness where he is allowed no linear direction nor clear spreading of civilization, where neither his inner restraints nor the external ones of his civilization are operating. For Kovic, this aspect of Vietnam asserts itself in his accidental shooting of one of his fellow soldiers:

He had panicked with the rest of them that night and murdered his first man, but it wasn't the enemy, it wasn't the one they had all been taught and trained to kill, it wasn't the silhouette at the rifle range he had pumped holes in from five hundred yards, or the German soldiers with plastic machine guns in Sally's Woods. He'd never figured it would ever happen this way. It never did in the movies. There were always the good guys and the bad guys, the cowboys and the Indians. There was always the enemy and the good guys and each of them killed the other. (pp. 194–95)

The Vietnam of *Born on the Fourth of July* inverts the forest of Cooper's *The Deerslayer* (1841), in which the prototypical American hero achieves manhood by shooting an Indian who with his dying breath renames the young title character Hawkeye. Kovic kills in the Vietnam woods only to lose his youthful illusions of personal power and righteousness.

In *If I Die in a Combat Zone* O'Brien depicts a Vietnam where one constantly moves in circles, with no visible enemy in front and surrounded by a hostile population. The protagonist trods upon a land that is sown with mines from which death may leap at any moment, literally in spring-loaded "Bouncing Betties." O'Brien's protagonist finds himself in this frontier unable to enter into or to avoid the identity his culture has taken on. Finding a group of boys herding cows in a free-fire zone, O'Brien's fellow soldiers fire at them, killing one of the cows. O'Brien says that he "did not shoot, but I did endure, without protest, except to ask the man in front why he was shooting and smiling" (p. 139). Earlier in the text O'Brien has commented that in the Vietnam bush each soldier finds the American "man in front" his personal representative of civilization; in this later passage the concept of American civilization is thus completely inverted, and O'Brien's own restraint does not remove him from complicity.

In this theme Caputo is again the most suggestive of the memoirists. Describing an operation south of Danang, Caputo says that the desolate area was "true Indian country, a region of fallow fields, sun-seared hills, and abandoned villages lying near a pale-green height called Charlie Ridge" (p. 104). But this "Indian country" appears an inversion of the wilderness to which the American frontiersman adapts in order to subdue. Earlier in the book Caputo has recounted his training in the counterinsurgency doctrine to which Kennedy had given "his imprimatur by sending the first Special Forces detachments to Vietnam, glamorous figures themselves in their green berets and paratrooper boots" (p. 16). Now he ruefully recalls how the manuals in those guerrilla-warfare courses had "cheerfully stated that the modern, civilized soldier should not be afraid of the jungle: 'The jungle can be your friend as well as your enemy.'" Showing himself gazing down from a helicopter, Caputo then juxtaposes this ideal of the American's relation to nature with his own response to Vietnam: "Looking at the green immensity below, I could only conclude that those manuals had been written by men whose idea of a jungle was the Everglades National Park" (p. 105). The reference to the national park turns the irony doubly back upon Caputo, who once dreamed in forest preserves of the "savage, heroic time" of the American frontier.

In the wilderness the contemporary American finds himself swallowed up and left without direction. Repeatedly in *A Rumor of War* Caputo describes this perception of the Vietnamese terrain as an overwhelming wilderness friendly only to the enemy. In one passage, he describes the terrain below his helicopter in images that could be coming from Filson's Boone standing upon an Allegheny peak: "An unbroken mass of green stretched westward, one ridgeline and mountain range after another, some more than a mile high and covered with forests that looked solid enough to walk on. It had no end. It just went on to the horizon" (p. 77). But he then proceeds to identify this natural westward expanse as manifesting, not a great destiny, but rather a ridiculous hubris. Realizing that "the whole North Vietnamese Army could have concealed itself in that jungle-sea, and we were going to look for a battalion," he "half expected those great mountains to shake with contemptuous laughter at our pretense" (pp. 77–78). Caputo's more specific target in this passage is the strategic folly of General Westmoreland's tactics of Search and Destroy; the larger target is America's belief in a destiny of ever adapting to and subduing the frontiers "stretched westward."

Indeed, throughout his descriptions of combat he emphasizes the Vietnam "bush" as a nature inherently hostile to the American character. He says that "It was the land that resisted us, the land, the jungle, and the sun" (p. 82); he wonders how "this sun could be the same one now shining gently in the cool midwestern spring back home" (p. 84); ambushed by an invisible enemy, he feels that "It was as if the trees were shooting at us" (p. 86). He sees "nothing friendly about the Vietnamese bush; it was one of the last of the dark regions on earth, and only the very brave or very dull—the two often went together—could look at it without feeling fear" (p. 105).

Having once hated the "drone of the power mowers" as the sound of the domesticated landscape of his suburban society, now he identifies gratefully with technology. After helicopters drop them off, he and his fellows feel abandoned: "Being Americans, we were comfortable with machines, but with the aircraft gone we were struck by the utter strangeness of this rank and rotted wilderness" (p. 79). At the time he articulated this foreboding in imagery of the American frontier ("I thought of that old line from the westerns: 'It's too quiet'"), but in his recollection as narrator he perceives the Americans' use of blind fire-power against the surrounding nature before moving into it to have been a "comforting racket" made in response to primordial human fears of wilderness, "as though rockets and machine guns were merely technological equivalents of the gourds and rattles natives use to chase away evil spirits" (p. 81). In the Vietnamese bush Caputo portrays an American protagonist returning to the frontier to find nature not the reinvigorating and renewing friend of Leatherstocking and the Green Beret, but rather the terrible haunt of devils once envisioned by the first Puritan settlers.

As the Puritans remaining in England had predicted would be the fate of those going to America, and as Conrad had claimed in *Heart of Darkness* (1899) would be the fate of a European idealist left alone in the African jungle, Caputo shows external wilderness calling forth the universal savage nature within man. He is careful to debunk the "frontier-heritage theory," widely held in the antiwar movement, that the American soldier "was inherently violent and needed only the excuse of war to vent his homicidal instincts" (p. xviii); after all, he points out, "twenty years of terrorism and fratricide had obliterated most reference points from the country's moral map long before we arrived" (p. xviii). He says that "the marines in our brigade were not innately cruel" (p. xviii), but that they responded to the conditions of the place they were in and the war they were fighting, developing the same ruthlessness practiced by both the communist and Saigon forces. Rather than a unique American capacity for evil, Caputo sees instead the lesson of American atrocities to be the utter lack of American uniqueness. In "the Indochina bush" the American soldier had returned further than the American frontier to "an ethical as well as a geographical wilderness" that is an equivalent to the "dawn of creation" (p. xx). Having escaped legal conviction for the murder of two civilians in

Vietnam, Caputo makes in his narrative the moral defense that he first outlines in his prologue: "Out there, lacking restraints, sanctioned to kill, confronted by a hostile country and a relentless enemy, we sank into a brutish state" (p. xx). Up until the main clause, this is of course a description of the frontier situation of the western hero and Green Beret. Caputo speculates that "Americans reacted with such horror to the disclosures of U.S. atrocities while ignoring those of the other side" because "the American soldier was a reflection of themselves" (p. xx). He himself leaves Vietnam rejecting forever the unique self-image represented by his ideal American "father": "I would never again allow myself to fall under the charms and spells of political witch doctors like John F. Kennedy" (p. 315).

Webb's *Fields of Fire* and Huggett's *Body Count* differ from the memoirs of Kovic, Caputo, and O'Brien in significant respects. Their protagonists Hodges and Hawkins restrain themselves from participating in atrocities yet remain pragmatically untroubled by the savage actions of their fellow soldiers. In both *Fields of Fire* and *Body Count* the protagonists, having willingly sought the challenge of war, thus demonstrate the classic character of the American hero, as originally defined by Cooper's Leatherstocking and embodied in Kennedy's Green Beret. Contemporary American society, however, proves unable to validate the heroic actions of Hodges and Hawkins, causing the achievements of both protagonists to lie suspended in an unfulfilled plot.

Webb's Hodges, for instance, swiftly establishes his contempt for regulation haircuts and appearance, while at the same time showing his skeptical men that he can accurately call in artillery (pp. 95–96). A natural warrior (he is interested in military service only in time of war), Hodges possesses civilized calculation combined with savage resourcefulness. Hodges' savage vitality is symbolized by the intuitive bond the new lieutenant quickly achieves with a violent proletarian sergeant called Snake. Snake, for all his viciousness, embodies a visceral purity that Webb clearly feels is necessary to a vital national character. Killed while trying to save a wounded Harvard dropout who has turned him in for murder of Vietnamese civilians, Snake is posthumously recommended by his commander for the Congressional Medal of Honor; the commander retracts the recommendation when he learns that Snake is also the man accused of the atrocity (p. 381). Hodges, also killed in the battle, and Snake both sacrifice themselves in the service of a society that has abandoned them. Dying for a society that cannot rid itself of its hypocritical self-righteousness in the face of moral ambiguity, Snake and Hodges embody for Webb a lost capacity of the American society to appreciate the character upon which its civilization has been built.

Huggett's *Body Count* shares a number of basic elements with *Fields of Fire*. The protagonist Hawkins also enters the Vietnam bush as a new lieutenant who must overcome the resistance of a "lifer" sergeant and the skepticism of his men. And, like Hodges, he does so by a savage instinct for primitive warfare combined with a civilized concern for the good of his men. Huggett, less mystical than Webb in his characterization of his protagonist, focuses in careful psychological detail on Hawkins' gradual growth into the position of company commander. Making *Body Count* more than a standard World War II story of growth into the "job," Huggett patterns a story of racial conflict and assimilation in which the simultaneous renewal and progress of American frontier landscapes is accomplished in Vietnam only to be unaccountably cut off from a larger pattern by a confused national strategy.

When Hawkins is at first sent into the Vietnamese bush to command a platoon, he is as yet too innocent of the savage conditions to establish his authority, a weakness represented by his objections to his sergeant's spreading of germs by passing around pickles with his hand, his mistake in setting up a perimeter position by the "book," and his disgust with his men for taking enemy souvenirs. But Hawkins is befriended by a full-blooded Indian with an inherited rapport with savage landscapes ("The jungle growth seemed to part and flow around him" [p. 47]). Like Snake, "Chief" is a primitive who recognizes in the protagonist "that unique ability for combat" (p. 67). He cautiously begins counseling Hawkins in the ways of the Vietnam wilderness, and after Hawkins kills his first "gook" the Indian ritualistically adorns his white, Princeton-educated friend with a trophy Hawkins is by then unabashedly ready to accept:

His eyes followed Chief as he turned and kicked over the dead sapper. Casually, but as if in a ritual, Chief stooped and smeared the belt in the blood on the gook's chest. Slowly straightening, he held it high over his head until it was dry.
  "Now, sir."
  Hawkins took it and snapped it on. The buckle glistened in the sun. He looked down once more, then back to the grinning men, and something passed between them.
  Then the Chief gave a silent nod and they snapped to attention.
  Their hands went up in unison. They saluted. (pp. 305–6)

Hawkins' triumph in combat, a triumph over both the savage enemy and the effeteness of his own corporate and academic background, is celebrated by his Indian friend as a regenerating return to the strife of primitive nature, which in the common salute of the rest of the men is identified with love of America.

Eventually triumphing over the career sergeant and captain to become himself the battle-tested company commander, Hawkins must continue the war while wrestling with racial division among blacks and whites. This conflict, toward which Hawkins shows egalitarian views in contrast to the racism of his former commander, is most pointed for him in the figure of a bitter young black soldier named Carlysle. In the climactic battle that concludes the novel, Hawkins savagely leads his men to a triumphant but bloody capturing of an important hill in the A Shau Valley. In the battle Hawkins fulfills his return to savage strength, leaping into an NVA foxhole, ramming a shotgun into an enemy's mouth, and feeling the enemy's brain matter splatter into his beard. After the battle, in striking contrast to his original squeamishness, he takes clear pride in presenting himself to two reporters as a wild man, blowing his nose with his hand while propping his shotgun beside him. Yet he also shows himself the wise liberal. He recommends Carlysle for a Silver Star in an egalitarian recognition of black valor (p. 444).

In these concluding pages, Hawkins is assured by his superiors of the importance of his triumph and of the medals he will receive. He has achieved the regeneration through violence at the basis of the frontier myth. At the same time he has, in a paradox brought forward from Cooper's and other frontier-romance writers' use of noble and evil Indian tribes,[10] won a measure of harmony with a noble racial Other by joining with him against another dark enemy representing the savage Other. Yet this fulfillment of the continuing march of an American frontier marked by a destruction and assimilation of darker races is ominously confused, for on the final pages of the novel Hawkins receives orders to haul down the American flag in deference to Vietnamese sovereignty and to withdraw from the hill in accordance with the strategy of attrition. *Body Count* ends with Hawkins' status as American hero an ironic identity. As the major who has brought these orders gives him a final leavetaking, he remarks to Hawkins, " 'Here comes the chopper. You explain—the men'll understand.' He bent against the wind, starting to run, then flung back, 'And congratulations again, Hero' " (p. 445). In Huggett's novel, as in the works of Webb, Kovic, O'Brien, and Caputo, Vietnam finally mirrors the American frontier in a strange and impossible configuration.

III

In the two most complex of the veterans' realistic accounts, Robert Roth's *Sand in the Wind* (1973) and John M. Del Vecchio's *The 13th Valley* (1982), we find the common tale underlying the memoirs and novels elevated into overt use of myth and symbol. Even in the realistic accounts of veterans the search for the meaning of Vietnam demands that American consciousness reexplore the experience in the same psycho-symbolic dimension in which it originally—if unconsciously—went there.

Sand in the Wind was little noticed when it was published. The author served as a Marine rifleman in Vietnam, and *Sand in the Wind* shares many of the particulars as well as the central preoccupations of other veterans' memoirs and novels. With its various characters of diverse social and regional background, its many episodes of harsh realism, and its exhaustive detail, it both resembles and surpasses *Fields of Fire* and *Body Count* as a naturalistic war novel. In its thematic development, however, it is considerably closer to *A Rumor of War, Born on the Fourth of July*, and *If I Die in a Combat Zone*, sharing the ambivalence of those works concerning the moral position of the American soldier. But *Sand in the Wind* is much richer and more complex than any of these works in its inventive elevation of realistic detail and personal experience into mythic symbol and allegorical journey.

Roth clearly perceives that the war was as disastrous an event in American mythic history as it was in the psyche of the combatant. He also sees that, since the combatant's psyche carried that mythic history whole to Vietnam, his inner psychological travail can be projected outward in the form of symbolic setting and mythic event. Roth's technique, not always fully controlled or realized but never less than provocative, is to develop the fragmentation, tension, and circularity of the Vietnam experience toward episodes evoking the nightmares of the classic American romances. Roth thus presents a faithful representation of the actual horror of the Vietnam experience while laying over it the mythic landscape of American culture. He gives us a landscape of war as credibly rendered as Dos Passos' World War I in *Three Soldiers* or Mailer's World War II in *The Naked and the Dead*, but one that has a tendency to resolve itself into the dreamlike terrain of Hawthorne, Poe, and Melville.

Set during the height of the war from the summer of 1967 through the 1968 Tet offensive, *Sand in the Wind* revolves for the most part around the experiences of two Marines serving in the same regiment in the northern part of South Vietnam called I Corps by the American military. In their psychological motivations these two characters symbolize the two halves of the American frontier impulse, and together their stories present Vietnam as a strange landscape where American history, having pushed into a truly alien terrain, becomes dark romance.

Chalice, quickly baptized "Professor" by his fellow soldiers in Vietnam, is an English major and graduate of Duke University serving as an enlisted man. As his name and nickname respectively suggest, he is a vessel carrying the sacred values of his culture as well as an obsessive thinker tortured by his attempts to make his actions correspond to his ideals. In a key episode late in the novel, Chalice searches in a fit of disillusioned anguish for "a target to renounce, to blame," and recalls the "cruel trick" represented by President Kennedy. Kennedy, with his image of "overwhelming sincerity," still seems to Chalice proof of the reality of American myth, of the "conceptions of his past,"[11] even as the fact of Kennedy's assassination seems proof before Vietnam of the utter self-delusion of American myth. That this has larger cultural implications is made clear in Chalice's attendant thoughts on the radicals he knew in college who would deride "things Kennedy had done and everything he represented, yet still squirm to avoid the mention of his name" (p. 454). Chalice perceives that their radicalism is actually American idealism wandering in despair in the aftermath of Kennedy's failure:

All their actions strived to retain the belief he gave them while discarding him and his myth—not refusing to be lied to, but insisting on being given different lies, still living with the myth, calling it by different names, refusing not to believe, the seed of all their hatred sown by a man they can never make themselves hate, knowing without admitting, that if he failed, no one can succeed. "There will always be someone," Chalice told himself, "who will refuse to believe, wait somewhere, patiently, with a rifle." (p. 454)

In *A Rumor of War* and *Born on the Fourth of July* Kennedy is the focus of the protagonists' outrage against their national mythology, and in *Body Count* the justification for the protagonist's conviction that he should follow the promptings of American myth; through Chalice in *Sand in the Wind*, Roth makes this need itself either to attack or invoke Kennedy the subject. While most of the veterans' works dramatize cultural disillusion and betrayal, *Sand in the Wind* gains a more self-conscious but less self-absorbed narrative perspective from which to explore the full measure of that trauma.

Chalice's trauma in Vietnam results from his loss of belief in a unique American relation to nature as the sign of a unique mission in the world. While portraying Chalice's participation in Search and Destroy operations in excruciatingly convincing detail, Roth attempts to suggest the larger cultural significance of these operations through ritualistic episodes of revelation and self-confrontation. During his first contacts with the Vietnamese bush, Chalice seeks communion with the natural landscape, but in each case his instinctual reverie is disturbingly disrupted. Swimming with his fellow soldiers in a stream, their rifles momentarily discarded, Chalice experiences the same "sense of freedom" and "relaxed excitement" he knew in similar moments with boyhood friends in "hidden

streams." His transcendent feeling, however, is broken by
yelling at the sight of "some naked men chasing a large
buck on the riverbank" (p. 67). Encouraged by many of his
fellows, one of the men draws a bead with his rifle. When
another prevents him from shooting the deer and asks him
why he wanted to kill it, the frustrated soldier replies
incredulously, "Whata you mean? That was a beautiful
buck. . . . Like to ride home with that thing tied to the
front of my car" (p. 68).

In a subsequent incident Chalice once again encounters
the Vietnamese landscape as innocent nature. Going down
to a river to bathe, Chalice sees little naked Vietnamese
children and huge water buffaloes frolicking in the water.
Attracted once again by this imagery of innocent harmony,
he moves closer, only to find Vietnamese nature instinctively rejecting him:

Captivated by the simple beauty of the scene, Chalice started to
walk towards it, as if to become a part of it. One of the water
buffaloes bolted to its feet, its formerly placid, bovine eyes now
locked in a suspicious, catlike stare. Chalice froze, then walked
back towards the rest of the men. (p. 124)

Having first observed the presence of the violent will of the
American hunter toward Vietnamese nature, Chalice subsequently finds that he cannot leave his identification with
that will to enter into harmony with the Vietnamese landscape.

Subsequently, Chalice does achieve communion with the
Vietnamese and their natural landscape. Hungry, isolated,
and brutalized in the bush, Chalice and several others face
a two-day trek back to the base without food when they
happen upon the corpse of an NVA soldier napalmed by an
American airstrike. With one Marine, allegorically named
Childs, acting as eager catalyst, all but two of the men
participate in a giddy act of cannibalism. The scene is brilliantly depicted as an act that, at this particular moment
under a thick jungle canopy, seems in the group contagion
a satisfaction of a natural appetite troubled only by aware-

ness of the civilized taboo. The scene has the tittering and guilty, yet innocent and passionate, quality of pubescent children crossing the barrier to sexual experience while hidden in blackness.

For the following 300 pages of the novel this scene will in Chalice's thoughts be "the canopy," a euphemistic cloaking even in his mind of the ultimate breakdown in civilized restraint. The term "canopy" also suggests that for Chalice the cannibalism is only explicable as an act he could have joined in while hidden from God and grace in a landscape of utter destruction. When moments earlier they had witnessed the airstrike, one of the men commented that it did not necessarily mean an enemy force had been sighted: "I was drinking with a few of them [American pilots] on my R and R and they were bragging about killing elephants, tigers, water buffaloes—they just like to drop bombs" (p. 201). The napalmed corpse thus embodies in microcosm the general torrent of wanton destruction American will has unleashed through its technology upon the Vietnamese landscape. Chalice, who had longed for communion with the landscape, enters into the savage communion of cannibalism of a Vietnamese. His special, if not fully realized, perception of the significance is clear when, with a "wild grin," he sticks his rifle barrel in the eye socket of the charred skull and laughingly holds it aloft before the "wild smiles" of his fellow communicants (p. 204).

Chalice is the vessel carrying the cherished value and ideal of American mission; temporarily overcome by his recognition that he is in Vietnam a force hostile to the landscape, his psyche turns completely over ("The Prof's really flipped his lid, now," one of the men says a moment later [p. 205]). More than a cannibal, he becomes a vaudevillian imitating a savage priest, a self-mocking obverse of the American Adam. This terrible moment symbolizes the traumatic fall of the American desire to return to natural virtue; this symbolism is ironically accentuated by the arguable rationality and self-recognition it involves when compared to the detached wantonness of the pilot who has first "cooked" the Vietnamese man from a technological remove.

After "the canopy," Chalice's second traumatic experience in Vietnam emerges in a similarly symbolic expression of the inverted American identity. While on a long, horrendous operation characterized by random death in the hostile area suggestively called by Marines (both actual and in the novel) "the Arizona," Chalice's company finds a growing excitement and sense of purpose after reported sightings convince them that they are pursuing an enemy force holding a Marine prisoner. This quest to save one of their own is soon overshadowed, however, by their desire to kill the Phantom Blooker, an NVA soldier who has killed many of their fellows with his extraordinarily cunning and skilled use of a captured M–79 grenade launcher. This dual quest to save and to revenge eventually breaks down when evidence causes them to suspect that the Marine captive and Phantom Blooker are the same person. When one of them asks, "How can anybody fight for the Gooks?" Chalice is consumed by rage: "That's what they tell us *we are* doing—fighting for the Gooks, except for the wrong fucking Gooks" (p. 383).

He now carries the company's own blooker, and his fellow soldiers have told him before they entered the Arizona that, since they superstitiously believe the Phantom Blooker must be killed by his own type of weapon, Chalice is their appointed champion. The Phantom Blooker—a Marine whom they first sympathize with as a helpless captive, then distance themselves from as a fool causing themselves to be endangered, and finally hate as a killer of Americans for Vietnamese—is the American identity lost, then derided, and finally in Vietnam conceivable only as an enemy. Chalice must necessarily slay him since he is the sole remaining vessel of that ideal. When he does, the Marines leave the Phantom Blooker's body unidentified in a cave, one of them furtively dropping the Phantom's Marine dog-tags into kneedeep water (p. 389). The killing of the Phantom symbolizes their repression of their own haunting ideal turned tormenting devil.

The second major character of *Sand in the Wind* is a lieutenant named Kramer. While the specific source of his grievances is never made clear, Kramer has requested service in Vietnam as an infantryman out of a desire to flee the "decisions" required at home. His only moment of regret occurs as he looks down from a plane taking him to Camp Pendleton on his way to Vietnam. A clear view of sea life through the water causes him to float metaphorically "towards the bottom" into "this quieter, simpler, more beautiful world" (p. 12). Kramer, though a humane and competent officer, represents another side of America's impulse to come to Vietnam, the desire to flee civilization that has always been the negative obverse of the mythic desire to enter nature.

Ironically, Kramer finds his desires as frustrated in Vietnam as does Chalice. Kramer originally perceives Vietnam as a "referenceless matrix" mirroring his own emptiness, but out in the Arizona (which of course is named after a land which once also appeared simply alien to entering whites) he is shocked to recognize a "valid, logical connection" (p. 292) of Vietnam to the historical conquest of America. One of his men, a fullblooded Indian named Redstone who will shortly be severed in two by a mine, tells Kramer that he and his three brothers have joined the Marines with the understanding that those who survive Vietnam will take the death benefits of the others in order to buy back some of the land their fathers lost to the whites. Kramer thus finds himself confronted in Vietnam with the Indians' view of the historical relation of the white American to the land: the white American brings the death that Kramer himself has chosen over life.

While recuperating from a wound Kramer meets a beautiful, enigmatic Vietnamese woman named Tuyen. Despite his desire to see her as a "bitch" he wants only to possess physically (pp. 396–97), Kramer is too impressed by her refinement and too sensitive to her aloofness to resist an involvement she herself seeks to avoid. Speaking with her in their shared French (she has spent a year at the Sorbonne), Kramer learns of her anticommunist father and Viet Cong husband, both dead. She enables him to see Vietnam through the eyes of ancient Vietnamese civilization, symbolized by her love for the old imperial city of Hue.

She and Kramer fall in love, an emotional connection that unblocks for him an incident that occurred out in the field and which he has been unable to remember. As the scene is vividly reenacted in his mind, he is walking with his men when a "tattered and mud-covered" NVA soldier staggers towards them across the rice paddies, at last drawing a knife and shouting "Kill me! Kill me! You're death! KILL ME!" as he comes straight toward Kramer (pp. 416–17). Unable even to unsling his rifle, he watches the soldier, torn apart by a fusillade from Kramer's troops, fall in his direction. Kramer remembers that one of the Marines had then pulled off a piece of the corpse's scalp. Traumatized by this memory, Kramer collapses to his knees in front of Tuyen, the Vietnamese dream-figure of civilized, feminine, domestic value who makes unbearable his identity as masculine American killer.

The Tet offensive soon follows, and Kramer hopes to find Tuyen in Hue as he participates in the destruction of the city. Roth reports the decision of the American military command to spare the lives of American troops by calling in the indiscriminate fire of artillery and bombers, a decision which inevitably sacrifices Vietnamese civilians along with the enemy, so that at last "the Marines no longer advanced upon a city, but instead upon its ruins" (p. 482). Unable to find Tuyen, Kramer stands amid the ruined city, an American finding in his meeting with the ancient civilization of Asia the utter folly of his own culture's belief in "progress":

Hue too had become a joke. But he remembered with pain Tuyen's description of it, and finally the myth that it had arisen from the ground as a lotus flower. "A lotus," he thought, "a lotus magically transformed into rubble." . . . "Why should Hue be any different?" he asked himself, realizing now that it was merely a city, and that no matter how beautiful it had once been, never was it anything more than the work of a destructive, brutal species that found it impossible to exist without destroying everything left behind by former generations, a species condemned to walk through the ruins of its ancestors. "The Ancient City," he repeated to himself, half laughing. (p. 483)

Kramer stands upon an Asian landscape a long way from that upon which Whitman imagined the American falling into the arms of his older Asian brother in a millennial embrace.

Kramer is forced into a nihilistic interpretation of man's history, while Chalice dies during Tet in a hopeless attempt to spare the civilians who are the supposed point of the Vietnam mission. The novel ends with Kramer, leaving Hue in a truck full of American corpses, taking a final look at the city "that had seemed so important once, promised so much," but now has revealed itself "merely the work of man, foredoomed to ruin by and despite him, fruit of his conceit, his enchanting delusions of creation—never destined to be anything more than sand in the wind" (p. 498).

Roth's purpose is never more clearly stated than in the thoughts of a decent, fatherly colonel who finds he must preside over a hopeless and deteriorating mission. Once, we learn, he had gained a tragic admiration for the doomed obstinacy of the Viet Cong (thus casting them in the role of the plains Indians in the American mythic landscape); subsequently, his "experiences and intuition" have overruled his "logic and all of his training" (p. 348) to convince him that he is in fact witnessing another tragedy altogether: "Now this destruction seemed no longer imminent, and was replaced by the destruction, not of his country, but of the myth that gave it life and in which he had once believed" (p. 349). Despite flaws of excessive length and digression, Roth's novel provides through allusive symbols a vision larger than personal pain. He articulates that pain as a death-agony of the American idea of itself.

IV

Like *Sand in the Wind*, John M. Del Vecchio's *The 13th Valley* transforms the author's personal experience into a work of broad cultural import by addressing Vietnam as an event in American mythic history. Del Vecchio, who was awarded a Bronze Star for heroism while serving in 1971 as a combat correspondent with the 101st Airborne, follows Roth in combining realistic detail with overtly symbolic elements. *The 13th Valley* has unique, interesting characters who gain symbolic import through traits they share with their mythic prototypes, and the narrative is skillfully orchestrated toward a furious climax in which language, feeling, and idea play off each other in complex counterpoint. In *The 13th Valley* a single operation late in the Vietnam War becomes a journey of American heroes into a frontier where they find themselves stranded from their society.

Like *Moby-Dick*, *The 13th Valley* is tragic epic, with Del Vecchio following Melville's strategy of having the commander of the operation see a cosmic significance in the objective. In a briefing to his officers and NCOs, the brigade commander, the Old Fox, describes the mission: to find, capture, and destroy a suspected NVA headquarters and communications center. He speaks in terms that endow the operation with epic significance, as he presents the mission as an extraordinary challenge, describing the tiny valley as one allied forces have never before searched because it is surrounded by "some of the highest mountains in all of Vietnam."[12] Finally, he offers the suspected NVA headquarters to his men as an ultimate objective of the American historical errand, an opportunity to at last attain the decisive victory that has seemed unreachable in Vietnam. Thus he describes the mission to the soldiers as nothing less than a quest to prove after all the historical validity of American destiny:

This is the last NVA stronghold in I Corps. We can kick the enemy out of our AO, out of this valley, out of I Corps and out of this country. Gentlemen, it is up to us. We are about to embark upon a historic mission. We must take the world, Gentlemen, as we find it and make it like we want it. We have the equipment, the mobility, the tactics. . . . Now is the time. Let us embark upon our rendezvous with destiny. (pp. 69–70)

While an entire brigade is being sent on this epic assault upon the world "as we find it" (wilderness) in order to "make it like we want it" (civilization), the reader goes with Alpha company, whose central characters embody the various aspects of the ideal American self-concept. As they are about to be lifted by helicopter into the valley, Del Vecchio explicitly dubs them as a group representation of their culture—superficially in the ethnic, regional, and class terms of Dos Passos' and Mailer's World War platoons, but ultimately in the terms of the mythic elements making up the culture's ideal character:

The restless infantrymen in the trenches and their clustered sergeants and lieutenants and captains on the landing strip represented a collective consciousness of America. These men, Chelini, Egan, Doc, Silvers, Brooks, all of them, were products of the Great American Experiment, black brown yellow white and red, children of the Melting Pot. Their actions were the blossoming of the past, blooming continuously from the humus of decayed antiquity, flowering from the stems of living yesterdays. What they had in common was the denominator of American society in the '50's and '60's, a television culture, the army experience—basic, AIT, RVN training, SERTS, the Oh-deuce and now the sitting, waiting in the trench at LZ Sally, I Corps, in the Republic of Vietnam. (p. 132)

This paragraph epitomizes the method of the novel. The characters carry in their minds the burdens of their national mythology. The operation takes place during the

Nixon period, when American soldiers came to Vietnam without illusions and without support at home. Sent on a mission which a distrusted institutional father, the Old Fox, has couched in grand terms of American progress and destiny, the men of Alpha company are the traditional small American band entering a wilderness landscape, "isolated and untouched" (p. 168) by Americans, to achieve a communal goal; in their minds, however, they are passionately pursuing their own quests. Those personal pursuits symbolically enact—in the seeming void of American mythic history that is Vietnam in this late phase of the war—the various cultural drives of the national quest.

Like the heroes of the Iliad, Del Vecchio's major characters are larger-than-life in their virtues and flaws while pathetically human in their entrapment in a fate they cannot comprehend or control. The commander of Alpha company—Lieutenant Rufus Brooks, called by his men the LT—is a young black officer with an M.A. in philosophy. Brooks is an original, complex creation: a warm, impressive, endearingly unpretentious and open character made up of many contradictory aspirations, strengths, and fears. Insufficiently appreciated by both his superiors and his wife, he is an ideal American leader. Moderate and controlled in his relations with both his men and his superiors (though tactfully disciplining toward the former and discretely rebellious toward the latter), Brooks combines a talent for practical action with a love for philosophical solitude. His leadership, while firm and calculated, is democratic and egalitarian; he carefully explains his decisions to his men and holds nightly meetings in which his subordinates are encouraged to voice and debate their views. Further, and in striking contrast to the army as a whole, under his command Alpha company has adapted to the requirements of Vietnam, learning the tactics of the enemy, confining drug use to the rear areas, and repressing racial tensions. Planning ambushes and searching for the enemy headquarters, Brooks uses the waiting periods to pursue an inquiry into the origins of conflict, personal and national, that eventually results in a utopian essay written in the field. He completes it shortly before his capture of the headquarters and his subsequent death. In his oddly heroic yet naïve character, this young black lieutenant brings to the Vietnam War the Enlightenment ethos of the forefathers (his troops believe he has "attained enlightenment" [p. 34]).

His right-hand man is Egan, a young Irish-American platoon sergeant who typifies the ideal American soldier in the mode of Davy Crockett and John Wayne: tough-talking (he tells another soldier to tell his children that "the night belonged to Egan—and he killed everybody" [p. 147]) but inwardly tender; always on the move while at the same time longing for the girl he keeps leaving behind; valuable in the wilderness for his self-reliance (the narrator tells us that the "jungle was his home" [p. 207]), but dangerously rebellious in the rear base areas. His frontier virtues leave his comrades, who say he is "beautiful" when in "contact" (p. 21), in awe of him. Egan is an American who has succeeded completely, in contrast to the general American presence, in adapting to Vietnam. He has come to know the land, to watch instinctively for its dangers, and to be indifferent to its discomforts.

Yet, in making this adaptation, he has not become a simple wild man, an anarch lacking civilized values. In addition to serving his lieutenant and his men, Egan insists that the American soldiers' "hearts are pure" and the American mission just, even if twisted and misrepresented by the politicians (p. 377). Egan is a killer but also an idealist, and his ideal is the American pastoral dream of a perfectly natural civilization, a perfectly benign nature. For this reason he cherishes the memory of his girlfriend Stephanie: "She was the antithesis of Nam. She was the good, the peaceful, the loving" (p. 279). And while he cannot rest in society or conform to rear-echelon restrictions and hypocrisies, he restrains himself in the jungle from descending into savagery. When one of his men props up an NVA corpse in an obscene position and severs an ear, Egan furiously stops him, denouncing him as a "savage" (pp. 227–28). Egan is consciously afraid only of spiders, perhaps a projection of an unconscious fear of entrapment in malevolent nature.

Each of the secondary characters making up the elite inner circle of Brooks' company embodies an aspect of the ideal American self-concept. Doc, a black medic who studies to improve his medical abilities and who is distraught over the inadvertent disruption of Vietnamese society by the American presence, has the intense compassion that has fueled American progressive, missionary, and reform movements. El Paso, son of a Mexican immigrant and student of history and law, spends his free time reading books on Vietnamese history. The arbitrator of the nightly debates, El Paso represents the American belief in constitutional law. Silvers, a Jew who asserts that America must honor its commitment to avoid finding itself wandering in a moral wilderness, retains the concept of Americans as a second Chosen People with a historical mission. Jax, a black tortured by injustice at home, voices the continuing presence of revolutionary impulses in the American character.

A major portion of the novel consists of these characters' contentious discussions on Vietnam and on race relations. Because they are both reasoned and passionate, and because they are always finally moderated by mutual respect and regard, these debates are a moving vision of American democracy. And, in their diversity of noble impulses and their representation of different races and peoples within American society, they offer a view of American mythic history strikingly attractive and even optimistic in the dark setting of the Vietnam night. Del Vecchio has taken the one continuous theme of moral affirmation found in the American literary narratives of Vietnam—the mutual loyalty and affection formed by the men in the field—and transformed it into a mythic representation of the living American ideal.

He structures the novel, however, around a character, Chelini, who stands outside of this group. The novel begins with Chelini's entry into Vietnam and ends with his attendance at a military ritual honoring those lost in the operation. As a soldier new to Vietnam, he is called Cherry, but he accepts this nickname as especially appropriate because he believes he has come to Vietnam simply "to observe" and tells himself that he is "totally naïve" and has "everything to experience and to learn" (p. 3). Cherry holds the American character's belief in its own innocence, while he longs for acceptance by Brooks, Egan, and the other experienced warriors. His psychological journey during the operation of *The 13th Valley* is thus set up to provide a measure of the distance, in a relative instant of its history, which the American self-concept traveled in Vietnam.

At first Cherry is caught between his enthusiasm for the camaraderie, excitement, and drama of the American presence in Vietnam and his moral doubts about its justification. When he kills, from only a few feet away, an unseeing NVA soldier who unwittingly walks up a trail into his sights, Cherry is profoundly shocked. Refusing the suggestion that he has earned a change in his nickname (the Deerslayer-becomes-Hawkeye pattern), Cherry at first is traumatized by guilt, convinced now that his coming to Vietnam to acquire experience has really been a willingness to kill. Soon this guilt inverts itself into an obsession with savagery. Quietly going mad, Cherry decides that "every man is part god" (p. 428). With this dark overturning of the transcendentalist notion of the shared divinity of nature, Cherry enters fully into Vietnam in a blasphemous, nihilistic love of destruction and death. Throughout the novel, Egan, who has constantly and furiously attacked Cherry for his innocence, is tormented by a dream of a Vietnamese sapper lifting a machete over him. The last time he has the dream the machete comes down before he awakes, and when his eyes open Cherry's face is above his (p. 541), the cultural brother who has taken on the savage identity projected upon the enemy.

At the end of the novel, in a powerfully dramatized scene, the survivors of the operation attend a ceremony in which the colonel of their battalion assures them that their sacrifices have kept South Vietnamese women and children safe and helped the young nation gain time in building its democracy. Cherry, completely dehumanized and lacking any moral center, mocks the tributes. Previous to this denoument, Brooks, Egan, and Doc die while lying atop one another in a protective embrace in the technological pyre of a burning helicopter. Throughout the novel Egan and the other enlisted men repeat a line expressing their determination to persevere despite the absurdities and sufferings of their situation, and to be loyal to each other despite their conflicts and disagreements: "Don't mean nothin'." When Cherry learns that Brooks, Egan, and Doc are listed as missing in action, he attempts to offer this refrain as a nihilistic final comment on their sacrifice, but is stopped by the new commander:

> "Well fuck," Cherry smiled. He was happy they were not listed among the known dead. In me, he thought. He laughed. "Fuck it. Don't mean . . ."
> Thomaston cut him off. "Don't say it, Soldier." (p. 589)

The 13th Valley thus ends with a traumatized American forced to regard the aspects of his ideal self-concept, the characteristics of his mythic heroes, as lost in the furious meaninglessness of Vietnam. Gazing at this spectre, the American consciousness can only blaspheme or deny.

V

The heroes of *The Ugly American* rebel against comfort-seeking careerists in the American foreign service; the Special Forces of periodical article and bestseller defy convention-bound Regular Army officers; the author-protagonists of *Hanoi* and *Trip to Hanoi* set themselves against the robot-like flyers who bomb North Vietnam; psychologically, all are seeking to leave civilization, the East, the city, the past, the conscious mind—Europe—to enter the wilderness, the West, nature, the future—America. Defying their contemporary society of organization men, affluence, and technology, they return to the virtues and mission of the frontier culture embodied in the pastoral heroes of American myth. The wish-fulfillment fantasy of these texts is consistently one of embrace with a virtuous natural man in common opposition to enemies personifying either raw savagery or exploitative civilization. In doing so the heroes find that they have returned to a duplication of the Old West, a pastoral landscape at a perfect moment—to the fantasy of the American protagonist—between primitive naturalness and civilized achievement.

In the veterans' memoirs and realistic novels, bound by the requirement of both forms to accurate representation, the authors cannot through fantasy remove their protagonists from their identity with their present society. Going to Vietnam on the same psychological and cultural quest as the protagonists of the earlier Vietnam literature, the protagonists of these works enter a true American nightmare: either the American hero is only everyman, anyman, lacking a unique ability to reject either savagery or civilization (as in *A Rumor of War*) or the culture is no longer capable of validating the hero's achievement (as in *Fields of Fire*). The pervasive sense in either case is of a loss of grace, of an abandonment by God, of living in a fable of the damned. A campus minister has written of his perception from ten years of working with Vietnam veterans, "Although therapy, jobs and benefits may be helpful in healing some of the hurt, the real source of the alienation and rage is gradually disclosed: it is the death of the national god."[13] Identifying the same wound in the culture as a whole, Andrew Young has spoken of Jimmy Carter's

failure, despite the several major successes of his administration, to answer affirmatively a traumatized people's
question, "Is God still on our side?"[14]

The significance of John F. Kennedy's role in so many of
the veterans' works, and of Kennedy's having succeeded
Johnson and Nixon in the culture at large as an ultimate
subject of passionate controversy, is that his image embodies the ideal self-concept from which Americans feel severed by Vietnam. For Kovic, for Caputo, for Huggett's
Hawkins, and for Roth's Chalice, Kennedy is the model of
revolt against the recent past of the immediate father,
against Eisenhower's complacent society. At the same
time, he is their contemporaneous image of the mythic
fathers, of the vigorous frontier culture uniquely defining
itself as mission. Believing that they are following his call,
the protagonists enter Vietnam after Kennedy's assassination. When the mission turns out in Vietnam to seem a
depraved joke, they look with pain, perplexity, and outrage, not at the President who has sent them there, but to
their original inspiration. In the same way, the culture that
first expunged Johnson and then Nixon, that would not
settle for Ford after he pardoned Nixon, and that angrily
removed Carter when he proved unable to renew their confidence, has found that it must simultaneously adore and
defile Kennedy in documentary, docudrama, revisionist
history, and tabloid gossip. Whether or not one believes
that Kennedy would have performed as did Johnson and
Nixon, once one has decided that the national self-concept
he projected has been proven a false idol, one must destroy
his image. More penetrating than Kovic, Caputo, and Huggett, Roth finds the central horror of Vietnam in its duplication of the mythic import of Kennedy's assassination:
either utter absurdity or the worst judgment upon the
worthiness of the people holding up such a wonderful image as their own.

During the 1970s no political leader was able to confront
this. Perhaps none could; certainly it would have taken

someone as perfectly attuned to this mythic dilemma as Lincoln, the two Roosevelts, and Kennedy himself had been to the psychological conflicts of their eras. The absence of such a figure in itself probably contributed to the sense of cosmic abandonment. So it was left to artists to take the American people on their second journey through Vietnam. In the best of their works, that meant finally moving back toward the realm of fantasy—of symbolic imagining—to discover the continuing dimensions of Vietnam as a terrain of the American psyche. Having entered Vietnam as a symbolic landscape, Americans would through highly imaginative narrative art have to find their way back out to American myth, enabling them to journey again forward into history.

CHAPTER FIVE

The Hero Seeks
a Way Out

THE THREE MOST highly praised of the literary works
to emerge from the Vietnam War—Robert Stone's *Dog Soldiers* (1974), Michael Herr's *Dispatches* (1977), and Tim
O'Brien's *Going After Cacciato* (1978)—are the least con-
cerned with a clear, sustained portrait of the war. Beginning where the veterans' memoirs and realistic novels
leave off, the protagonists attempt to free themselves from
this fallen landscape of American myth. In Stone's novel,
this takes the form of an allegorical "thriller" in which two
Americans move from Vietnam to the California desert
with a dark grail of smuggled heroin; in Herr's journalistic memoir, the narrator takes us on an intensely self-
conscious exploration of his memory of Vietnam, a search
into his own unconscious for the war's "secret history"; in
O'Brien's novel, the soldier-narrator flees the reality of
Vietnam on an imagined journey across Asia to Paris. In
contrast to the veterans' realistic narratives, these works
focus not on the journey into Southeast Asia but rather on
its legacy, on what it means to be an American after Vietnam. Their protagonists seek new symbolic landscapes
where they can attempt to reassert the ideal American
identity in the aftermath of Vietnam.

I

Robert Stone went to Vietnam in 1971 for approximately
two months, working as a journalist but actually motivated by a felt need to include the war in a novel he was

trying to write.[1] An award-winning first novelist, Stone came to his researches in the Saigon drug-trade from his own involvement with the psychedelic experiments of Ken Kesey and the Merry Pranksters in the San Francisco Bay area, chronicled in Tom Wolfe's *The Electric Kool-Aid Acid Test* (1968). Drawing on both experiences, Stone produced *Dog Soldiers*, a tale of heroin-smuggling that begins in Saigon and ends in the desert surrounding a failed California commune. Critically acclaimed, in the words of reviewer Thomas Powers in *Commonweal*, as the "best book so far about the spiritually corrupting effect on the United States of the war it fought in Vietnam,[2] *Dog Soldiers* sold modestly but was accorded the National Book Award. Since the renewal of interest in Vietnam, writers in popular periodicals and literary journals have consistently cited *Dog Soldiers* as one of the finest novels of the war.

At the opening of the novel Converse, a burnt-out writer and idealist traumatized in Vietnam, has "in the absence of anything else"[3] devised a plan to enlist his former Marine buddy Ray Hicks, now a sailor for the merchant marine, to deliver three kilos of heroin to Converse's wife, Marge, in Oakland. Converse receives the heroin from Charmian, the beautiful daughter of a former Southern governor with powerful "friends" in both Washington and Saigon. Marge is to hand the heroin over to people who Converse believes are linked to the CIA. When the "people," two thugs working for Antheil, a corrupt regulatory official in league with Charmian, try to steal the heroin from Hicks and Marge, they flee down through California until their pursuers catch up with them at the remnants of a desert commune. This thriller, reversing the westward direction of America's journey to Vietnam, suggests the mythic legacy of Vietnam for American consciousness. In Stone's novel Vietnam is the murderous field that has finally forced frontier-marching America to gaze upon its self-projected image, stripped of its dreams and myths, and find nothing but brute behavior.

To convey this vision, Stone uses the tension between the realistic credibility of the thriller (its authentic locale, reportorial detail, topical references, and plausible motivation and behavior) and the popular fantasy it provides through characters who live life "on the edge" and through a melodramatic plot of flight, pursuit, and climactic shootout. Stone's manipulation of these elements undermines the expectations created by the thriller genre, which Stone values for its mythic element (he sees it as "an irreverent echo of the epic,")[4] and so the form of the novel itself configures into a failed fictive landscape in which a reader follows the lurid dreams of the popular culture into a final frustration. Stone achieves this effect through a complexly compressed modulation of the terse, "hardboiled" prose of the thriller, of the allusions and symbols with which Joseph Conrad and Graham Greene have already invested the genre, and of the parodic devices characteristic of contemporary American "fabulist" fiction by such writers as Thomas Pynchon and Kurt Vonnegut.

Set late in the war, *Dog Soldiers* leaves Vietnam after the first few chapters, but Stone's brilliantly atmospheric portrait makes it an enduring psycho-symbolic presence. Stone introduces us simultaneously to Vietnam and to the traumatized journalist Converse, letting the consciousness and setting reflect each other for the first sixty pages. So sensitive to suffering that his father kept the newspapers concerning Hiroshima away from him, Converse is a "moralist" and "world-saver" (p. 55) as well as a failed playwright. He has come to Vietnam to escape the paranoid confusion of reality with the fantasies he writes for a sensationalist tabloid ("Skydiver Devoured by Starving Birds"; "Mad Dentist Yanks Girl's Tongue"), and in hope of producing a valid book or play. Converse has thus conceived of his journey to Vietnam as a Hemingwayesque literary version of regeneration on a violent frontier. There his encounter in Cambodia with an Elephant Bomb dropped mistakenly by the South Vietnamese Air Force

leads him instead to retreat into dope, fantasy, and ultimately the smuggling scheme. Discovering in Vietnam
that the fantasized tabloid horrors of his culture have been
projected into actual atrocities, he dwells with dark romanticism upon such bizarre images of the war as the
Great Elephant Zap, the killing of elephants with helicopter gunships when the American command "decided that
elephants were enemy agents because the NVA used them
to carry things" (pp. 41–42). Listening to the stoned fantasies of MP's about skin-diving girl sappers and porpoises
trained as guards, he enjoys this vision of Vietnam as lurid
comic book: "He was picturing the silent depths of the Bay,
Navy-gray porpoises with spiked collars locked in combat
with knife-wielding sloe-eyed sapper girls. The Battle of
My Lat Bay, illustrated by Arthur Rackham" (p. 46).

A bitter parody of the American liberal, Converse has
projected his dreams of revivified will and mission into
Vietnam only to find them revealed to himself as paranoid
brutality. Finding spots on the wall of his Saigon hotel
room left by the previous tenant's crushing of harmless
house lizards with a framed tintype of Our Lady of
Lourdes, Converse perceives a mirror image of his and his
nation's projection of its terrors upon the Vietnamese: "It
was just as well not to wonder why. There was never any
satisfaction in that. Perhaps the man had thought they
would bite him. Or perhaps they had kept him awake
nights, whispering together" (p. 22). Toward the end of the
novel, the last mention of Vietnam is Converse's comment
on why Hicks helped them escape: "Nobody knows. . . .
That's the principle we were defending over there. That's
why we fought the war" (p. 305). Despising his "liberal
sensitivity" (p. 22), he has lost his belief in the reality of
moral distinction and thus of valid action. Converse himself links his traumatic self-discovery in Vietnam to that of
the nation at large. He tells Hicks that Vietnam "is the
place where everybody finds out who they are." When
Hicks ironically responds, "What a bummer for the gooks,"

Converse answers: "You can't blame us too much. We didn't know who we were till we got here. We thought we were something else" (p. 57).

Converse smuggles heroin into his own society to act upon his perception that the American mythic landscape of unique character and mission overlays a moral desert. His various self-justifications all suggest this bitter denial of idealism: a cynical reenactment of the white man's errand in America implicit in his quoting a conquistador ("I desire to serve God. . . . And to grow rich, like all men" [p. 15]); a desperate pursuit of a goal that is not illusory ("I feel like this is the first real thing I ever did in my life. I don't know what the other stuff was about" [p. 57]); a quest for regeneration through erotic communication with the beautiful, soulless Charmian ("He had tried it in order to do something dangerous with her" [p. 181]). As for moral compunctions, Converse finds them made absurd by the Great Elephant Zap: "If the world is going to contain elephants pursued by flying men, people are just naturally going to want to get high" (p. 42).

Made impotent by his traumatic self-discovery in Vietnam, Converse cannot stop desiring certain women who represent contemporary images of a lost past: a missionary woman he encounters in Saigon, who with her "gray . . . waxen coloring" (p. 2) elicits "a small rush of admiration, desire, and apocalyptic religion . . . subverting his common sense" (p. 7); Charmian, who "had taken leave of life in a way which he found irresistible" (p. 25), a "ghost" who "belongs to a vanished era in American history . . . at the age of twenty-five" (p. 30); and June, who with "her eyes . . . fouled with smog and propane spray" elicits his sudden desire "beyond perversity" for "a speed-hardened straw-colored junkie stewardess, a spoiled Augustana Lutheran" (p. 181). Converse's failure to complete his fumbling approaches to these women, each a grotesque image of a lost American ideal, represents his inability either to stop pursuing or to vigorously desire fallen American dreams. Converse, and post-Vietnam liberal American self-consciousness, is the "converse" of traditional American belief in the American's special character and destiny, a loathing of America as a beautiful object of desire revealed as decayed, soulless, and artificial.

With Converse's transfer of the heroin to Ray Hicks at the harbor of My Lat, the setting shifts across the ocean to California and the narrative focus to Hicks. While in the Marine Corps together in a time before the novel, Converse had exposed Hicks to Nietzsche. But Converse has provided Hicks only with an intellectual framework and impetus. Before Nietzsche, the only books Hicks had ever finished were Ray Bradbury's *The Martian Chronicles* and Mickey Spillane's *I, the Jury*, and Hicks is driven by American dreams of utopia and fantasies of righteous violence. Converse's relation to Hicks thus symbolizes the relation in America of intellectual emphasis upon the power of individual consciousness and will to the heroic fantasies of the culture at large.

When we meet Hicks he is an aspiring hero trapped in a disillusioned culture that, like Converse, has come to view the total commitment of a warrior as the behavior of a "psychopath" (p. 55). Stone has made his American hero the "tough guy," the disinherited descendant of Leatherstocking first appearing in the Depression novels of such writers as James M. Cain. Stone thus makes the specific prototype for Hicks the most diminished and alienated version of the basic archetype beginning with Cooper's frontiersman and continuing through the western cowboy and urban hardboiled detective. In doing so, Stone transforms the alienated Vietnam veteran into a symbolic figure of American heroic virtue disowned by his culture; Hicks' tragedy results from his seeking the higher roles of the western hero and hardboiled detective, a "tough guy" seeking to find a traditional American mission worthy of his heroic attributes.

In sharp contrast to Converse's protected youth, Stone tells us that Hicks began life as an orphan, eventually finding community in the Marine Corps. At the same time he met Converse he also discovered Japan, and from it he took a wife, the ideals of Zen, and a concept of himself as a samurai, a drawing upon the strengths and virtues of an Asian way of life duplicating that which Leatherstocking draws from the forest Indians. The Vietnam War at first offered him a fulfilling social role in which he could use the skills he learned from Asia against Asians in the service of his society: both his subordinate teenaged riflemen and former commander "expected that he be better and more professional at war than themselves, and he had been" (p. 75). But while he had declined to act upon the larger moral uneasiness the war presented to "a man who maintained a spiritual life, and who had taken an Asian wife" (p. 75), an institutional betrayal of the men he served eventually forced him to acknowledge the bankruptcy of his community by quitting the Marines. That betrayal was, as he bitterly terms it, the Battle of Bob Hope. In a minor dereliction resulting from "a mood of vague disgruntlement" (p. 76), Hicks violated orders by allowing some of his men to see the entertainer. In an undesirable patrol assigned in retaliation, every man who attended the show was killed and he himself wounded.

As a result of this absurdist wasting in Vietnam of heroic sacrifice, Hicks is an alienated Leatherstocking without a community to serve or mission to pursue. Reduced to drug-dealing, Hicks is nevertheless repelled by the decadence around him and sporadically seeks to counter it. In the first episode after his smuggling of the heroin into America, he sits in an Oakland bar he once valued for its good Italian food and pool table but which now features topless dancers in a cage. Disgusted by its coldness, he lashes out at those around him, makes fitfull calls to his former Japanese wife Etsuko and his former girlfriend

June, and tries to avoid knowledge of the pervasive decadence (informed that an executive-looking man with a brahmin-looking East Indian woman are a sadomasochistic couple, he replies, "I don't want to know all this shit, man . . . I don't want to know it" [p. 81]). The scene is reminiscent of the fictional hardboiled detective Philip Marlowe's journeys through 1940s Los Angeles. Like Raymond Chandler's hero, Hicks responds to the sordid landscape of American society by trying to be a solitary white knight. For instance, he warns a man that he has just pretended to go along with a scheme to terrorize him. When the man immediately suggests that they do the same to the schemer, Hicks furiously gazes at the sign over the bar: "Today is the First Day of the Rest of Your Life" (p. 90). His attempt at a valid act leaves him despairing that there is "no place for me" (p. 90).

When Stone moves Hicks out of the urban landscape, he switches from mocking associations with the hardboiled detective to images of the western hero. At the suburban home of the Hollywood hustler Eddie Peace, Stone describes Hicks as bearing two pistols "before his shoulders with the barrels raised like a movie-poster cowboy," causing Peace to deride him as "Buffalo Bill" (p. 187). And later his former Countercultural guru Dieter, speaking from a mountaintop in the southeastern California desert, says that Hicks is "trapped in a samurai fantasy—an American one," in which "he has to be the Lone Ranger, the great desperado—he has to win all the epic battles single-handed" (p. 270). Just as Converse represents the liberal self-consciousness of late-Vietnam America lost in the void of its shattered mythology, Hicks embodies the predicament of the heroic "will to power" of that mythology, orphaned by the exposure of false mission and community.

Hicks represents the late-Vietnam-era disillusionment of American mythic aspiration, not only with the nation-building efforts of the liberal American establishment but with the utopian dreams of the opposing Counterculture as well. In addition to his disillusioning service with the Marines in Vietnam, Hicks is a former member of Those Who Are, a Countercultural commune led by Dieter. When Hicks, fleeing the pursuing criminal-cops, takes Converse's wife Marge to the remnants of the mountaintop commune, he repeatedly makes sarcastic references to its illusory utopianism. Showing her a ruined garden, he tells her how originally they spent hours spreading chickenwire in order to avoid poisoning gophers because "it was the time of peace and love and all that lives is holy. . . . In the end somebody got drunk—I don't remember who—and came down here with a shotgun and blasted all the gophers they could find" (p. 219). When Marge responds to the sound-speakers and lights Dieter has spread through the forest by asking "Doesn't he like trees?" Hicks sarcastically identi-fies the guru with the mythic-historical American fathers: "Not him. He's a pioneer" (p. 220). Eventually killing his former guru, Hicks laments this culmination of the ruined Countercultural experiment as an absurdity at one with Vietnam: "Lousy stupid thing. Like the Battle of Bob Hope. Like everything else" (p. 313).

Bereft of any community or ideal he can serve, Hicks has in the course of their flight together committed himself to the drug-addicted Marge, even though he objectively rec-ognizes her to be "some junkie's nod, a snare, a fool catcher" (p. 169). Telling himself that "if the serious man is still bound to illusion, he selects the worthiest illusion and takes a stand" (p. 168), he makes it his mission to save her when she goes down the mountain to surrender the heroin to the besieging criminal-cops who have Converse as host-age. He rejects Dieter's arguments that he can't win by saying "real life don't cut no ice with me" (p. 290), ordering the guru to light up his forest and use the sound system as soon as the shooting begins: "Get on the mikes—I want a real deluge of weirdness. I want an opera" (p. 290). While this idea is on one level a practical tactic to create confu-sion among the villains, it also suggests Hicks' decision to attempt to force his need for a heroic mission upon actuality.

As the novel moves toward the climactic confrontation between the "good guys" and "bad guys," the looming presence of Vietnam comes into focus. While in Vietnam, Converse ironically watches a scene of the television western *Bonanza*, a "shoot-out" among desert boulders between a sharply contrasted hero and villain (pp. 37–38); now Hicks himself participates in that ritual of American popular culture in an attempt at overcoming the meaninglessness left by his Vietnam experience. As he moves forward Hicks recognizes that he is reenacting his disillusioning Vietnam experience with the original roles reversed:

The folly and complacency of the smoker in the truck were a great comfort to him.

I'm the little man in the boonies now, he thought.

The thing would be to have one of their Sg mortars. He was conceiving a passionate hatred for the truck—its bulk and mass—and for the man who sat inside it.

The right side for a change. (p. 294)

In this scene Hicks, the disinherited but still idealistic hero, simultaneously reenacts two experiences: the mythologized American history ritualized in westerns and other popular genres, and the recent American trauma to those assumptions embodied in Vietnam. That Hicks can relive his Vietnam experience in the configuration of American myth only by imagining himself as the American enemy is very much the point *Dog Soldiers* has to make. The American hero at last finds a satisfactory role by becoming a Viet Cong, acting out a self-created role that brings him back to his lost mythic-historical position as a solitary frontier individual fighting an enemy identified with the machine. In the ensuing "shoot-out" Hicks saves Converse, Marge, and the heroin but is badly wounded. He sends his friends off with a promise to meet them with the heroin out on some tracks running through an expanse of dry washes and salt.

Hicks kills Dieter, mistaking his attempt to throw the heroin into an abyss for theft, and walks into the salt land, trying to control the pain of his wound and imagining that he is heroically taking upon himself the pain of innocent victims in both Vietnam and America. He dies in the expanse of flat salt land that to Converse seems to come "out of nothing to nowhere" (p. 330), the landscape of American history now that its phantasmagoric mythic overlay has been removed by the revelations of Vietnam. Hicks' death follows the tragedy of the disinherited "tough guy" that David Madden has traced in the literature of the Great Depression, an earlier shock to American mythic assumptions: "The sentimentality that sometimes surprises us in the tough guy is partly a betrayal that the hard-boiled attitude is a willed stance, taken for daily occasions, that often gets set as self-delusion."[5] Marge ties a white kleenex onto the heroin pack, surrendering the heroin while leaving Hicks as sacrificial victim.

The end of the novel brings no optimism; that defining trait of the American is instead rendered obscene in the ruthlessly banal "when-the-going-gets-tough-the-tough-get-going" musings of the corrupt Antheil. Hicks' death resonates with our mythic images of noble sacrifice, but it is the result of a quest he has deluded himself into seeing as worthy. Marge, who weeps over him and sees his act as one of love, admits that it runs counter to sanity and intelligence (p. 305). And Converse refuses to see any significance in it at all. At the beginning of the novel he responded to the American missionary woman's tale of her husband's execution by the Viet Cong with an ironic expression of Biblical acceptance: "God in the whirlwind" (p. 7). As Converse and Marge flee the surrendered heroin and sacrificial corpse of Hicks, their final view of the pursuing Antheil, and metaphorically of their past experience, is a nihilistic, phantasmagoric vision of an absurdist whirlwind: "The column rose, a whirling white tower with a dark core, spewing gauzy eddies from its spout, its funnel

curving to the shiftings of the wind—the gross and innocent measure of some drugged, freakish process" (p. 335).
With the will of Hicks lost, Marge and Converse are left
only with her futile "fuck you" and his passive "let it be" (p.
335). In *Dog Soldiers* Stone presents Vietnam as an awful
spectre from which Americans return to a mythic landscape itself now experienced as an anti-frontier.

II

No other literary work to emerge from the Vietnam War
has been as widely and enthusiastically acclaimed as
Michael Herr's journalistic memoir *Dispatches*. Nomi-
nated in the nonfiction category for the 1978 National
Book Award, *Dispatches* became a bestseller and was
greeted by reviewers as both a literary masterpiece and a
definitive portrait of the American involvement. Writing
in *Harper's*, Michael Malone stated flatly that "Herr has
told the truth of the war in Vietnam, and asked us to face
it." William Plummer wrote in *Saturday Review* that *"Dispatches* is, hands down, *the* book about Americans in Vietnam," and in *Newsweek* Peter Prescott suggested that it
"may be the best book any American has written about any
war." Commentators suggested that Herr had journeyed
beyond the old hawk–dove positions and political-
historical explanations to probe something obscurely at
the center of America's involvement in Vietnam. Favorably
contrasting the ambiguity of *Dispatches* to Frances
FitzGerald's confident historical analysis in *Fire in the
Lake: The Vietnamese and the Americans in Vietnam* (1973),
Roger Sale asserted in the *New York Review of Books* that
"Herr at his best hurls one into his experience, insists an
uninitiated reader be comforted with no politics, no certain morality, no clear outline of history." In *Time* Paul
Gray most succinctly stated the theme that critics were
finding so persuasive: "Deep in the heart of all the years of

debate was the conflict itself, beyond the grasp of logic. Herr dared to travel to that irrational place and to come back with the worst imaginable news: war thrives because enough men still love it."[6]

A 27-year-old freelance writer, Herr persuaded *Esquire* magazine to send him to Vietnam in 1967. Quickly giving up his original idea of writing a regular column, Herr convinced the editors to let him cover the war as he saw fit, and during his eleven-month stay he moved about the country by helicopter in search of the war, witnessing the siege of Khe Sahn and the Tet offensive at Hue. While he published some early articles, Herr underwent psychiatric analysis before being able to complete the book.[7] The result is an intensely fragmented, self-absorbed work in the genre of literary reportage developed in the 1960s by Mailer, Hunter Thompson, and Joan Didion. Written in a highly wrought yet urgently spontaneous prose, *Dispatches* is less a book about Herr's journey in Vietnam than about his subsequent exploration of that experience. Herr himself has called it "a book about writing a book."[8] By focusing not on an objective portrayal of the people and events of Vietnam, but rather on the characters and images of Vietnam residing in his retrospective consciousness, Herr imaginatively embraces the multiplicity of the American experience there. Through this strategy, based on an unblinking willingness to face the idea that "you were as responsible for everything you saw as you were for everything you did,"[9] Herr attempts in *Dispatches* to explore his own complicity in the war to discover its deepest meaning.

Herr's claim for the credibility of this technique is that he achieved complete empathy with all aspects of the American effort in Vietnam: "After a year I felt so plugged in to all the stories and the images and the fear that even the dead started telling me stories" (p. 31). Further, Herr insists that deep below the separate perspectives of the many Americans he met in Vietnam "somewhere all the

mythic tracks intersected, from the lowest John Wayne
wetdream to the most aggravated soldier-poet fantasy, and
where they did I believe that everyone knew everything
about everyone else, everyone of us there a true volunteer"
(p. 20). He finds this place where the "mythic tracks intersected" during shared drug experiences with various irregular soldiers, loner-descendants of the Leatherstocking
prototype for the American hero:

> In Saigon and Danang we'd get stoned together and keep the
> common pool stocked and tended. It was bottomless and alive
> with Lurps, seals, recondos, Green-Beret bushmasters, redun-
> dant mutilators, heavy rapers, eye-shooters, widow-makers,
> nametakers, classic essential American types; point men,
> *isolatos* and outriders like they were programmed in their genes
> to do it, the first taste made them crazy for it, just like they knew
> it would. You thought you were separate and protected, you
> could travel the war for a hundred years, a swim in that pool
> could still be worth a piece of your balance. (pp. 34–35)

Herr's identification with these "classic essential American types" is crucial to the book in both its interior and
exterior landscapes. In its interior landscape, Herr's remembered eleven-month experience in Vietnam, he connects his participation in the war as unconventional
"Apache" journalist to that of such solitary adventurers as
Green Berets and Lurps (Long Range Recon Patrollers),
suggesting that he is intimately connected to them in motivation and attitude. In its exterior landscape, the surrounding consciousness of Herr's remembering perspective, he connects his mission as self-probing author to the
characteristic mission of these irregular soldiers, scouts
who dared to enter the jungle alone in order to bring out
information useful to the regular military. Herr thus pro-
poses that the central drama of *Dispatches* is his daring to
enter deeply into his memories of the war. There he risks
confrontation with the most dangerous truths of his
psyche, American truths of an American psyche, to bring
back to the culture needed information for its survival of

the Vietnam experience. Turning early in the book to the question of when the war started, what its root causes were, Herr concludes that the history of the American involvement resists conventional history, that "you couldn't use standard methods to date the doom" (p. 49), since "for all the books and articles and white papers, all the talk and the miles of film, something wasn't answered, it wasn't even asked" (p. 49). Herr reveals his lonely, self-assigned mission in his claim that "hiding low under the fact-figure crossfire there was a secret history, and not a lot of people felt like running in there to bring it out" (p. 50).

The "secret history" which Herr perceives as "hiding low under the fact-figure crossfire" begins in an unconscious desire which the culture projected onto Southeast Asia. In Herr's view, the Green Berets and irregular adventurers embody pure projections of that desire. Immediately after his assertion of a "secret history" to the war, Herr sketches 1963, the last year Kennedy directed his counterinsurgency experiment, as a time "when a dead American in the jungle was an event, a grim thrilling novelty." Vietnam was then an "adventure" participated in by "Irregulars, working in remote places under little direct authority, acting out their fantasies with more freedom than most men ever know" (p. 50). Saying that "they never became as dangerous as they'd wanted to be, they never knew how dangerous they really were" (p. 51), Herr sees these counterinsurgency experts as carriers of American mythic expectations who were unable to force Vietnam into the configuration of the inner romance they projected upon it; instead, they led the country across their imagined mythic landscape into a history that overwhelmed the American idea of frontier: "Their adventure became our war, then a war bogged down in time, so much time so badly accounted for that it finally became entrenched as an institution because there had never been room made for it to go anywhere else" (p. 51).

As Herr presents his past version of himself moving through Vietnam, the inner landscape of the book, he periodically shows this "innocent" Herr encountering Americans from whose actions and attitudes he attempts to separate himself. As probing narrator, journeying through the exterior landscape of his memory of those experiences in Vietnam, Herr reverses this process by moving closer and closer to acknowledgment of his complicity with these characters. This movement is embodied in the narrator's progression from the unstated connections silently suggested by juxtaposed episodes to the negative implications of self-irony, finally to fully articulated grasping of the experience. Herr's narrative form—seemingly a chaotic assemblage of episodes and vignettes—actually represents a "howling" mental wilderness through which a heroic narrator journeys toward the grail of self-knowledge. Since this self-knowledge will be found where the "mythic tracks" intersect in the "common pool" of American types, it will be the grail of the culture as well. Like the Green Berets and Lurps, Herr journeys through woods that conventional journalists and historians will not enter in order to bring back essential information; however, Herr journeys in his consciousness through a darkly ambiguous landscape infinitely more frightening, in psychological terms, than the black-and-white New Frontier across which the Special Forces and other counterinsurgency irregulars sought to extend a "classified universe" (pp. 51–52).

The first section of the book, the long "Breathing In," takes the reader on an intensely compressed version of the larger journey making up the book as a whole. Since Herr's journey is psychological, this repetitious pattern, in which the discovery of the book must be made more than once, works because it represents the psychological reprobing and reconsideration of a traumatic experience until it can be fully articulated and accepted. As in the book as a whole, two journeys simultaneously take place in the

"Breathing In" chapter: the correspondent Herr's journey to war, and the narrator Herr's journey toward frank acknowledgment of the first journey's implications. After a prefacing vignette focusing on an army information officer unable to report or even see the true landscape of the war, Herr begins the chapter with a portrait of a Lurp immediately followed by a portrait of his close friends in the press.

Herr portrays his observation of the Lurp as his own nightmarish American dream of becoming like a savage to defeat the savage Other. Looking at the Lurp's face "painted up" for a mission, Herr sees it as a seeming projection of his own darkest imaginings, "like a bad hallucination," that he contemplates in awe: "In the coming hours he'd stand as faceless and quiet in the jungle as a fallen tree, and God help his opposite numbers unless they had at least half a squad along, he was a good killer, one of our best" (p. 6). The Lurp's face is a reverse mirror image of another American face, that of the Countercultural "freak" or "hippie" back in California ("not like the painted faces I'd seen in San Francisco only a few weeks before, the other extreme of the same theater"), and Herr implies that the Lurp sees Herr as that opposite face ("he thought I was a freak because I wouldn't carry a weapon"). Fascinated by the sight of the Lurp walking with his team "into the treeline" at nightfall, Herr is as quick to turn away from the reality of his reflection's violence when after dawn he reemerges from the night's adventure:

I never spoke to him again, but I saw him. When they came back in the next morning he had a prisoner with him, blindfolded and with his elbows bound sharply behind him. The Lurp area would definitely be off limits during the interrogation, and anyway, I was already down at the strip waiting for a helicopter to come and take me out of there. (p. 7)

Herr depicts himself as having fled the Lurp, but this assertion of separateness is subtly belied by the immediately succeeding fragment. Without explanatory transition, Herr jumps to a portrait of himself and his journalist friends Tim Page, Dana Stone, and Sean Flynn. That group portrait mirrors the Lurp and his team. Just as the Lurp is a glamorous irregular who expresses his half-savage individuality through "a gold earring and a headband torn from a piece of camoflauge parachute material" (p. 6), Herr describes how Page "liked to augment his field gear with freak paraphernalia, scarves and beads" (p. 7), and how Flynn would sometimes look "like Artaud coming out of some heavy heart-of-darkness trip . . . combing his mustache through with the saw blade of his Swiss Army Knife" (p. 8). Herr also depicts the Lurps and correspondents as sharing the freedom of the irregular from institutional authority: "since nobody was about to tell [the Lurp] to get his hair cut it fell below his shoulders, covering a thick purple scar" (p. 6); Herr and his colleagues dismiss regular soldiers' comments about their long hair with swaggering claims of being the Rolling Stones and successfully confront an angry officer who wants to know why they did not salute. When the officer learns that they are correspondents, they have to flee in order to frustrate his desire to "crank up his whole brigade and get some people killed" in quest of publicity (p. 7). While seemingly asserting their opposed natures, Herr's juxtaposed portraits silently sketch the deeper common face of the Lurps and the correspondents, both adventurers finding excitement and independence on the edge of the regular war.

As the chapter continues, Herr introduces his nonlinear passage through Vietnam by helicopter as a metaphor for the probing, repetitious, obsessive journey of his remembering consciousness:

it started out sound and straight but it formed a cone as it progressed, because the more you moved the more you saw, the more you saw the more besides death and mutilation you risked, and the more you risked of that the more you would have to let go of one day as a "survivor." Some of us moved around the war like crazy people until we couldn't see which way the run was even taking us anymore, only the war all over its surface with occasional, unexpected penetration. (p. 8)

As Herr takes the reader on the "collective meta-chopper" (p. 98) of his recollecting consciousness, he continually probes for "unexpected penetration" into the secret meaning of his memories. With remembered extremes dominating the organization, he characterizes the collective meta-chopper itself as

in my mind . . . the sexiest thing going: saver-destroyer, provider-waster, right hand-left hand, nimble, fluent, canny and human; hot steel, grease, jungle-saturated canvas webbing, sweat cooling and warming up again, cassette rock and roll in one ear and door-gun fire in the other, fuel, heat, vitality and death, death itself, hardly an intruder. (p. 9)

The greatest contrast Herr sets up is between the grunts who fight the war and the noncombatant "Dial Soapers" who sit in comfort in Saigon and other urban base areas. Herr opposes these two aspects of the American mission in terms of frontier vitality versus urban decadence:

It seemed the least of the war's contradictions that to lose your worst sense of American shame you had to leave the Dial Soapers in Saigon and a hundred headquarters who spoke goodworks and killed nobody themselves, and go out to the grungy men in the jungle who talked bloody murder and killed people all the time. (p. 42)

Herr's portrait of these noncombatants suggests his own underlying motivation in seeking the war, a desire to escape the spiritual decay of an affluent, bureaucratic, inauthentic society. Saying that "for the noncombatants stationed in Saigon or one of the giant bases, the war wasn't much more real than if they'd been getting it on TV," he detects "the common failure of feeling and imagination compounded by punishing boredom, an alienation beyond tolerance and a terrible, ongoing anxiety that it might one day, any day, come closer than it had so far" (p. 44). Here Herr detects in these bureaucrats the frustrated fantasy-life of a frontier society become corporation land that Mailer had presented in *Why Are We in Vietnam?*:

And operating inside of that fear was the half-hidden, half-vaunted jealousy of every grunt who ever went out there and killed himself a gook, furtive vicarious bloodthirsting behind

10,000 desks, a fantasy life rich with lurid war-comics adventure, a smudge of closet throatsticker on every morning report,
requisition slip, pay voucher, medical profile, information hand-
out and sermon in the entire system. (pp. 44–45)

Herr's loathing of this secret lust for the war provides
"unexpected penetration" into his own consciousness. Earlier Herr has quoted a soldier who responded to the official
rationales for the war as "just a *load* man. We're here to kill
gooks. Period." At that time Herr commented: "Which
wasn't at all true of me. I was there to watch" (p. 20). The
target of Herr's self-irony is uneasily close to the "vicarious
bloodthirsting" he condemns in the Dial Soaper.

As Herr closes the opening chapter, he at last confesses
the complicity he has previously only suggested. After evoking his transcendent sensations during combat, he says
that "Maybe you couldn't love the war and hate it inside
the same instant, but sometimes those feelings alternated
so rapidly that they spun together in a strobic wheel rolling all the way up until you were literally High on War, like
it said on all the helmet covers" (p. 63). Speaking of the
soldiers' brutality, he says that "I stood as close to them as I
could without actually being one of them, and then I stood
as far back as I could without leaving the planet" before
telling "one last war story" (p. 67). This story is his confession that during Tet he gave up his pretenses as detached
observer to enter fully into a desired mythic-historical
American role: "we were in the Alamo, no place else, and I
wasn't a reporter, I was a shooter" (p. 68). Finding a dozen
dead Vietnamese across the field the next morning and the
empty clips around his feet, he "couldn't remember ever
feeling so tired, so changed, so happy." Later, however, he
throws away the fatigues he was wearing. The next six
years, he tells us, were "years of thinking this or that about
what happens when you pursue a fantasy until it becomes
experience, and then afterward you can't handle the experience" (p. 68). Herr's personal pursuit of "a fantasy until it
becomes experience" exactly parallels his analysis of the

national pursuit in Southeast Asia of an adventure until it becomes a war.

The rest of the book never expands beyond the insights of this opening chapter; rather, it continues to move over the same themes and subjects, representing the action of a mind obsessively re-probing an experience in search of clearer comprehension and finally acceptance. Late in the book, Herr forces himself to confess in yet more explicit terms what he had revealed at the end of the first chapter:

All right, yes, it had been a groove being a war correspondent, hanging out with the grunts and getting close to the war, touching it, losing yourself in it and trying yourself against it. I had always wanted that, never mind why, it had just been a thing of mine . . . and I'd done it. (p. 206)

In the last chapter, "Breathing Out," Herr describes the trauma he suffered in trying to return to civilization from the personal frontier Vietnam embodied for him. After describing a night spent in a fresh landing zone, "in the heart of Indian country," he tells us that the Marines later named it LZ Loon and that Flynn said "That's what they ought to call the whole country"; Herr reflects that it would be "a more particular name than Vietnam to describe the death space and the life you found inside it" (p. 255).

In the interior landscape of *Dispatches* Herr depicts himself taking the same journey into Vietnam that America took with the Green Berets, suffering the same trauma of lost innocence and romantic illusion. In the exterior landscape of his remembering consciousness, however, Herr retakes the journey into a dangerous frontier, becoming a solitary hero whose accomplished mission is not to map the wilderness for a marching civilization but rather to illuminate the murky ambiguities of a wilderness interior to the civilization itself. Herr takes as his subject the "turnaround point" (p. 45) of the American drive westward, and finds in his literary exploration of that awful terrain his opportunity for heroic action on the American mythic landscape. The excitement of *Dispatches* for the post-Vietnam American is that it suggests Vietnam may yet be transformed into a frontier landscape affording a meaningful errand for the culture, an errand of self-examination.

III

Five years after his memoir *If I Die in a Combat Zone,* Tim O'Brien returned to his experience as a combat infantryman in Vietnam with his novel *Going After Cacciato.* O'Brien had developed his craft with an intervening first novel, *Northern Lights* (1974), about a returned Vietnam veteran's relationship with his brother, and had broadened his perspective through graduate study in government at Harvard University and work as a National Affairs reporter for the *Washington Post.* The complex vision O'Brien brings to the Vietnam subject in *Going After Cacciato* received enthusiastic acclaim in major magazines and newspapers across the country. In *Commentary,* for instance, Pearl K. Bell favorably contrasted *Going After Cacciato* with fellow veteran Winston Groom's *Better Times Than These* (1978), an authentically detailed but unfocused and formulaic imitation of James Jones' and Irwin Shaw's novels of World War II. She observed that "Instead of slogging inch by inch through the same muddy jungle that television transformed into an instant cliché, O'Brien stands the war on its head and turns it into a picaresque fantasy." Writing in the *New Yorker,* John Updike found that "the ambitious structure of the novel bespeaks an earnest intelligence that wishes to confront a traumatic experience on an ideological and moral level." In a cover article for the *New York Times Book Review,* Richard Freeman claimed O'Brien's combining of fantasy and realism in the novel to be "a major achievement and possibly the only way to deal with the truths of Vietnam."[10] Such praise was capped by the 1978 National Book Award for fiction, and the intricate structure of the book has made it a subject of continued analysis in literary journals.

Going After Cacciato is a novel within a novel, written in the mind of protagonist Spec 4 Paul Berlin while he stands guard one night from midnight to dawn on the Pacific shore of Vietnam. The chapters are divided into three categories: the periodic "Observation Post" chapters, in which Berlin reflects upon the fiction he is creating; the "memory" chapters, in which he recalls, with no particular chronology, the previous events of his tour in Vietnam; and the "fantasy" chapters, in which he imagines a journey of his squad all the way to Paris in pursuit of the deserter Cacciato. In the remembered realm of the book Cacciato "actually" does desert, and the mystery of his fate serves as the inspiration to Berlin's imaginative "dream." *Going After Cacciato* dramatizes the heroic pathos of a youth struggling in his mind toward some viable escape from the landscape of a seemingly meaningless war.

The realistic novels and memoirs of Caputo, Kovic, Huggett, Webb, Roth, and Del Vecchio (as well as the earlier memoir of O'Brien himself) tell a common tale in which the youthful protagonist leaves behind the society of his immediate father to connect with the cultural father by entering the frontier in Vietnam. There he suffers the traumatic shock of finding that he has instead entered a crazily inverted landscape of American myth frustrating all of his expectations. The protagonist of *Going After Cacciato* begins in this anti-frontier utterly separated from his proper mythic role, and imagines himself into a frontier stretching west from Vietnam all the way back to the Europe where the American errand commenced. Paul Berlin optimistically seeks through his imagined journey to Paris to work out what possibilities may remain for the aspiring American hero separated in Vietnam from the ideal self-concept of his culture.

In contrast to the escape from the immediate father (the present society) in search of the true father (the cultural mythos) found in the opening chapters of the veterans' memoirs and realistic novels, Berlin looks back from Vietnam at a single father who embodies at once the mythic concept of a good society and a good war. Significantly, Berlin closely associates his father with the landscapes of American myth. He recalls that his father fought "in France, knowing certain things certainly,"[11] the landscape of World War II in which the American enjoyed the role of rough but benign liberator of an effete but grand European civilization. His father also represents the American as yeoman validating the American frontier impulse by extending civilization to the west. Berlin dreams of returning home to the resonantly named Fort Dodge, winning an approving nod from his father by showing his medals, and then "they would go out to where his father was building houses in the development west of town . . . and his father would explain . . . how it took good materials and good craftsmanship and care to build houses that would be strong and lasting" (p. 68).

Berlin locates the important moments he has shared with his father in symbolic frontier settings of a preserved wilderness. On leave before going to Vietnam, "he'd gone camping with his father along the Des Moines River," where his father has assured him that "It'll be alright. . . . You'll see some terrible stuff, sure, but try to look for the good things. Try to learn" (p. 272). On an earlier trip to this preserved spot of American wilderness his father had taught him the names of the stars and their constellations, as well as the valleys of the moon as "guideposts, he'd said, so that no matter where in the world you are, anywhere, you know the spot" (p. 40).

The one fully presented episode from Berlin's youth is a sojourn he makes with his father to Wisconsin as members of Indian Guides "to camp and be pals forever." In the camp they ritualistically take the Indian names of Big Bear and Little Bear, don headbands and feathers, join in group powwows around a campfire, and race with canoes. But the trip culminates traumatically when Berlin gets lost in the woods trying to follow his father's tracks in a Guide Survival game. Found "lost, bawling in the big Wisconsin woods," Berlin recovers from his failed frontier initiation when he and his father share "hamburgers and root beer on the long drive home, baseball talk, white man talk, and he remembered it, the sickness going away" (pp. 59–60). This episode, movingly presented in a single paragraph set off by itself, establishes Berlin's deep desire to succeed at the frontier experience in order to feel that he deserves the comradeship and approval of his father.

In the "bad time" in which the book opens, Berlin is sick once again, this time deep in the woods of Vietnam, desperately seeking some way to follow in the steps of his father. In this anti-frontier he is trapped in the realization that he cannot here make the passage that would elevate him from a loved child to an approved son, and thus successfully bring him into the American mythic landscape. The Vietnam landscape collapses the progressive time and space of the American mythic landscape into a suspended world where "the war was always the same" and the features blend "into a single gray element" (p. 13). Later in the book Berlin contrasts Vietnam to the changing colors of the seasons back along the Des Moines River, the symbolic frontier landscape of his wilderness camping trips with his father, lamenting that here there is "nothing to gauge passage by" (p 67).

Vietnam is a mystery in which, a fantasized VC officer tells him, "the land is your enemy" (p. 67). Doc Peret, a fellow squad member, tells Berlin that Vietnam is "your basic vacuum. . . . So here we are . . . nothing to order, no substance. Aimless, that's what it is: a bunch of kids trying to pin the tail on the Asian donkey. But no fuckin tail. No fuckin donkey" (p. 131). Berlin sees in the hedgerows of Vietnam the alien relation of the culture to the American:

So where the paddies represented ripeness and age and depth, the hedgerows expressed the land's secret qualities: cut up, twisting, covert, chopped and mangled, blind corners leading to dead ends, short horizons always changing. It was only a feeling. A feeling of marching through a great maze, the feeling that mice must have as they run mazes. A sense of entrapment mixed with mystery. (p. 300)

Subsequently, Berlin lists what is mysteriously missing for the American soldier in this Asian landscape, the features of direction and clarity his father knew in the mythic landscape of World War II:

They did not know even the simple things: a sense of victory, or satisfaction, or necessary sacrifice. They did not know the feeling of taking a place and keeping it, securing a village and then raising the flag and calling it a victory. No sense of order or momentum. No front, no rear, no trenches laid out in neat parallels. No Patton rushing for the Rhine, no beachheads to storm and win and hold for the duration. They did not have targets. They did not have a cause. They did not know if it was a war of ideology or economics or hegemony or spite. On a given day, they did not know where they were in Quang Ngai, or how being there might influence larger outcomes. They did not know the names of most villages. . . . They did not know how to feel when they saw villages burning. Revenge? Loss? Peace of mind or anguish? They did not know. . . . They did not know good from evil. (pp. 320–21)

In this landscape, Berlin can only feel his separation from his father as well as the unfairness of it.

Entrapped in an anti-frontier of no direction and no meaning, Berlin conceives of his imagined journey after Cacciato. Cacciato serves in Berlin's fantasy as a kind of brotherly substitute for his father, a "guide" and "scout" (p. 81) who can lead Berlin's consciousness across a frontier of independent thought toward new comprehension of his situation. Cacciato is an ultimately unresolvable mystery of contradictions just as is the journey the squad takes after him. Those contradictions are the two opposing possibilities of the American character and history laid bare in Vietnam. Cacciato is on the one hand the quintessence of the desired American self-concept: a solitary, independent, innocent, benign, optimistic, and determined character who, having set for himself a goal, exhibits on his journey west cunning self-reliance while stripping himself of the baggage of his past identity, his "armored vest and bayonet, then his ammo pouch, then his entrenching tool and ID card" (p. 32), leaving behind maps for those who would follow his lead. Yet, as Berlin and other members of the pursuing squad assert repeatedly, Cacciato and his journey are also clearly "dumb" (p. 31) and "foolish" (p. 20). In appearance Cacciato seems "curiously unfinished" and characterized by a "boyish simplicity" (p. 21), and if he is Emerson's American Adam freeing himself of the encumbrances of an old world for a fresh start in a new one, he poses the problem of whether this new man is boldly showing the way to a better world or regressing into the self-indulgence of childhood.

Berlin's fantasized journey in the footsteps of this odd, dubious descendant of Leatherstocking creates an alternative landscape to the anti-frontier of Vietnam that, as Berlin repeatedly asserts to himself, restores the sense of "possibilities." Approximately a dozen times during the first quarter of the book the journey is described as a movement "west" or to the "Far West," with an emphasis on the changing terrain as they pass through the "wilderness." But at the heart of this restoration of the mythic American journey is a paradox. Cacciato has planned his frontier adventure by "thumbing through an old world atlas" (p. 21) and seeks not entry into nature or the founding of a New World but an escape into a city, Paris, that is a symbol in the American imagination of civilization at its most cultured and decadent. (Berlin's middle-aged lieutenant says, "So Cacciato's gone off to gay Paree—bare ass and Frogs everywhere, the Follies Brassiere" [p. 17]).

Berlin and his squad escape the directionless, passageless vacuum of Vietnam in their pursuit of Cacciato, following the essential American impulse to leave complication and corruption behind, but they themselves cannot decide if they are pursuing a mission (to bring him back) or an escape. The novel suggests that after Vietnam American consciousness can continue to follow the impulse of American myth only by abandoning the logic of American history. In the anti-frontier which American history has reached in Vietnam, Cacciato is all Berlin can imagine from the mythic traits of the American hero, an innocent and self-reliant Leatherstocking who can continue the optimistic trek westward only by dumbly and paradoxically leaving American mission in a self-indulgent regression back to the Old World. This paradox is perfectly presented in the imagery with which a member of Berlin's squad is described driving a cart: "Oscar shook the reins, hollered gid'yap, and soon they were riding westward along the rolling plains to Paris" (p. 76). When Berlin at last confronts Cacciato in Paris, he sees "a baby's smile, beguiling and meaningless" (p. 372).

Ultimately, in the realm of his imagined fantasy, Berlin must face the realization that his frontier journey brings him as a deserter to the landscape where his father came as a heroic savior. Looking at a newspaper, Berlin finds two photographs of Eisenhower accompanying a story of his death. One shows Eisenhower as a cadet at West Point, the other "showed him riding into Paris, the famous grin, his jeep swamped by happy Frenchmen" (p. 356). Berlin concludes that "an era had ended" but that it was difficult for his generation to feel much, "maybe his father would feel the right things" (p. 356). The protagonists of the realistic novels and memoirs go to Vietnam believing they are answering Kennedy's call to reenter the frontier of American mission, following the young President's example of replacing the old Eisenhower as heroic figure of a new generation. In *Going After Cacciato* the youthful protagonist gazes at the two images of a youthful and subsequently triumphant Eisenhower, makes no mention of Kennedy, and contemplates his own utter separation from any pos-

sibility of ever achieving the status of the previous generation, of his father.

Along the way to Paris Berlin has acquired a companion,
a young Vietnamese woman who is a projection of his desire to leave the war. In Paris she urges him to step fully
into his fantasy, leaving the war and the past behind. In a
scene mimicking the Paris Peace talks, Berlin rejects her
position, insisting that peace comes not simply from
"pursuing one's own pleasure" but "within the context of
our obligations to other people." Berlin gives up his fantasy with the conclusion that "imagination, like reality,
has its limits" (pp. 377–78). The novel returns to the
"actual" moment when Cacciato escaped the squad's ambush and they gave up the pursuit to remain in the war,
with Berlin on the last page contemplating the possibility
that Cacciato could "maybe" make it to Paris (p. 395). The
novel thus ends ambiguously with the boundless optimism
of the continuing frontier impulse contradicted by the
seeming lesson of Vietnam: that even the American must
accept limits.

IV

With the war over, the enduring problem of Vietnam for
America is its legacy for the story by which Americans
have shaped their understanding of their place in geography and history. Thus the three Vietnam works that have
been most widely received as important literature have
been less interested in a sustained portrait of the war than
in an exploration of its implications for American myth. In
some sense, each of these texts leaves Vietnam for another
landscape: *Dog Soldiers* for California; *Dispatches* for its
author's consciousness as he writes back in New York;
Going After Cacciato for a fantasized journey to Paris. All
three of these movements into a landscape providing an
alternative to Vietnam are made by protagonists seeking a

heroic role on personal new frontiers permitting them to achieve the traditional American self-concept. In *Dog Soldiers* Ray Hicks attempts to act out the redemptive roles of the heroes of his popular culture, and at last sacrifices himself while feeling the ironic satisfaction of being the lone, skilled, determined "little man in the boonies" against the superior force appearing in a machine. Michael Herr, as the narrator-protagonist of *Dispatches*, transforms his Vietnam experience into a mental wilderness through which he may journey on a valid mission for his culture, taking the risks entailed in his quest for the "secret history" of his and his nation's involvement in Vietnam. The need to create an alternative landscape to Vietnam becomes most overt in *Going After Cacciato*, in which Paul Berlin uses his imagination to leave the mysterious anti-frontier of the war behind to pursue to its logical conclusion the conflict between the boundless possibilities represented by the American frontier and the inescapable limits represented by the Vietnam experience. These three works powerfully portray an irresolvable tension between the memory of Vietnam and the memory of the previous mythic American landscape.

In these works the legacy of Vietnam appears to be the denial of a myth that nevertheless has lost none of its beauty or allure. That this seeming denial of the nation's understanding of its unique character and destiny has not been accompanied by any truly catastrophic effects on America's position in the world only increases its haunting aspect as evidence of something more deeply, mysteriously wrong. *Dog Soldiers*, *Dispatches*, and *Going After Cacciato* show the self-conscious American, burdened with the experience of Vietnam, attempting to escape this communal meaninglessness by entering a mental terrain with the configuration of the past mythic landscape. Writing from and for a modernist literary sensibility already emphasizing the ironic and pathetic in a broken world, Stone, Herr, and O'Brien present us with the cultural dimensions of a national myth fragmented by Vietnam. But they can thus offer Americans only journeys away from their myth that ironically re-create it within personal consciousness while denying its larger cultural, historical validity. In the two epic films about Vietnam, *The Deer Hunter* and *Apocalypse Now*, artists working in the ritualistic arena of the popular movie theater would turn the journey around in the other direction, sending the American mythic hero himself, the ideal self-concept of the culture, through a Vietnam mythicized into an overtly symbolic landscape of American memory.

In the iconography of *The Empire Strikes Back*, the frontier youth, wearing a holster on his hip, contends with an image of the dark past of Europe, wearing Nazi helmet and medieval robe.

CHAPTER SIX

Epic Return

O F THE FILMS which suddenly renewed interest in the
Vietnam War during the late 1970s, Michael Cimino's *The
Deer Hunter* (1978) and Francis Ford Coppola's *Apocalypse
Now* (1979) were by far the most ambitious. Instead of following the conventions of either the war or antiwar genres, the two directors based their films on genres of
American popular romance and explored the implications
of America's Vietnam experience for the mythic conceptions carried by those genres.

A 1959 graduate of Hofstra University, Coppola had entered film school at UCLA and then become the first of a
new generation of younger, film-school-trained directors
who would come to dominate contemporary American
film. With the immense artistic and commercial prestige
he gained from the two *Godfather* films, he decided in 1975
to direct a screenplay that adapted Joseph Conrad's classic
novella of European imperialism in the Congo, *Heart of
Darkness*, to a Vietnam setting. He pressed forward through
a series of crises (including a set-destroying typhoon in the
Philippines and the heart attack of starring actor Martin
Sheen) that made the film famous long before it appeared
in theaters.

The Deer Hunter was filmed in relative obscurity.
Cimino, a New Yorker in his late thirties with an M.F. A. in
architecture from Yale, was a screenwriter who had directed only one previous film, *Thunderbolt and Lightfoot*
(1974), which starred Clint Eastwood. Seemingly from
nowhere, Cimino's film appeared several months before

Coppola's notorious work-in-progress, accompanied by a promotional campaign successfully designed to overcome anticipated resistance to the Vietnam subject matter by emphasizing its epic human drama.

Such smaller films as *Go Tell the Spartans* (1978), *Coming Home* (1978), and *Who'll Stop the Rain?* (1978), a simplified adaptation of *Dog Soldiers,* more consistently pleased film critics and Vietnam doves, since they were more "realistic" and adopted clearer political stances. The extraordinary cinematic power and invention of *The Deer Hunter* and *Apocalypse Now* won the two films both major box-office success and many critical awards (*The Deer Hunter* received both the Academy Award and the New York Film Critics' Circle award for best picture of 1978; *Apocalypse Now* shared the grand prize at the 1979 Cannes Film Festival). Nevertheless, they were widely attacked in reviews and articles for being implausible and incoherent. In the *New Yorker,* for instance, Pauline Kael snidely compared *The Deer Hunter* to "boy's adventure classics" while complaining that "the film's point of view isn't clear." And in *Commonweal* Colin Westerbeck similarly derided the film's "level of contrivance" while attacking it as a "Western in which the Vietnamese Communists are the Indians, the vicious savages who have to be mowed down." In the *Atlantic,* Ward Just echoed many critics in calling *Apocalypse Now* "arguably the most wonderfully photographed cartoon in film history, but still a cartoon." Comparing its violations of verisimilitude to the Russian roulette in *The Deer Hunter,* he said that "I am puzzled and appalled at the need for inventing a metaphor for the Vietnam War."[1]

The parallel attacks on the two films inadvertently pointed to their shared approach: neither film attempts a literal depiction of the war in Vietnam. Like the classic American "romancers" of the early American novel, Cimino and Coppola transform their subject into mythic allegory. To use Hawthorne's term, they "spiritualize" Vietnam into a symbolic landscape. On a far more overt and far higher artistic level, *The Deer Hunter* and *Apocalypse Now* return the American public to Southeast Asia in the same psycho-symbolic dimension in which Americans originally dreamed Vietnam in *The Ugly American* and the legend of the Special Forces. In both films the journey of the main character deep into the wilderness of Vietnam is a journey by the idealized American hero deep into his inner nature, long since projected upon Vietnam, to confront his traumatized mythic values. While disparate in texture and theme, both films render Vietnam into a nightmare journey of the American hero through an inverted landscape of American myth and dream.

Each of the films patterns its narrative along the lines of a heroic quest. In each case that quest is drawn from a genre of popular American romance. In the case of *The Deer Hunter,* with its allusion to *The Deerslayer* (Cooper's "Leatherstocking" novel that depicted a youthful initiation into Indian fighting), the inspiration is obviously the western's frontier mythos. *Apocalypse Now* adapts the Conrad novella to the specific conventions of the hardboiled detective story—itself a twentieth-century urban outgrowth of the western. These two enduring genres of American pulp literature provide the two directors the contexts within which they can explore Vietnam on the fundamental level of. American cultural myth.

I

Despite its decline in recent years, the western has been the major formula story of American popular culture over the last century and a half, establishing its central significance as American myth. The western is defined, not by a single pattern of action, but by the influence of its symbolic frontier landscape upon a lonely hero.[2] The confrontation of these basic forces creates a sharply delineated conflict resulting in a variety of stock characters and plot configurations. With its emphasis on the relation of the hero to a frontier, the western deals with the conflict created by the dominant direction of American experience, the flight from community (Europe, the East, restraint, the conscious) into a wilderness (America, the West, freedom, the unconscious).

In *The Deer Hunter* Cimino, who in the subsequent *Heaven's Gate* (1981) turned directly to the genre, presents America's experience in Vietnam through the major elements of the western. As Leslie Fiedler has shown, the "low" forms of fantasy literature, particularly those emphasizing violence and terror, have provided the classic authors of the American novel with symbolic vehicles for the exploration of basic conflicts within American consciousness.[3] Although the function of the popular western, as John Cawelti has observed, is "to resolve some of the unresolvable contradictions of American values that our major writers have laid bare,"[4] the genre has in the hands of literary practitioners such as Owen Wister and film-makers such as John Ford served as a vehicle for sophisticated popular art. In addition, it has also provided an important influence and impetus for the more disturbing explorations of American culture found in Hawthorne, Melville, Twain, Hemingway, and Faulkner. The western formula affords Cimino the strengths of the central national myth in dealing with Vietnam as a collective American trauma. At the same time, *The Deer Hunter* achieves more than a perpetuation of past myth by its understanding of the essence of the myth and its critical examination of it. Unlike *The Green Berets*, in its novel and especially its film version an unthinking use of the western formula, *The Deer Hunter* is a western affected by the shift in landscape. *The Deer Hunter* is an important artistic interpretation of the war precisely because it so fully comprehends the essence of its source and self-consciously explores its meaning in reference to recent American experience.

In *The Deer Hunter* the actions and character of a lonely hero, Michael Vronsky (Robert De Niro), are closely associated with wilderness landscapes, the basis for a structure of violent conflicts and sharp oppositions. The film turns on such characteristic devices of the western as male-bonding, the repressed love of the hero for a "good woman," the terror of confrontation with savage denizens of a hostile landscape, dancehall girls, even a "shoot out" across a table in a crowded gambling room. But even as Cimino thus sets the Vietnam experience squarely in the context of the dominant American historical-mythic tradition, he turns the genre upside down. Assimilating the Vietnam experience into the western formula, Cimino substitutes for its traditional plot motifs, implying the inevitable triumph of white consciousness, a story of traumatic captivity.

The accusations of racism made against *The Deer Hunter* are not correct in a political or social sense; Vietnamese are shown as among the victims of the Viet Cong in the Russian roulette captivity scenes, a black American soldier without arms in the military hospital is one of the most vivid statements against war in the film, and white Americans are prominently shown placing bets in the final Russian roulette scene. But the film does employ the imagery that has traditionally obsessed American popular culture and which was projected upon Vietnam in *The Ugly American*, the legend of the Green Berets, and in reverse fashion the rhetoric and writings of the antiwar movement: a violent confrontation between the conscious and unconscious, civilization and wilderness, played out in the white imagination as a struggle between light and dark. *The Deer Hunter*, through the western formula, presents Vietnam as a historic projection of an internal struggle of white American consciousness, but one where the dream (inherent in the western) of mastery over nature and the unconscious, or alternatively of benign communion with them, is turned upside down into a nightmare of captivity.

The defining elements of the western are first present in *The Deer Hunter* in a timelessly mythic configuration: the hero Michael lives on an edge between civilization, the Pennsylvania steel town named Clairton representing both European tradition and modern industrialization, and nature, the surrounding mountain forest embodying the original American wilderness. Cimino has written that he explained to his director of photography "at the beginning my feelings about location, my feelings about the importance of size and presence of landscape in a film—and the statement that landscape makes, without anyone realizing it."[5] His symbolic intentions are asserted by his representation of an "ideal" Pennsylvania steel town with a composite of eight separate locations from Cleveland to Pittsburgh, of the Alleghenies with the more magnificent Cascade Mountains of Washington state, and of the deer with an impressive stag imported from a wildlife preserve in New Jersey. In each case Cimino sacrifices authentic setting to achieve a more powerfully mythic landscape.[6]

The deer hunter himself has the salient traits embodied in his Cooper-prototype and in virtually every western hero to follow. Living on the outer edge of the town in a trailer, he is a part of the community and yet is clearly separated from it by his alienation from its corruption and by his strict adherence to a personal code closely associated with the uncorrupted wilderness. For example, he despises all of his friends except Nick (Christopher Walken) for their inability to understand the ritualistic importance of killing a deer with "one shot." And at the wedding reception he responds to whispers from Stanley (John Cazale) about the actual father of the pregnant bride's unborn child by running down the street stripping off his clothes, a compulsive flight from social corruption. Finding little relevance in the old European traditions of the community, Michael has, like his literary ancestor, turned to nature. In the opening sequence he perplexes his companions by insisting that they go on a hunt that night because the "sun dogs" he sees in the sky are an old Indian sign of "a blessing on the hunters sent by the Great Wolf to his children."[7] And in strong contrast to his detachment from the elaborate rituals of the Russian Orthodox wedding, which he knows are mocked by the pregnancy of the bride, he is intensely involved in the proper preparation, practice, and culmination of the hunt. Finally, the taunts of Stanley that Michael does not take advantage of opportunities with women clearly set Michael in the tradition of the celibate western hero.

Michael is also characterized as separated from his community by the more disturbing traits of the western hero. Suggestively, the characters regard Michael with both respectful awe and uneasy perplexity, finding his omen-reading crazy and his hunting prowess extraordinary. From the viewer's perspective also, Michael's characteristics have contradictory significance. His need to prove self-reliant control results in reckless activity, as in the scene in which he risks his own and his friends' lives by passing a truck on the inside merely on a casual bet. And his deer hunting, attractive for its skill and sense of value, results in the image of a gutted deer sprawled across his old Cadillac's hood as it speeds down the mountain road to drunken singing. Even Michael's distaste for the practice and consequences of sexual promiscuity is set off against his repressed passion for Nick's girlfriend Linda (Meryl Streep), revealed in his courting of her during the wedding reception.

Indeed, the narcissistic, promiscuous, and pistol-flashing Stanley, who is Michael's antagonist, is also the dark reflection of his repressed self, just as the outlaw is the mirror image of the western hero. Michael's flight down the street from Stanley's whispers about the corrupted bride is also a flight from the chivalrous advances he himself has made to his best friend's girl. And when Michael, deriding Stanley's womanizing and carrying of a handgun, holds up a bullet and says, "*This* is *this*, this isn't something else," his insistence on the bullet's lack of symbolic significance while he himself cradles his deerslaying rifle must be ironic for the viewer. Michael, like the western hero, is a man of extraordinary virtues and resources that are dangerous unless properly channeled into a role protective of the community.

While the defining elements of the western are those of *The Deer Hunter*, they are conceived in more complex psycho-symbolic terms. The western has conventionally projected the conflicts of American consciousness in characters representing either pure good or pure evil (hero versus outlaw, lawmen versus rustlers, cavalry versus Indians, noble Indian tribes versus threatening tribes) in a single landscape. Cimino uses the same psycho-symbolic method and terms, but dramatizes the conflicts within the consciousness of the hero and projects them in a division of both characters *and* landscape. Like *The Ugly American* and the various tales making up the legend of the Green Berets, the film develops through the stock oppositions and melodramatic confrontations of the western, but they are presented more explicitly as external images of the protagonist's consciousness, projections of his impulses and thus of the national consciousness he represents as mythic hero. As a result, Vietnam functions in the film as a mirror image of America, a dark landscape turning upside down the benign landscape of Cimino's mythic Alleghenies.

This relation of Michael as western hero to the landscapes and secondary characters of *The Deer Hunter* is brilliantly embodied in the remarkable cut with which Cimino abruptly moves the film from America to Vietnam. One moment Michael, after returning to the bar from the mountain hunt, is in a quiet reverie as he listens with his male friends to melodic piano; the next, surrounded by dead American soldiers, he lies unconscious amid the exploding horrors of Vietnam. The effect of the cut is to have

Michael wake up from his dream of the deer hunt to a nightmare inversion of the landscape and its relation to the hero and community. The first third of the film shows Michael in flight to nature and away from a strained, corrupt, but strongly bonded community. But, as Michael recovers consciousness, that flight has taken the viewer into hell. From a high angle the camera looks down on Michael as he struggles to lift himself from the jungle grass, a sharp contrast to the low angle from which the camera set Michael against the sky during the deer hunt. The community, a small Vietnamese village, is surrounded, not by snow-capped, pine-forested mountain peaks, but by dark jungle foliage. In contrast to the opening shots of the film, which showed Michael and his friends at the mill harnessing fire to make steel, now helicopters destroy the village with incendiary bombs. Steven's pregnant bride metaphorically, and his mother literally, dragged him from the male haven of the bar; now a grinning North Vietnamese cadre tosses a grenade into a shelter full of women and children. Michael and his friends found satisfaction in hunting and gutting a deer; now pigs fight over the entrails of dead American soldiers. Nature and civilization are the dominant terms of both the American and Vietnamese settings, but in Vietnam the asylum of nature has become an invading hell.

Yet Michael is revealed as in his element here, for his influence and impulses have been unleashed in this frontier landscape. His countenance immediately verifies this, for the hunter who guided himself by Indian lore now wears a cloth headband about his head and has war paint (for camouflage) streaked on his face. He is, in fact, a Green Beret Ranger in an advance reconnaissance unit, and both his appearance and his professional identity link him to the tradition of Indian fighters who used Indian skills, became like Indians, to protect the community from Indians. Michael, who like Deerslayer and other western heroes could only flee the internal threat of corruption inherent in social relations, responds to the external threat of a darker-skinned man firing on a woman and child by literally purging him from the earth with fire. Michael's intense compulsions in the first third of the film were manifested in reckless driving, excessive drinking, flight from women, and a hunt resulting in the image of a gutted deer. Michael, like the western hero, finds a place for his violent impulses only in a threatened community. This scene classically parallels the image of a frontier hero protecting innocent settlers by killing the savage Indian. But Michael's method, a furious blast from a flamethrower, visually asserts the deeper ambiguity of the scene; it opened with women and children fleeing to an underground shelter as American helicopters descended to blow apart their village with napalm. The North Vietnamese soldier is only an undisguised version of the evil that Michael's "good" forces bring to the community. And both the "evil" North Vietnamese and "good" American helicopters act out the repressed hatreds against community found in the male culture of Clairton's bars and hunts.

This ambiguity, based in a visual presentation of the "good" and "evil" elements of the western in clear mirror relation to each other, is brought to its fullest implications in the central sequence of the film, the forced Russian roulette scenes. This sequence has been the focus of the most outraged attacks on the film, for to such critics of the war as Jane Fonda and Gloria Emerson it has seemed to present a white America as innocent victim of a savage Viet Cong.[8] And, indeed, it is a portrayal of America's experience in Vietnam out of that earliest source of the western, the Indian captivity narrative in which innocent whites are subjected to hideous tortures. But there are deep ambiguities within this apparent confrontation between innocent whites and dark savages. The Viet Cong, as they grin, drink beer, and bet money while forcing their captives to play Russian roulette, display the same impulse and even the same iconography as did Michael and his friends in the bar in Clairton when they drank and bet on televised football. And the one-shot nature of Russian roulette is a parallel to the one-shot value of Michael's hunt. Finally, just as Michael has been the restrained, intense leader of loutish companions, the Viet Cong have the look of grinning, stupid brutes except for the impassive, controlled visage of the leader.

The effect is that the Viet Cong function as demonic images of the dark impulses of American culture, particularly as found in the western hero Michael. The Indians and other darker races, closely associated with the wilderness landscape in which the white culture confronts them, have functioned in the myth and literature of American culture as symbols of forces in the unconscious. The larger symbolic design and implications of the film are a continuation of those elements of the western: the Vietnam jungle and its savage Viet Cong denizens are the nightmare inversion of the American forests and beautiful deer. Nightmare and dream, both landscapes and their inhabitants are projected aspects of the unconscious, a region beyond the confines, restraints, and limits of the conscious mind embodied in the community. The captivity scene, as did the Puritan narratives of Indian captivity, embodies a nightmare journey into the darker implications of wilderness. If the wilderness landscape (the unconscious) is a place to which the hero goes in order to dominate his passions without external restraints, it can also be the place where he may find himself captive to those same passions. The hunter becomes the hunted, the one shot of complete control an emblem of self-destruction.

By making a captivity narrative the central episode of the film, Cimino inverts the terms of the western formula. While the captivity narrative was a major nonfiction genre of early American writing, the western employs its horrors only to set the revenge-quest plot in motion; in effect, the western substitutes a fantasy emphasizing the eventual assertion of white power and value for a historical genre that

had emphasized the experience of complete passivity before an alien culture. Conceiving of the Vietnam War as a
western in which the captivity experience is the pivotal
episode, Cimino makes *The Deer Hunter* deeply disturbing
on the most resonant level of cultural myth.

The trauma of the captivity experience is foreshadowed,
and its full resonance prepared, earlier in the film when
Michael confronts a Green Beret who unexpectedly appears at a bar in the American Legion hall during the wedding reception. In a scene that takes place earlier in the
day in Michael's trailer as he prepares for the deer hunt
that night, former-President Kennedy looks out from a
photograph on the wall as Michael and Nick discuss the
hunt and their imminent departure for Vietnam. When the
Green Beret responds to Michael's question that night
about what Vietnam is like by answering "fuck it" and
taking a shot of whiskey, the traumatic fall of the Kennedy-
version of the frontier hero is foreshadowed. The hunt,
Vietnam, Kennedy's New Frontier, and the Green Beret all
come together in the western hero Michael. In the Green
Beret at the wedding reception, Michael confronts the
trauma of the American hero in Vietnam that he himself
will experience there in captivity. The western hero looks
forward in history to his descendant, the Green Beret, but
from his position of innocence cannot perceive that he is
gazing at the crisis toward which he is moving.

The final third of the film develops the consequences of
the captivity experience. *The Deer Hunter* presents Vietnam as a frontier landscape so hostile that America, having come as hunter with dreams of omnipotence, is held
captive and forced to confront the full implications of its
own impulses. There is no revenge-quest in *The Deer
Hunter* because it would be beside the point; the point is to
determine how a culture proceeds once it has experienced
the inversion of its central assumptions about itself.
Michael's resourcefulness as western hero enables him to
lead Nick in killing their captors, but not before they have

suffered captivity to unrestrained violence. Nick, who called Michael a "control freak" and resisted his obsession with killing the deer with "one shot" in favor of "thinking about the deer" and "the way the trees are in the mountains," is psychologically destroyed. In the Puritan narratives of Indian captivity, as Richard Slotkin has pointed out, "captivity psychology left only two responses open to the Puritans, passive submission or violent retribution.[9] Nick in effect follows both courses. He first has to be restrained by Michael from repeatedly beating a Viet Cong corpse, but then turns the unleashed impulse to destroy back upon himself. Unable to call Linda, then lured into the Russian roulette of Saigon, fading into dope and finally death, Nick represents an innocent acceptance of nature that cannot survive the dark revelations of Vietnam. Michael, the hunter who dominates nature (his unconscious) through controlled violence (repression), discovers in captivity that he cannot be omnipotent.

For both of these Adamic characters Vietnam is a "fall," but for Michael it is a fortunate one. In the second deer hunt of the film, which follows the Vietnam captivity experience, he does not shoot the deer despite his increasingly frantic pursuit of it. Instead, when the deer faces him, he shoots into the air and says "Okay," then sits by a stream and angrily shouts the word, which is this time echoed back by the mountains. "Okay" is of course an expression of acceptance, and Leo Marx identifies the echo as a standard device of pastoral literature representing the establishment of a reciprocal relationship with nature, the "pastoral ideal" of locating a "middle ground somewhere 'between,' yet in a transcendent relation to, the opposing forces of civilization and [primitive] nature."[10] When at the climax of the film Michael once again faces Nick across a table at a Russian roulette game, he is desperately attempting to bring Nick back from his captivity in the violent compulsions once present but "controlled" in Michael and subsequently transferred to Nick in the first Russian roulette scene. While Michael has responded to the trauma by moving toward a cautious version of the acceptance of nature that Nick had, Nick has become the alienated nihilist Michael potentially could have become. Nick had abandoned the "one-shot" obsession of Michael for simple primitivist communion with his benign ideal of nature, but the traumatic experience of captivity has turned his innocence into the opposite extreme of an obsession with a "one-shot" submission to passivity. The same experience has led Michael to abandon his "one-shot" obsession with control, instead accepting a balance, or "middle ground," between the conscious and unconscious.

A common device in such Hollywood westerns as *The Searchers* (1956) and *The Magnificent Seven* (1960), perhaps originating in Cooper's use of Natty Bumppo and Duncan Heyward in *The Last of the Mohicans* (1826),[11] is the "doubling" of the hero. Typically, the experienced hero rides off at the end, "free" but alone, and the "novice hero" settles down with a woman, domesticated but "happy." This gives both forces of American consciousness mythic affirmation and thus avoids a cultural choice. Cimino has reversed the usual fates of the two heroes, with the experienced hero giving up his lonely freedom in order to "settle down" in the community and the novice hero now finding himself unable to return to it. In addition, Cimino has substituted for the ambiguous image of riding-off-into-the-sunset a clear image of self-destruction in an alien landscape.

In settling down, Michael does not abandon the personal code of the western hero based on the hunter myth;[12] he instead brings it to the protection of the community from a threat he now recognizes, however inarticulately, as internal, a dark compulsion holding both himself and his culture in captivity. The first third of the film portrays Clairton as a world of strong male-bonding in which women, like the deer in the forests, are objects upon whom a principle of nature is projected and subdued. Michael's passionately restrained courting of Linda during the wedding reception is an attempt to express and at the same time control the passion for her that threatens to corrupt his "pure" love for Nick; this frustration contrasts with the spiritual satisfaction he finds shooting the deer with "one shot" in the company of his male friend. The cultural implications are darkly, if also comically, mirrored by Stanley's response to another man's sexual advances to his girlfriend: he punches the girl. Even the sensitive Steven, who is willing to marry the woman he loves when he knows she is carrying another man's child, is accused by his mother as she takes him from the bar of burdening her with his family while he goes off to Vietnam with "these bums." The eventual results of this stance are apparent in Linda's alienated father, drunkenly threatening on the morning of the wedding to give the whole town "flat tires" before greeting his daughter with a blow to her head and a declaration that all women are "bitches."

Initially confused and passive upon his return to Clairton, Michael, after his climactic acceptance of the freedom of the deer (a traditional symbol of the feminine principle in the unconscious),[13] can act as hero in freeing his community from its captivity by a self-destructive cultural impulse. That night in the mountains he returns without his rifle to his male companions to find Stanley, in response to sexual taunts, pointing his chrome-plated pistol at their friend Axel. In a rage at this reflected image of the compulsion he has just thrown off, Michael uses Russian roulette to purge Stanley of his dark obsession with male sexual power, and then throws Stanley's talisman of destructive potency out into the night. With this purgation of his darker self, Michael is able to go back down into town and in effect "rescue" a weeping Linda from the exclusion represented by Axel's declaration that on the hunt there would be "no women." He then takes the crippled Steven from the veterans hospital, where old men run bingo games for maimed young men in a parody of the final sterility of men without women. Michael restores Steven to his wife, who waits in bedridden loneliness, and to the young boy, who plays with a toy pistol in an innocent promise that without new example the future will follow the nightmare of the past. Finally, Michael returns to Vietnam in an attempt to bring back Nick.

Michael's return is set against the background of America's flight from Vietnam during the fall of Saigon. Despite the terrible failure of his quest to save Nick, *The Deer Hunter* suggests it is a journey America must make, a return to its Vietnam experience to face its destroyed innocence and the consequences of its prior obsession with control. When Michael, after failing to convince the drugged Nick to return home, resorts to substituting for Nick's opponent in his next game of Russian roulette, he tries to convey to Nick the lesson he has learned from his intense struggle with their traumatic experience. As he saved Nick physically in the first Russian roulette game by convincing him to risk death in order to outwit their captors, now he attempts to save Nick from the resulting obsession by trying to persuade him not to risk death senselessly. "Is this what you want?" Michael asks as he places the pistol to his own head, and accompanies his agonizingly slow pulling of the trigger with, "I love you." When Nick, thus far showing no recognition or response, then places the pistol to his own head, Michael desperately asks if he remembers the "trees" and the "mountains," only to see Nick, with a moment's apparent recognition, smilingly answer "one shot" before blowing his head apart.

This final conversation is a reversal of the ideas they exchanged in Michael's trailer before going to Vietnam, with the implications of "one-shot" control revealed as containing those of "one-shot" self-destruction. When he holds Nick's bloodsoaked head Michael faces, and thus can fully recognize, the result of his prior obsession. Crying "Nicky" in hysterical despair, he must realize that, through the legacy of his earlier drives, he has killed Nick.

This scene is followed by actual footage of a network news correspondent, on an aircraft carrier off the Indochina coast, reporting the end of the American involvement in Vietnam while in the background a helicopter from Saigon is pushed wobbling into the sea. The parallel implies that America, like Michael, must make the connections between its failure in Vietnam and the drives of its triumphant past.

The controversial ending of the film is thus neither jingoistic absolution for America's Vietnam involvement nor an ironic commentary. All the surviving characters, male and female, have been brought together by the hero to a table in the former male haven of the bar. Close shots of setting plates, lifting chairs, and making room around the table emphasize the daily heroism involved in preserving a community. Accepting loss and trauma, the western hero has taken a place in his society. In joining in the spontaneous singing of a tearful "God Bless America," concluded with a smiling toast to Nick, Michael also joins his community in asserting the continuing value of the ideal embodied in a simple love for America, for the dream of a benignly magnificent landscape, but with a full awareness both of the dangers of chaotic nature and of a person's, or society's, obsession with self-reliant control. In contrast to the proud assertions of "The Star-Spangled Banner" and "My Country, 'Tis of Thee," "God Bless America" is a humble acknowledgment that the divine favor seemingly manifest in the American landscape can be achieved only if a spiritual consciousness will guide America on its uncertain nighttime journey. Michael and the other characters make a half-conscious call for grace, a parallel to the Puritan settlers' anxious renewals of their special covenant with God, the compact which in secular form has been central to the idea of America. With this startling, intensely moving ending, Cimino suggests that America can benefit from Vietnam if as a result it assimilates the resourcefulness and adaptability of its frontier character to the intense self-examination and communal obligation associated with its Puritan heritage.

The basic impulse of the western has been the concept of regeneration through violence. In *The Deer Hunter* this concept is reversed, for the regeneration results from the inner-directed response of the hero to violence turned back on him. Purgation is replaced by shock, and then acceptance. Vietnam is viewed as the self-projected historical nightmare through which America can awaken from its dream of innocent mastery into a mature consciousness.

II

The opening scenes of *Apocalypse Now* quickly disabuse the viewer of any expectations that the film will attempt a faithful adaptation of *Heart of Darkness*. Recalling the highly literate language of Conrad's narrator Marlow, a number of reviewers noted with bemusement or dismay the similarity between the voiceover narration of Captain Willard (Martin Sheen) and what Veronica Geng, who was substituting for Pauline Kael, called in the *New Yorker* the "easy ironies, the sin-city similes, the weary, laconic, why-am-I-even-bothering-to-tell-you language"[14] of Raymond Chandler's private eye Philip Marlowe. Combined with the opening shots showing Willard with a cigarette hanging out of the side of his mouth, rotating ceiling fan above and a revolver and bottle of liquor at his side, this language signals the development of the broad symbolic outline of *Heart of Darkness* through the specific ethos, imagery, and pattern of the hardboiled detective genre. In this way *Apocalypse Now* transforms Conrad's classic English novella of nineteenth-century European colonialism into an American journey.

The hardboiled detective genre, which originated in the *Black Mask* pulp magazine in the 1920s, is a distinctly American version of the classic detective story. It was raised to a high artistic level by Dashiell Hammett and Chandler in fiction and by John Huston and Howard Hawks in film. The private eye, unlike the brilliantly analytical classic detective, is a twentieth-century urban, and thus more sophisticated and cynical, descendant of the western hero. He combines the tough attributes necessary for survival in his environment with a strict integrity based on a personal code of ethics. The setting is a modern American city, most often in Southern California, an urban wilderness or "neon jungle" that is geographically, historically, and mythically correct for the genre because the hardboiled detective moves through a corrupt society that has replaced the frontier.

There are important similarities, reflecting the common source in a single pattern of myth, between *Heart of Darkness* and the hardboiled detective formula. Both have isolated protagonists on a journey of mystery and adventure who are employed by others while actually preserving their personal autonomy of judgment. In both works the protagonist encounters revelatory scenes of the depravity of his society. And the final apprehension of the criminal, while on the surface restoring moral order, actually ends in dissolution, with the protagonist more cynical about his world than before. Thematically, both Conrad's novella and the hardboiled detective genre are generally understood to be journeys through a symbolic underworld, or hell, with an ultimate horror at the end providing a terrible illumination. In method both combine the classic motif of a quest for a grail with a modern, geographically recognizable locale. And while the clipped, slangy style of the hardboiled genre has on the surface little in common with the obscure, evocative style of *Heart of Darkness*, they pursue similar purposes in the dreamlike (or nightmarish) effect with which they render reportorial detail.

The essential patterns of *Heart of Darkness* and the hardboiled genre separate only in the relation of the protagonist to the criminal. The detective, despite his similarity to the underworld in speech and appearance, remains sharply distinct from the murderer, for in not only exposing but also judging the murderer he embodies the moral order of the ideals of his society not found in its reality; Marlow, in contrast, comes to identify with Kurtz, finally admiring him as much as he is repelled by him, thus making *Heart of Darkness* ultimately a psycho-symbolic journey to the unconscious. While the hardboiled formula asserts lonely integrity as an alternative to a corrupt society, Conrad's novella implies a universal darkness in man.

In *Apocalypse Now* Coppola uses the hardboiled detective formula to transform the river journey of *Heart of Darkness* into an investigation of both American society (represented by the army) and American mythos (represented by Colonel Kurtz [Marlon Brando]). The river journey in *Apocalypse Now* is full of allusions to Southern California, the usual setting of the hardboiled genre, with the major episodes of this trip through Vietnam centering on the surfing, rock music, go-go dancing, and drug-taking associated with the west-coast culture of the time. As a result, the river journey drawn from *Heart of Darkness* takes the detective and viewer, not through Vietnam as a separate culture, but through Vietnam as the resisting object of a hallucinatory self-projection of American culture.

Captain Willard's river journey is both external investigation of that culture and internal pursuit of its ideal. Willard is a hardboiled detective hero who in the Vietnam setting becomes traumatized by the apparent decadence of his society and so searches for the grail of its lost sense of mission. Kurtz represents that mythic ideal and finally the horrific self-awareness of its hollowness. In the hardboiled genre the detective hero, denied by his pervasive society even the refuges of nature and friendship with a "natural man" available to the western hero, is forced by his investigation of a corrupt society to retreat into his own ruthlessly strict moral idealism; *Apocalypse Now* forces the detective into a quest for that idealism itself.

From the beginning of the film it is clear that Willard lacks the genre-detective's certainty of his own moral position. Willard has already been to Vietnam, and upon going back to America has found that he would "wake up and there'd be nothing." Further, he is unsure of his purpose in returning to Vietnam: "When I was here I wanted to be there, when I was there all I could think of was getting back into the jungle." While the opening imagery establishes Willard's detective identity, it also asserts his diminished version of that figure. The closeup shots of letters from home and of a photograph of his ex-wife, to which he places a lit cigarette, represent what he has had to abandon. His drunken practice of Oriental martial arts, as opposed to the controlled drinking and solitary chessplaying of Chandler's Philip Marlowe, represents a shift from troubled purpose to self-destruction. And Sheen's taut characterization invests this deterioration of the detective's cynical armor with the explosive alienation of a James Dean. Similarly, Willard's voiceover narration, written by *Dispatches* author Michael Herr and widely derided as a banal parody of Chandler's prose, evokes the sardonic perspective of a Philip Marlowe without the strong sense of personal identity conveyed by that detective's penetrating wit. But it is immediately apparent that this detective suspects *he* is a criminal. When the soldiers come with his orders to report to the military command, for what as it turns out will be an assignment, Willard responds drunkenly, "What are the charges?" Since it comes after weeks of "waiting for a mission," Willard accepts the assignment to assassinate Kurtz as a murderer, but he asserts in voiceover that "charging a man with murder in this place was like handing out speeding tickets at the Indy 500." He knows that he could also be called a murderer, for he has a record of unofficial assassinations.

As guilty detective, Willard is a portrait of the traumatic fall the American self-concept has experienced in Vietnam. The torment that has driven Willard back to Vietnam in flight from himself is dramatized in the claustrophobic Saigon hotel room scenes. After first viewing his mental image of American civilization burning lush Asian jungle, we watch Willard descend into a drunken madness, accompanied by the Doors acid-rock group playing "The End," that culminates when he cuts himself while smashing a mirror in which he has observed his image. After the drunken nightmare, as Willard sits screaming and bent on the floor smeared with blood, the film begins the story proper with the appearance of the soldiers bringing him his orders. This psychological descent into personal annihilation presents the same imagery as that at the end of the film in Willard's climactic confrontation with Kurtz, when—once again accompanied by the Doors' song— Willard is splashed with blood as he cuts a man who has become an image of his hidden self. The implausible events, the surreal and often religious imagery, the eerie music used to punctuate key scenes, the pervasive dissolves, the statement to Willard in the General's quarters that "this mission does not exist, nor will it ever exist," the portentously retrospective voiceover narration, all contribute to the experience of the film as a journey into the self that is both nightmare and revelation.

The narration also suggests that this journey into the self has strong symbolic dimensions for the American culture. As the soldiers come up the stairs, Willard's retrospective voice comments: "Everyone gets everything he wants. I wanted a mission, and for my sins they gave me one. Brought it up to me like room service." His desire for a "mission" to provide justification for his continued existence resonates with the American view that its identity results from its special mission, and his receiving it in punishment for his "sins" echoes the agonized need of the Puritans for purgative self-condemnation when they sensed that they had fallen from their "errand." The resulting journey appears as though simultaneously summoned by his own nightmare and sent by a judging God. Willard, as a diminished hardboiled detective hero representing the contemporary American ideal experiencing traumatic self-doubt, goes on a mission through the mean streets of American culture and his own soul to confront the original American mythos, his double. His subsequent telling of the tale, the film itself, is the means by which American consciousness may admit its former self-delusion in a search for salvation: "It was no accident that I got to be the caretaker of Colonel Walter E. Kurtz's memory, anymore than being back in Saigon was an accident. There is no way to tell his story without telling my own, and if his story is really a confession, then so is mine."

In melding *Heart of Darkness* and the hardboiled detective genre into this psycho-symbolic journey through Vietnam, *Apocalypse Now* draws more of its particulars from the latter. Willard, having been summoned from his Saigon quarters, an equivalent to the private eye's seedy downtown office, receives his assignment from the General, who clearly evokes the manager in *Heart of Darkness* by speaking of "unsound" methods while engaging in the brutal exploitation of a country. The specific development of the scene, however, as the General tells Willard that Kurtz had disappeared with his Montagnard army into Cambodia when he "was about to be arrested for murder," suggests a conventional episode of the hardboiled formula. Sitting over an elegant lunch in the elaborately furnished trailer serving as his headquarters, and with a melancholy expression listening to Willard's record as an assassin before having him assigned to "terminate" Kurtz, the General is, in the context of the Vietnam War, a military version of the powerful client who receives the detective with palpable distaste in his impressive mansion. Marlow's private aloofness from his employers in *Heart of Darkness* becomes in *Apocalypse Now* the hardboiled detective's retention of his self-reliance and judgment while ostensibly working for his client: "I took the mission. What the hell else was I gonna do? But I really didn't know what I'd do when I found him."

Likewise, while the journey downriver in *Apocalypse Now* adopts the parallel development in *Heart of Darkness* of the protagonist's growing repulsion from his society and increasing attraction to Kurtz, this pattern is once again specifically presented according to the hardboiled formula. In that formula the detective, while pursuing the murderer, uncovers such pervasive corruption in the society that his final isolation and judgment of the criminal is undercut. A commentator on the genre characterizes the portrayal of the official representatives of society, the police, as "incompetent, brutal, or corrupt."[15] These traits are the point of the three major discoveries Willard makes on his journey about how the army is "legitimately" fighting the war. Witnessing Colonel Kilgore's use of overpowering technology to slaughter a Viet Cong village full of women and children for the prize of a surfing beach, Willard says in voiceover: "If that's how Kilgore fought the war, I began to wonder what they really had against Kurtz. It wasn't just insanity and murder. There was enough of that to go around for everyone." After leaving the USO show where he has seen profiteering and dehumanized sex, the glamorous corruption typical of the detective novel, he comments: "The war was being run by a bunch of four-star clowns who were going to end up giving the whole circus away." And his reaction to the futile and apparently endless battle of the Do Lung bridge, fought merely so the generals can say the bridge is open, is a disgusted, "There's no fuckin' CO here."

Chandler's detective often nostalgically contrasts his perverse twentieth-century environment with the vision of a noble nineteenth-century past. Willard encounters in his Vietnam journey a contemporary American mission unsuccessfully cloaking itself in references to the American heritage. The invocation of Lincoln by the General, the

cavalry hat worn by Kilgore, and the costumes of cavalry-
man, Indian, and cowboy adorning the playmates all represent attempts by the society to place Vietnam on a
continuum with American historical myth. These attempts only make more grotesque the moral and military
failure in Vietnam while also suggesting disturbing questions about the American heritage itself. Indeed, Willard's
last view of the American mission in Vietnam before crossing into Cambodia to find Kurtz is of a black soldier, primitive necklace around his neck, trapped in the endless
killing of the Do Lung bridge. He has been returned by
American society to both slavery and savagery. In these
symbolic visions Coppola plays the nostalgic idealism of
the hardboiled detective genre off against the exposure of
the "rapacious and pitiless folly"[16] of the colonial ideal in
Heart of Darkness. He thus dramatizes the problem Vietnam presents for America's view of its "redemptive" history.

Alternating with these shore scenes of a damned society,
the scenes on the river show Willard relentlessly pursuing
the American ideal that is his desired self. The pattern of
Marlow's growing attraction in *Heart of Darkness* to the
hearsay he gathers concerning Kurtz is developed through
a stock device of thrillers: a dossier full of fragments of
evidence that the detective must sort through and inter-
pret. Willard, repelled like Conrad's Marlow and the hardboiled detective by the depravity of his society, recognizes
in his "investigation" of Colonel Kurtz that this "murderer" is a fulfillment of his own inner ideals. Kurtz has
openly asserted the purposeful action, ruthlessness, autonomy from considerations of personal gain, and adherence
to a personal code that are the hardboiled characteristics
of Willard. As a result Willard, like Marlow, finds himself
attracted to the murderer.

In the voiceover narration, as he looks through Kurtz's
dossier, Willard speaks of how the more he learned of
Kurtz the "more I admired him," how Kurtz made a report

in 1964 to the Joint Chiefs and Lyndon Johnson that was restricted because "It seems they didn't dig what he had to tell them," and how later Kurtz returned to Vietnam as a member of Special Forces to win unique success. Here again Coppola follows the hardboiled formula while pushing its significance into the more disturbing investigation of the self adapted from *Heart of Darkness*. The detective often has a friend or is attracted to a woman who turns out to be the murderer, but he discovers this later and is only then confronted with the dilemma; Willard is attracted to Kurtz *after* society has identified him as a murderer. Like Conrad's Marlow, he consciously moves away from a corrupt, inefficient society toward an idealistic, efficient outlaw. By the time he approaches Kurtz's compound Willard has made Marlow's "choice of nightmares":[17] "Kurtz was turning from a target into a goal."

The oppositions between Kurtz's approach to Vietnam and that of the official command represent the oppositions of American mythic value brought forward to the Indochina landscape. Willard is disgusted by the official American mission because, with its technology, hypocrisy, and decadence, it is an extension of a decadent society. He is drawn to Kurtz because he has left that society to go alone into a wilderness landscape—the mythic journey by which the western hero continually regenerated the American identity. Willard discovers that Kurtz, who was being "groomed for one of the top slots in the corporation," insisted on joining the Special Forces even though that decision ensured he could never go beyond colonel. In essence, Kurtz heroically renounced the aristocratic privilege of his West Point background along with the "other-directed" ambition of the contemporary "organization man" for the idealistic autonomy of the frontier hero: "He could have gone for general but he went for himself instead."

As he reads how Kurtz has stripped himself of his former life through the physical trials of airborne and Green Beret training, Willard discovers his own dream of a return to

the strength of nature. In Saigon Willard had been obsessed with his knowledge that "every minute I stay in this
room I get weaker, and every minute Charlie squats in the
bush he gets stronger." Bringing to Vietnam the reaffirma-
tion of American mythic values envisioned by President
Kennedy when he first sent in the Special Forces, Kurtz
has demonstrated self-reliance (without authorization, he
conceives and executes a hugely successful military operation), adaptation to indigenous tactics (fighting in guerrilla fashion, he uses the methods of "hit-and-run" while
operating with native forces), and pragmatic ruthlessness
(he identifies and has assassinated enemy agents among
the South Vietnamese allies). Reading in Kurtz's dossier
the record of a renegade criminal from American society,
Willard finds the mythic American character and mission.[18]

This identification of the detective figure with the murderer, never allowed in the hardboiled formula, is brought
to its disorienting climax in the scene which Coppola has
called the most important in the film,[19] Willard's shooting
of the wounded Vietnamese woman, followed by his explicit explanation: "We'd cut'em in half with a machine
gun and give'em a Band-Aid. It was a lie. And the more I
saw of them, the more I hated lies." Later, just before
Willard kills Kurtz, the Colonel says that there is nothing
he "detests more than the stench of lies." By developing
Apocalypse Now according to the defining elements of the
hardboiled formula, but extending the investigation into
the self, Coppola shocks the audience. No longer a witness,
through the detective-figure, of the external horror of his
society, the audience is forced into a questioning of the
formula's normal source of order: the moral idealism, the
uncorrupted honesty, the purposeful efficiency of the detective himself. This scene prepares the viewer to experience the confrontation between Willard and Kurtz as a
meeting of the detective-figure with the final implications,
and hollow basis, of the American mythos. Thus *Apocalypse*

Now shows Vietnam forcing the hero into the psycho-symbolic investigation of the ideal self provided by *Heart of Darkness.*

The final scenes of the film, set at Kurtz's compound in Cambodia, represent the most visible use of Conrad's novella. Here again, however, the particulars owe considerably more to the hardboiled detective formula. In many works of the genre the murderer turns out to be a "magical quack," a charlatan doctor or mystic presiding over a cult or temple.[20] Free of social restraint, Colonel Kurtz has, like his literary namesake, set himself up as a god among primitive tribesmen, becoming a ghastly figure of evil. The Russian "fool" in *Heart of Darkness*, now a Countercultural American photojournalist (Dennis Hopper), still praises Kurtz mindlessly in mystical terms. But these elements are presented within a more detailed portrayal of Kurtz as the magical quack the hardboiled detective tracks down to his Southern California headquarters, a significance first suggested by allusions to Charles Manson in a newspaper story about the Sharon Tate slayings, and in the similarity of the "Apocalypse Now" graffiti at Kurtz's compound to the "Helter Skelter" scrawled at the LaBianca home.

This portrayal is even clearer in the plot development, for whereas Marlow confronts a pathetic Kurtz crawling away in the grass, this Kurtz, if psychologically "ripped apart," is nevertheless still a powerful, controlling figure who has Willard brought to him. Like the magical quack, he sneeringly taunts, tempts, and intimidates Willard. The murderer often scorns the detective for his low socio-economic position and quixotic quest (Kurtz tells Willard, "You're an errand boy sent by grocery clerks to collect the bill"), has him held captive and drugged or beaten (Kurtz has Willard caged, brutalizes him by leaving him exposed to the elements, and drives him into hysteria by dropping the severed head of a boat crewman into his lap).

In the hardboiled formula the spiritual desperation of a corrupt world is suggested by the magical quack's success in acquiring mindless followers (represented here by the worshipping photojournalist and by Willard's converted predecessor on the assassination mission, the zombie-like Captain Colby). Even more important is that the trappings of a cult, with its strange rituals and temples, heighten the pattern and atmosphere of the grail quest in the hardboiled detective story, making more explicit the symbolic role of the private eye as knight journeying to an evil place to vanquish the champion of Darkness.[21] The explicit use of Weston's *From Ritual to Romance* (shown by the camera as one of Kurtz's books) in the final confrontation between Willard and Kurtz involves precisely this ritualistic pattern. Once again, however, the implications are of the confrontation with the self brought from *Heart of Darkness*.

The hardboiled formula is completed with Willard's rejection of Kurtz when he sees that Kurtz is indeed a murderer without "any method at all," and with his resistance to Kurtz's intimidation and brainwashing in order to fulfill his mission. Nevertheless, he himself knows that his slaying of Kurtz is done with the latter's cooperation: "Everyone wanted me to do it, him most of all." The ritualized assassination, with its psychologically resonant images of Willard rising from the river, entering a long corridor, and meeting a similarly painted Kurtz face-to-face, further suggests that the detective-figure is in fact killing not an external evil, but his unconscious self.[22]

Willard's discovery of the moral chaos that has resulted from Kurtz's pursuit of American mission has led him to see the darkness that pervades not only the hypocrisy of the army, but also the darkness at the heart of his own pursuit of an honest war. The indulgence in death and depravity, of total power, that Willard finds in Colonel Kurtz's display of severed heads, his reading of selected lines from Eliot, and his parable of a Viet Cong atrocity is a devastating illumination of the same hollowness, the darkness, that in *Heart of Darkness* Marlow finds in the figure of Kurtz. Here the Vietnam context and hardboiled detective persona of the protagonist give it a specific commentary on the American identity: not just the corrupted American reality, but the American self-concept of a unique national virtue and destiny drawn from original nature is itself a fraud. Just as Marlow discovers in Kurtz the essential lie of European imperialism to be the idea of civilization itself, Willard finds in Colonel Kurtz the essential lie of his own and his nation's Vietnam venture to be the American myth of special character and mission.

Both Willard and Kurtz, discovering the inherent weakness and corruption of their society, have turned to the enemy they identify with the jungle landscape. Willard speaks admiringly during the film of "Charlie's" purity and strength, observing that the Viet Cong soldier doesn't "get much USO" and has only "victory or death" as routes back home. Kurtz tells Willard that his illumination came when he realized, "like I was shot with a diamond . . . bullet right through my forehead," that the Viet Cong's cutting off the children's arms was a stronger act than his inoculation of them: "You have to have men who are moral and at the same time who are able to utilize their primordial instincts to kill without feeling, without passion, without judgment—without judgment—because it's judgment that defeats us."

As a Green Beret, Kurtz originally sought to bring to Vietnam the American "middle landscape" represented by the "flower plantation" he saw as a young boy journeying up the Ohio River, where it appeared that "for about five miles heaven had just fallen to earth in the form of gardenias." This millennial vision of nature touched by a blessed civilization is symbolically "all wild and overgrown now," for in Kurtz's mind Vietnam has revealed it as a weak, naïve unwillingness to see that the opposing forces of nature and civilization can possess their full strengths only if both are followed to their extremes. Kurtz has pushed himself out onto an ultimate frontier, the "edge of a straight razor" on which he says he saw a crawling snail surviving: "That's my dream, it's my nightmare." The "horror" Kurtz has become is a "ripping apart" of the contradictions in the American mythic ideal of turning away from civilization to nature to find the strength and virtue to redeem nature to civilization. As renegade Green Beret, Kurtz represents the Adamic innocence of its death-dealing heroes brought to its tragic "apocalypse" in this Asian jungle; as hardboiled detective, and thus descendant of the western hero, Willard represents the self-contemplation of that nightmarish discovery.

This is the significance, a virtually explicit reference to the role of the genre-detective, of Kurtz's telling Willard, "You have a right to kill me . . . but you have no right to judge me." When he goes to kill Kurtz, Willard is accompanied in voiceover by his implicit assertion, echoing the hardboiled detective's bitter autonomy from his society, that he is not acting as an "errand boy": "They were going to make me a major for this, and I wasn't even in their fucking army anymore." In killing Kurtz, he sacrifices instead the self-concept of natural virtue and divine errand that has been revealed in Vietnam to be the pretentious, bloated, and hollow false idol erected by American consciousness: "Even the jungle wanted him dead, and that's who he really took his orders from anyway." Willard then refuses the temptation to replace Kurtz as "god" to the Montagnards, and just as significantly, he does not answer the code-named "Almighty," who over the radio demands the coordinates that would enable the American command to bring down their fiery "judgment" of an airstrike;[23] instead, he looks up to the heavens as an absolving rain washes from his skin the paint and blood that completed his "doubling" of Kurtz.

But, as he moves back toward civilization with Lance, the American innocent traumatized into mindless savagery, and Kurtz's book (an elaborate explanation of his actions over which Kurtz finally scrawled "Drop the bomb" and "Exterminate them all!"), what revelation can Willard

bring? Coppola suggests only that America must return
from its Vietnam experience without the myth of American exceptionalism inherent in its idea of natural virtue
and special mission. Returning to Vietnam through the
cultural "dream" represented by a popular narrative
genre, perhaps America can realize that it has confused
natural will with divine calling: "It was a real choice mission. And when it was over, I'd never want another."

III

The different interpretations of the Vietnam War provided by *The Deer Hunter* and *Apocalypse Now* flow
logically from the different meanings of the western and
hardboiled detective genres. Since the western is a nineteenth-century myth looking forward to a new civilization,
and the detective formula a twentieth-century myth looking around at a failed society, the visions that *The Deer
Hunter* and *Apocalypse Now* bring to the Vietnam experience are literally a century apart. In *The Deer Hunter*
Cimino assimilates Vietnam to a regenerative myth that
makes the traumatic experience a conceivably fortunate
fall for the American Adam; in *Apocalypse Now* Coppola
presents Vietnam as a nightmare extension of American
society where only a marginal individual may preserve the
American ideal. But beyond these implications the films
also differ in their relations to their respective sources. *The
Deer Hunter* stands the western myth on its head, retaining
its central elements while showing that the Vietnam landscape inverts its meaning; *Apocalypse Now* follows the pattern of the detective formula but extends the area of
investigation into the self, merging the genre with the
theme of *Heart of Darkness*. The result is that *The Deer
Hunter* insists that Vietnam can be encountered in strictly
American terms, while *Apocalypse Now* undermines the
one dependable source of American order, the idealistic

self-concept embodied in the American hero. Cimino sees the Vietnam involvement as a projected mirror where Americans can recognize their darkest impulses but in response return once again, though with a new self-awareness, to the original promise Cooper had recognized in the prerevolutionary days of the young Deerslayer. Coppola views Vietnam as the projection of Southern California into an alien landscape where even the American ideal stands at last exposed.

The Deer Hunter and *Apocalypse Now*, while presenting distinctly different interpretations of the Vietnam War based in the separate genres shaping their structures, also have an underlying relation resulting from their common use of genres. Each of the films takes a hero who is a version of the national archetype and sends him on a quest in which the aberrant, fragmented, hallucinatory Vietnam experience inverts or subverts the cultural assumptions carried by the familiar structure of a popular genre. In this way the western and hardboiled detective genres provide collective dreams which, disrupted, suggest the significance of Vietnam as a pivotal experience for American consciousness.

The major flaws critics found in the two films, their implausibility and ambiguity, are essential aspects of the romance mode by which the major American narrative tradition has dealt with extreme experience revealing basic cultural contradictions and conflicts. The unusual difficulty presented to a viewer by these two "popular" films strengthens their significance for the culture. *The Deer Hunter* and *Apocalypse Now* have a powerful impact, as evidenced by their commercial success and critical controversy, upon initial viewing. But the mystery created by their complex, ambiguous layerings of symbolic patterns demands a sustained engagement through repeated viewing, reflection, and discussion. Ridiculed by viewers understandably wishing clear confirmation of their own views, *The Deer Hunter* and *Apocalypse Now* become, as the great American romances have been, rituals in which a cultural tragedy may be contemplated, the terror re-enacted, and the meaning probed.

Thus the war may possibly be assimilated as a source of new myth, and thus we may finally leave Vietnam through the symbolic dimension in which we entered it. But to return where? That is a remaining question that tragedy cannot answer.

CHAPTER SEVEN

Toward New Myth

IN 1982, in a lead article of *Foreign Affairs* entitled "The Care and Repair of Public Myth," historian William H. McNeill focused attention on the inadequate response academic historians, preoccupied with the "revisionist" debunking of old myths, were making to the loss of culturewide belief: "A people without a full quiver of relevant agreed-upon statements, accepted in advance through education or less formalized acculturation, soon finds itself in deep trouble, for, in the absence of believable myths, coherent public action becomes very difficult to improvise or sustain." Without specifically referring to Vietnam, McNeill argued that the diminishing wealth and power of the United States since 1945 should stimulate "thoughtful men of letters" to provide a modified myth that could replace "both the original Puritan vision of creating a 'city on the hill' uniquely pleasing to God, and its variously secularized versions that continue to dominate our national self-image."[1]

McNeill's article addressed a growing concern among intellectuals and other commentators in the early 1980s that Americans were moving incoherently into the future from a past they no longer found intelligible. In the last summer of the doomed Carter administration, *Time* ran a six-page cover story by Lance Morrow on American history and myth that deplored the "millennial chill" that since Vietnam had taken hold of the American psyche, concluding that "The nation, like the profession of history, needs someone with the intellectual power to devise a new myth or revive the old." A year and a half later, historian C. Vann Woodward wrote in the *New Republic* of how a myth of collective guilt had resulted from the Vietnam experience:

Still draped in legends of national infancy, myths of innocence, success, invincibility, and righteousness . . . we were caught short a decade or more ago at the climax of our own mythic national pretensions and exposed in deeds and failures that mocked all the old myths. It was then that the obsession with guilt took hold.

Woodward deplored as equally simplistic the revisionist interpreters of American history and President Reagan's and pollsters' assertions that "Americans have made a sudden recovery from their malaise, restored their self-esteem and self-confidence, and now face the future and a skeptical world with old-time assurance." Both of these extremes suggested to Woodward that Americans were proving unable to move beyond their deeply embedded concept of the national character as a new Adam, with the result that the national psyche continued to oscillate between self-perceptions of unique innocence or unique evil. A few months later in the conservative *National Review,* Charles Burton Marshall rejected President Reagan's and Norman Podhoretz's recent claims that Vietnam had been "a noble cause," pointing out that they were ignoring the hubris of an American leadership that had never doubted "the susceptivity of remote realities to U.S. designs." Explaining that "hubris includes the assumption of having luck on one's side," and noting that Podhoretz's *Why We Were in Vietnam* traced the consistent dependence of Presidents Kennedy, Johnson, and Nixon upon luck in their Vietnam policies rather than upon calculated strategic assessment, he concluded that America's discovery that it was no longer lucky was "hard for the nation to get used to."[2]

"Getting used to" moving through the perils of time without the assurance of luck, without the conviction of a special grace conferred by a special geography, is precisely the function of the literary and cinematic narratives which American artists have produced in response to the Vietnam experience. The stories through which we have retaken the Vietnam journey—the veterans' realistic novels and memoirs, the literary works about trying to move on after Vietnam, the two epic films—have presented a Southeast Asian landscape that overturns the meaning of the previously known landscapes of American myth. These narratives purge us, forcing the reader or viewer to reexperience, this time self-consciously, the tragic shattering of our old myths. This process may prepare the culture to accept a significant alteration of our view of ourselves and of our world, a new mythic interpretation of our historical experience that will intelligibly include the experience of Vietnam.

Along with these purgative works, there may also be a different kind of narrative art, one that will prepare us for an eventual embracing of an altered American myth. In *America Revised* (1979), Frances FitzGerald has documented that after Vietnam, textbook publishers no longer dare to present school children with a coherent vision of American history.[3] Perhaps this explains why the simultaneous growth in the popular culture of fantasy has been necessary. While the facts of our history remain heated from the backward-burning fires of the Vietnam-era controversies, it may be that no political leader or historian can successfully create a new synthesis from those facts. Working with historically removed yet allusive symbols, however, fantasists may be able to make us "used to" the adjustments in our mythic patterns required by Vietnam. By this indirect narrative route, they may be already altering the mythic patterns of our minds, preparing American consciousness to restructure its story.

Thus our fantasists may be operating as messengers from our collective unconscious, carriers of personal dreams that temporarily substitute for the role more properly played by social myth. In *The Hero with a Thousand Faces* (1949), myth-scholar Joseph Campbell discusses evidence that dreams take over the role of providing guiding patterns to an individual psyche passing through a crisis for which its society affords no relevant myths:

Apparently, there is something in these initiatory images so necessary to the psyche that if they are not supplied from without, through myth and ritual, they will have to be announced again, through dream, from within—lest our energies should remain locked in a banal, long-outmoded toyroom, at the bottom of the sea.[4]

In a 1984 interview with *U.S. News and World Report*, Campbell argued that the unprecedented rate of technological change had destroyed our mythology, and speculated that "poets" such as filmmaker George Lucas in his *Star Wars* trilogy were rearranging our old images to deal with our new anxieties about our machines.[5]

America's discomfort with its transformation into a technological society was crucially bound up in its initial dreams and eventual nightmare of Vietnam. In dealing with this tension between previous American myth and the fear of the machine, Lucas has constructed a fantasy that ushers Americans through a traumatic experience, analogous to Vietnam, toward a reconception of their character and destiny. Lucas' *Star Wars* trilogy represents the first significant step in moving beyond the purgation of our old myths to the synthesizing of an energizing new myth of America, a dream in which Americans may secretly—even to themselves—reexperience the horror of their Vietnam self-discovery and emerge from it not only regenerated but transfigured. When such a mythic pattern has been assimilated into popular consciousness, the way may be prepared for a visionary politician or historian to restructure American history according to that pattern. Then Americans will once again see themselves in a narrative that they can both believe and act upon. We need then to explore just how a work of post-Vietnam popular culture may be altering, as does a dream, our understanding, on a level deep below our rational perspectives, of our past experience and thus of our intuitive impulses toward the future.

I

Lucas, only 39 when the third of the *Star Wars* films was completed, grew up under the influence of both the Protestant-ethic values of his father, a prosperous storeowner in Modesto, California, and the fantasies provided by popular culture in comic books, television shows, and movies. After graduating in 1966 from the film school of the University of Southern California in Los Angeles, he made an antiutopian vision of a grimly bureaucratized future, *THX 1138* (1971). He then made the enormously successful *American Graffiti* (1973), a look back at the high school world of the Kennedy era as a lost world of innocence. A coda stated that one of the main characters was later killed in Vietnam and another fled to Canada in opposition to the war. For a time he planned to direct *Apocalypse Now* for Coppola, who owned the original script written by John Milius. After Coppola decided to direct the Vietnam film himself, Lucas made a dramatic break with the movies he and others had been producing for the disillusioned youth culture:

After I finished *American Graffiti*, I came to realize that since the demise of the western, there hasn't been much in the mythological fantasy genre available to the film audience. So, instead of making "isn't-it-terrible-what's-happening-to-mankind" movies, which is how I began, I decided that I'd try to fill that gap.[6]

The reception of the original *Star Wars* film in the summer of 1977 certainly suggests that Lucas filled a painful gap left in American consciousness by the loss of the western and its frontier mythology during the Vietnam era. The film instantly became a major event in the popular culture, comparable to the advent of the Beatles more than a decade earlier. Lines of ticket buyers stretched around buildings, and favorite characters and lines of dialogue appeared on T-shirts across the country.

Most of the critics were similarly enthusiastic. Writing in *Newsweek*, Jack Kroll welcomed it as badly needed escapism in an era of tragic self-revelation: "The fairy story, the comic strip and *Star Wars* are anti-tragedies—they tell their heroes 'you don't deserve misfortune, go get the rats.' It's the last chance for kids to have fun before they grow up to be Oedipus." David Brudnoy welcomed it in the conservative *National Review* as "unashamedly a fantasy, and if the pollsters haven't yet caught on, America appears sated with reality and wants some magic again." In the *New Republic* Stanley Kauffmann presented the slightly more reluctant view of many liberals that "Flash Gordon, Buck Rogers and their peers guard the portals of American innocence, and *Star Wars* is an unabashed, jaw-clenched tribute to the chastity still sacred beneath the middle-aged spread." Pauline Kael summed up these responses in September when she wrote in the *New Yorker* that "The excitement of those who call it the film of the year goes way past nostalgia to the feeling that now is the time to return to childhood."[7]

For the public at large, *Star Wars* has grown into an ever-larger and more pervasive phenomenon. The original film and the sequels *The Empire Strikes Back* (1980) and *Return of the Jedi* (1983) occupy, at the time of this writing, three of the top five positions on the list of all-time box-office successes. *Star Wars* toys, books, and other items have become a major industry.[8] The three films have been extremely successful at drawing audiences back for repeated viewings, and through cable broadcasts and video cassettes continue to reinforce their imprint on American consciousness. Beyond its own success, the *Star Wars* phenomenon has spawned a pervasive turn toward adventure and fantasy, from Lucas and Steven Spielberg's

Indiana Jones films to the many animated television series creating mythological universes.

As the *Star Wars* saga became unexpectedly darker and more complex in theme, however, reviewers in journals of political opinion separated themselves from the mass enthusiasm. In his review of *The Empire Strikes Back* in neoconservative *Commentary*, Richard Grenier attacked Lucas for living "in the dream world of the child, where the relationship of action to consequence is fuzzy at best—a state of impaired perception widespread in the so-called counterculture." From the left Robert Hatch, reviewing *Return of the Jedi* three years later in the *Nation*, cautioned that "Fairy tales no doubt embody our fears and aspirations; how reliable they are as moral guides is another question."

Significantly, writers in religious publications were among the most receptive to the latter two films of the trilogy, perceiving that spiritual allegory could probe contemporary concerns deep below specific political positions or even ideologies. Reviewing *The Empire Strikes Back* in *Christian Century*, Gerald E. Forshey found the sequel to *Star Wars* possessing "both universal appeal and political contemporaneity" in its dramatization that "innocence has ended, and responsibility has become the watchword." In his review of the last film of the trilogy, Harry Cheney in *Christianity Today* found that "Lucas and his talented artisans have constructed an extravagant cathedral of dreams" in which viewers and characters "have aged together as good friends, weathered the terrible truths of self-knowledge, and arrived with hope intact."[9]

Lucas pleased all but the most solemn with the first *Star Wars* film by answering the need of a national consciousness deep in the collective amnesia of the post-Vietnam era for escape into a fantasy world that could substitute for the lost landscape of American myth. As long as Lucas' fantasy appeared to be only inspired nonsense, critics of opposed political perspectives could gratefully drop their Vietnam-era attitudes to share the popcorn-eating enjoyment of the mass moviegoer. The dark surprises of *The Empire Strikes Back* and the portentous triumph climaxing *Return of the Jedi* caused them to draw back and fragment in their responses. For the public at large, who did not have to consciously think about the relation of fantasy to political concerns, the adventure was apparently both too pleasurable and too resonant to be abandoned when it deviated from expectations. Free of the historical controversies that now attended any portrayal of Americans in their Old West or even in Europe or Asia during World War II, Lucas could in his fantasy take Americans down their familiar mythic tracks toward a finally altered drama of their mind. The secret subject of the *Star Wars* trilogy is the traumatic passage of the American self-concept through the self-discovery of the Vietnam horror, and its potential power is to energize Americans to move forward from that experience with a modified conception of their ideal character and destiny.

II

The opening words of *Star Wars* set the trilogy not in the posited future of science fiction but rather in a distant landscape of the remote past, "A long time ago, in a galaxy far, far away . . ." After the Saturday-afternoon-serial–style block letters have left the screen the film begins, following a brief pause of eerie "once-upon-a-time" music, with the camera suddenly descending to reveal a huge spaceship bearing down upon a smaller, clearly vulnerable one. This opening presents the ensuing narrative as our dream, and the images that will soon confront us have the impact of a dream arising from the collective memory of our culture. Lucas gives us in *Star Wars* a story and images drawn from our myths, thus achieving the powerful resonance evoked by our feeling that, despite the strangeness of this setting, we dimly remember having been here before. By setting the film not in a historical past, but rather in a vaguely distant past located somewhere else that is really the remembered landscapes of American myth, Lucas gives himself the freedom of dream to rework our collective beliefs about ourselves in the light of a new and terrible experience. A conscious mind may enter sleep to confront, through oblique symbol, a traumatic personal experience that cannot successfully be endured in waking contemplation; the national consciousness may enter the dark movie theater to confront through an artist's symbolic fantasy an otherwise unendurable and debilitating recent historical experience. Like a sleeping psyche guided by messages from the unconscious, the audience may work its way along the fantasized passages laid out by the artist toward an altered vision with which it may reenter the streets of its waking reality.

The ancient, distant galaxy that is the setting for *Star Wars* is a symbolic landscape duplicating in strangely fantastic forms the familiar elements of the American mythic landscape. The opening sequence vividly establishes this surrealistic collapsing of our remembered past. From within the smaller spaceship we watch a door being burned open, waiting anxiously with a small band of generally middle-aged men who appear to be ordinary, frightened, but determined citizen-soldiers. Soon they are overrun by a force of facelessly uniform, helmeted drones who crush the rebels by the sheer overwhelming force of Empire. The enemy are at once the British Redcoats and the German Storm Troopers (they are called "Imperial Storm Troopers"). Their leader, Darth Vader, is a black-clad figure whose masking helmet shows us at once the visage of a medieval lord, a Nazi commander, a corrupting insect, an inhuman machine. With the puny rebel forces of the Republic, we stand against a composite of our culture's darkest images of Europe. As Vader's Imperial Storm Troopers brutally take over the small ship, this mythic memory turns into impossible nightmare: the Redcoats have crushed the Minutemen, the Nazis have wiped out the GI's, the dark father of Europe has come back from our haunted psyche to triumph over our fathers after all.

The unfolding galactic "starscape" of Lucas' trilogy elaborates on this imagery to present us with a definitive evocation of the mythic American landscape as it has appeared in the images of succeeding eras. The central figure, Luke Skywalker (Mark Hamill), is an innocent American Adam in the mode of Huck Finn and the young Deerslayer. Han Solo (Harrison Ford), his experienced big-brother figure, is indeed in the history of American popular culture a more experienced version of Luke, the twentieth-century urban popular culture's reimagining of the pastoral frontier hero as a wisecracking, hardboiled but still pure-of-heart "tough guy." The doubled hero Luke and Han, accompanied by a Wookie as the traditional Noble Savage representing their closeness to nature, move across a frontier landscape between the utterly corrupt, rigidified, exploitative, unnatural world of the Empire's metallic Death Stars and the chaotic, wild, threatening, savage planets of desert Sand People and forest Ewoks. They fight of course for the threatened but growing community of individualists who are the Rebel Alliance, and who occupy a symbolically middle landscape in their base on a lushly green planet dotted by starkly functional shelters making up a version of a pioneer settlement. These dreamed versions of our preferred images of ourselves fight the apocalyptic war that American myth has perceived as the drama of world history: a war against an evil, bureaucratic empire revealed to us through its various villainous leaders as at once the pompous monarchy, the faceless corporation, the darkly mystical Nazi totalitarianism, the palely ruthless Soviet presidium—a Europe that conservative and liberal Americans can once again join in loathing as the true Other.

New myth, if it is to be firmly grounded, can develop only out of old, deeply rooted ones, and the success of

Lucas' underlying scheme in the trilogy depends on his holding back during the first film the alterations of previous American myth that will occur later. In that way both the hero Luke and the audience can at first operate in the innocent, psychologically safe world of previous American genres of popular culture. In the original *Star Wars* Luke's story exactly follows the mythic traces of the ideal pre-Vietnam American self-concept. Apparently orphaned, and possessing a youthful desire for adventure coupled with a natural virtue protected by rural innocence, he is guiltlessly set free from the benignly restrictive domesticity of his Uncle Owen when Storm Troopers destroy his home and foster parents. The old Obi-Wan-Kenobi (Alec Guinness), who tells Luke that he was a friend of Luke's father (who has been killed by Darth Vader) is a grandfather-figure who presents Luke with the values and tutelage that his true father would have passed on. Telling Luke that he is now needed to take up the light saber of his father in opposition to the Empire, Obi-Wan passes to Luke the "torch" of his true father, the ongoing cultural mission that validates his impulses to leave the domestic duties of home for adventures across the galaxy. At the end of this first film, Luke has destroyed the first Death Star through a natural skill with his small fighter ship, in which he climactically gives up the computer targetting-system to feel the Force that links his spirit to nature as a whole, an event that is continuous with the frontier sharp-shooter's sign of natural virtue. The imagery of the easy triumphs in *Star Wars*, including (except for the symbolic Wookie) strictly white-Anglo-Saxon-looking compatriots and cherished American mythic evocations of western shootouts and World War II dogfights, reinforces the characterization of Luke. The first *Star Wars* film beautifully compresses America's mythic memory of its pre-Vietnam time.

With the second film, *The Empire Strikes Back*, Lucas lets his American Adam rush into an experience for which he is as utterly unprepared as was the original audience by its expectations that this fantasy was simply following the familiar patterns of American popular culture. The ancient Jedi teacher Yoda expresses skepticism at Luke's potential, regarding him with that worst of contemporary American self-suspicions, that he is "too old" to progress, and yet critiquing his character in terms that dismiss the American frontier vision as inadequate because immature: "This one a long time have I watched. All his life has he looked away, to the future, to the horizon. Never his mind on where he was, on what he was doing. Adventure, excitement. A Jedi craves not these things!"[10] When Luke, ignoring Yoda's warnings that he is not yet ready, tries to save Han and Princess Leia, without first calculating the odds against his success and acquiring a fuller self-knowledge, he duplicates the essence of the American error in Vietnam of making a momentous decision on the basis simply of right intention and past luck. In his confrontation with Vader he thus suffers the essential trauma which the American self-concept underwent in Vietnam. Unable to defeat Vader, Luke suffers a devastating discovery of unexpected limits, symbolized by the loss of his hand to Vader's light saber, and a devastating discovery of his possibly evil nature, embodied in Darth Vader's revelation to Luke that he is Luke's true father; the traumatized American Adam leaps into an abyss, a metaphorical equivalent to the chaos into which the post-Vietnam American psyche leapt as it fled the spectre of impossible failure and self-revelation. Luke survives, terribly chastened and forced to return to Yoda, the teacher of universal self-knowledge and ancient wisdom.

In the first film, Luke left behind the domestic world of a restraining "false father" (Uncle Owen) to answer the call of his "true father" (the dead Jedi knight, sworn to guard the Republic, whose light sword Obi-Wan-Kenobi tells Luke he must take up against the Empire). In the second film Luke has been devastated by the discovery that this true father, from whom he has derived both his natural traits and his mission, has actually been corrupted into the very principle of exploitative power that Luke thought he was opposing. This unexpected dark grail, seemingly overturning the basis of both his self-concept and his quest, parallels that found by the protagonists of the veterans' memoirs and novels: a traumatizing denial of the mythic assumptions with which the contemporary sons sought to reject the enervating and self-seeking concerns of their suburb-dominated society to fulfill the call of their mythic fathers' historic errand. At the conclusion of *The Empire Strikes Back,* the *Star Wars* saga is left at essentially the same tragic moment of mythic self-discovery portrayed in *Apocalypse Now* when Willard confronts his mythic ideal Kurtz. Luke has faced both his enemy and his father, and finding them to be the same has had the basis of his self-concept exploded by terrible doubt. The American Adam has learned that his parentage ties him to a fallen past, that he is not an exception to history and the fallen world of time, but is rather a limited, fallible person whose destiny is in profound doubt.

In the last third of *The Deer Hunter* another incarnation of the American hero struggles with a similar self-discovery from his Vietnam experience, eventually to transform himself and heroically seek to preserve his community by communicating the message he has grasped. His mixed success leaves the film, and the filmgoer's consciousness, in a state of purgative pity and terror mixed with hope. As a mythic rather than finally tragic work, the *Star Wars* trilogy moves forward from traumatic self-discovery to energizing triumph. At the opening of the third film, *Return of the Jedi,* Luke returns from his completed training, armed this time with a power of self-knowledge that disciplines his youthful idealism, vigor, and natural skill into a mature—which is to say chastened—assuredness, command, and acquired craft.

Lucas sends his American Adam not in flight from his corrupt and exploitative father, the central thrust of previous American mythic story, but rather back to him on a mission of both acceptance and redemption. In a second symbolic combat, Luke finally overcomes the Empire by overcoming the dangers he now recognizes in his own natural virtues. Renouncing at last the use of his light sword against his wounded father, he pulls back from the will to power he has inherited from his corrupted parent, in effect pulling back from the tendency of self-righteous pursuit of mission to become only a self-deluding version of pursuit of domination. Recognizing in his son his lost self, the dying Vader in turn saves Luke by destroying the Emperor who tries to torture his son into submission.

The unmasking of Darth Vader at the end so that we may hear the true voice of the father, free of machine-amplification, reveals the deepest meaning of the trilogy. Like the "grandfather" Obi-Wan-Kenobi, Luke's father speaks in an aristocratic English accent. The story of Luke is the story of an American rebellion against a British father to preserve the father's lost ideals (the American myth of national birth in a virtuous separation from a corrupted English parent [the tyrannical King] in order to carry forward the threatened English heritage of liberty) that reverses direction to become a return to, acceptance, and redemption of that parent. This central motif in turn connects to Lucas' embedding of American myths within the English context of medieval Arthurian romance. In the *Star Wars* trilogy Americans are allowed to retain their ideas of national uniqueness and special mission, but are carried forward to a new acceptance that those concepts should shed the notion of a virgin national birth excepting their nation from the universal fallibility of human character and history. Rather than only moving west in flight from the consciousness of his European past, the American hero must first turn from new frontiers to confront a dangerous tendency inherent in his European origins.

While this symbolic confrontation is in progress within the Death Star, final battles with the Empire's Storm Troopers are underway in space and on a forested planet.

In space an armada of the Rebel forces, now including many strange-looking creatures, duplicates our mythic memory of the great air and sea battles of World War II. On the ground, Han and Leia enlist the forest Ewoks in a successful guerrilla war against the Empire's drones, fulfilling American frontier dreams of having the natural man join with the American against the European. When all three battles have ended in the decisive victory of good, the viewing audience can bask in the reflected light of a screen that has dreamed the longed-for cosmic apocalypse at the end of American history.

Yet, even as the imagery of the battles duplicates past mythic American triumphs, it also reconceptualizes that vision. In contrast to the simple reprise of American myth climaxing the first *Star Wars* film, the rebels are not simply or even primarily white Anglo-Saxon in visage. While Luke fights the symbolic battle representing the internal psychological struggle of our culture, Han, Leia, and other whites—even other "humans"—appear in the broad panoramic battles as only a vital part of a huge alliance of diverse creatures united by their common opposition to the principles of the Empire. At the concluding celebratory feast around campfires in the Ewoks' forest, the vision of a post-apocalyptic millennium of universal harmony and love distinctly places the American visage as one among many equal brothers and sisters. In addition, the apocalyptic and millennial finale of the *Star Wars* trilogy is really not apocalyptic and millennial at all, since the celebration of victory ends the film on a note of anticipation as much as resolution. The scene is exultingly cacophonous, a dynamic moment of unstructured equilibrium from which there is clearly a possibility either of progress or of lapse. The *Star Wars* trilogy, only a middle third of Lucas' fantasized galactic history (which may or may not be given complete form on film), ends on a note of triumphant completion that includes a sense of terrible passage and renewed possibility.

The *Star Wars* trilogy has it both ways, repeating and altering American myth, but such contradiction lies at the basis of mythmaking. Through image and story, myths enable us to perceive the world from a deeper dimension in which seemingly opposing values can coexist. By the same process, new myth can grow out of old through the introduction of new elements that can cohere with previous elements within the ambiguous workings of symbolic narrative. Thus we can retain the best of the old while moving forward to a new vision.

The fantasy Lucas has presented Americans in *Star Wars* is a redreaming of American memory that includes the Vietnam experience as a traumatic passage to a higher plane of understanding. As true myth, it presents not a tragic vision of idealism destroyed by reality, of aspiration diminished by fallibility, but rather an energizing vision of what can be attained in the world of time, if only for a moment before the struggle must begin anew, by pursuing the timeless quest. As a fantasy constructed out of a free use of previous myths, the *Star Wars* trilogy perhaps offers on another plane a more energizing vision yet: a vision of Americans' opportunity, in the midst of a fallen mythic landscape, to take control of their destiny by taking control of their national consciousness, and thus self-consciously to work out the implications of the Vietnam experience for their larger journey through history. Americans can seek, through the mental rehearsal of art, a meaningful structure for the narrative of actual experience they will make their future.

Epilogue

EMERGING FROM World War II, America had seemingly stood on the edge of completing the redemptive mission handed down from the Puritans. Yet its citizens soon found their will stalemated by a revolutionary ideology. Calling the United States an "old," "decadent," and "imperialistic" power, the Soviet Union asserted that communism was the wave of the future. The United States, in unaccustomed alliance with the old colonial powers of Europe, became a guardian of the status quo. By the late 1950s, many Americans suspected that they had indeed become "ugly." With John Kennedy as their youthful yet sophisticated image, they dreamed in the early 1960s of carrying forth their revolutionary heritage into the frontier of the emerging nations.

Vietnam was bound up in those expectations of returning to the landscape of American myth. Thus the enduring trauma of Vietnam has been the disruption of the American story. The war was a lost crusade, the costs of which were obscenely high. South Vietnam had been conquered (or liberated) by the North; America had abandoned its many works of engineering, a scarred countryside, and a host of orphans. The Montagnards and others who had listened to Americans' promises had been left to the communist future. Cambodia had become a new synonym for holocaust. If the United States could not fairly be made to bear the full guilt for these consequences, Americans could not deny that their efforts had brought only disaster to Southeast Asia. For Americans, those efforts included the sacrifice of 58,022 American lives. Another 303,704 Ameri-

cans had been wounded. According to the Veterans Administration, 23,104 of them would live out their lives
completely disabled.

Yet the dominoes, at least after Cambodia, have not
fallen. Domestic institutions were shaken but have survived. While the "Vietnam syndrome" has made American
foreign policy alternately blusterous and skittish, its
premises have not drastically changed. In their personal
lives, most Americans pursue "fulfillment" in a plethora of
"lifestyles." It is an ironic source of our anxiety that for
most Americans the tangible consequences of the debacle
in Southeast Asia seem inordinately slight. The enduring
legacy has been psychological, cultural, spiritual; Vietnam, like Kennedy's assassination, remains a spectre. In
that context, the renewal of spirit achieved by President
Reagan, although desperately needed, feels more like bra-
vado. The doubts of an unexplained national nightmare
linger.

No nation can survive without a myth; no nation profits
from holding onto a myth that cannot plausibly include
recent historical experience. The respective results can
only be a cynical "realism" or a self-deluding fantasy.
American narrative artists thus have sought to find the
implications of the Vietnam failure for a nation that has
conceived of itself as a frontier extending to the culmination of world history. The memoirs, novels, and films of the
Vietnam experience explore the war as a symbolic landscape inverting America's frontier mythos. These works
constitute a phantasmagoric literature of strange errands,
haunted doubles, and fated encounters. From the meta-
physical searches of *Dispatches*, to the dreamed flight in
Going After Cacciato, to the nightmarish mission of
Apocalypse Now, their protagonists wander over the landscape of a Vietnam that exists now in American minds.

Throughout these narratives, the hero of the New Frontier makes his appearance. Such works as *A Rumor of War*,
Sand in the Wind, and *Dispatches* see Kennedy as a false
father, or deluded son, or both. With his empty rhetoric,

Kennedy sends thousands of young men to die even after his own absurd death should have revealed the young hero's illusions. More subtly, Kennedy is seen in the ghostly apparitions of the Green Berets that figure in *The Deer Hunter* and *Apocalypse Now*. Both films warn Americans that not even the ideal American can control all. Not even he can be like God. In attempting to assimilate this lesson to a hopeful new vision, Lucas' trilogy takes the American Adam through a traumatic fall. To that youth, the "torch" of his father is passed, as it was passed to John Kennedy. At first, we love his readiness and his luck. When the protagonist discovers his limits and his intimate relation to evil, he accepts the need for self-examination. He returns chastened but determined to pursue right as he can see it.

Kennedy is already a hero of American myth. Those psychohistories, docudramas, and tabloid features which have surrounded his image with gossip and Freudian innuendo have only confirmed our fascination. His place is not the settled one of Washington, Lincoln, or even Franklin Roosevelt. These three "great" presidents each represent a crucial historical passage that America completed. In Washington we find our independence and righteousness, in Lincoln our democracy and continued union, in Roosevelt our commitment to social justice and global responsibility. In Kennedy we find our aspiration. Whatever his actual flaws and limitations, he projected our dreamed self so artfully that we take from his story both the measure of our desire and of our despair. Americans cannot forget the New Frontier, though the meaninglessness of the assassination and of Vietnam seems to have forever severed us from it. Yet Kennedy remains a memory both energizing and cautionary. He created not only an administration but a powerful tale; through that story, Kennedy still provides direction.

What should be the meaning of Vietnam for American myth? Surely America should not give up its sense of uniqueness and see itself as an ordinary country. There is, in any case, no such entity. Every nation has its special identity, flowing from its unique circumstances, history, and traditions. The United States certainly has had reason to feel a special obligation to the rest of the world. Its geography long left it remote from entanglement with other nations. It allowed the young nation to expand to frontiers easily defended and yet opening upon trade and commerce. It allowed the modern world's first republic to settle its major issues, develop its institutions, and form its character without interference. In the process, America became a nation identified, at its best, with possibility and freedom and progress. But without a conqueror, festering compromise, or major failure, it was also able to ignore its guilts and flaws.

America has yet to be conquered, but it has inflicted upon itself a failure so spiritually wounding that its citizens have been compelled, of their own will, to open the landscape of the nation's capital with a Vietnam memorial that is a symbolic grave. In that memorial, and in the literature, we can search out the terrors of our own nature. We can see that the deeply flawed past, from which the nation began by declaring its independence, is truly our father. But we can also see that only a second failure, of nerve, would cause us then to draw back from the American frontier, from our own better dreams. Mythmaking is an active, not a passive, process. Perhaps, from the landscape of our Vietnam failure, we can find a new determination to brave the opening expanse.

Notes

1. "An Angry Dream"

1. William J. Lederer and Eugene Burdick, *The Ugly American* (New York: Norton, 1958), p. 24. Subsequent references are to this edition and included within the text.

2. J. Hector St. John de Crèvecoeur, *Letters from an American Farmer* (1912; rpt. New York: Dutton, 1926), pp. 40–44.

3. For my understanding of the meaning of Asia for America, I am particularly indebted to Henry Nash Smith, *Virgin Land: The American West as Symbol and Myth* (Cambridge: Harvard University Press, 1950); Harold R. Isaacs, *Scratches on Our Minds: American Images of China and India* (New York: John Day, 1958); Michael Schaller, *The United States and China in the Twentieth Century* (New York: Oxford University Press, 1979); and James C. Thomson, Jr., Peter W. Stanley, and John Curtis Perry, *Sentimental Imperialists: The American Experience in East Asia* (New York: Harper and Row, 1981). For my summaries of the American concept of its world mission, I draw primarily on Ernest Lee Tuveson, *Redeemer Nation: The Idea of America's Millennial Role* (Chicago: University of Chicago Press, 1968); and Edward McNall Burns, *The American Idea of Mission: Concepts of National Purpose and Destiny* (New Brunswick, New Jersey: Rutgers University Press, 1957).

4. Timothy Dwight, *Greenfield Hill* (New York, 1794), book VII, lines 303–10.

5. Frederick Jackson Turner, *The Significance of the Frontier in American History*, Harold P. Simonson, ed. (1893; rpt. New York: Ungar, 1963), p. 28.

6. 18 Cong., 2 Sess., *Register of Debates in Congress*, Senate, 1, cols. 712–13 (March 1, 1825).

7. "Pioneers! O Pioneers!" in *Leaves of Grass*, Harold W. Blodgett and Sculley Bradley, eds. (New York: Norton, 1965), lines 13–16, p. 229; lines 93–96, p. 232.

8. "Passage to India," in Blodgett, lines 169–74, p. 418; lines 219–23, pp. 419–20.

9. Ralph Waldo Emerson, *Complete Writings* (New York: Wise, 1929), p. 1193.

10. "Text of the Two Addresses Before Congress by Mme. Chiang Kai-shek," *New York Times*, Feb. 19, 1943, sec. L+, p. 4.

11. Thomas A. Dooley, Dr. Tom Dooley's Three Great Books: Deliver Us from Evil, The Edge of Tomorrow, The Night They Burned the Mountain (New York: Farrar, Straus and Giroux, 1968), p. 44.

12. Graham Greene, The Quiet American (1956; rpt. New York: Penguin, 1977), p. 18.

13. See Edward Geary Lansdale, In the Midst of Wars: An American's Mission to Southeast Asia (New York: Harper and Row, 1972).

14. The Quiet American, p. 32.

15. Nathan A. Scott, Jr., "Catholic Novelist's Dilemma," Christian Century, Aug. 1, 1956, p. 901; James Ramsey Ullman, "A Skillful Tale of Adventure and a Burlesque of Yankee Innocence," New York Herald Tribune Book Review, March 11, 1956, p. 3; A. J. Liebling, "A Talkative Something-or-Other," New Yorker, April 7, 1956, p. 136.

16. Sales figures are from Alice Payne Hackett and James Henry Burke, 80 Years of Best Sellers: 1895–1975 (New York: R. R. Bowker, 1977), p. 12.

17. Robert Trumbull, "The Ambassador Who Didn't Read Sarkhanese," New York Times Book Review, Oct. 5, 1958, pp. 5, 38; Jim Walls, "A Damning Indictment of Americans Abroad," San Francisco Chronicle, "This World" Section, p. 18; Percy Wood, "Angry Novel Exposes Our Errors in Asia," Chicago Sunday Tribune, "Magazine of Books" Section, p. 1.

18. Rev., Catholic World, April 1959, pp. 64–65; Margaret C. Scoggin, rev., Horn Book, Aug. 1959, p. 320.

19. "The White Man's Burden," Time, Oct. 6, 1958, p. 92; Delia W. Kuhn, "Bagging Asia," Saturday Review, Oct. 4, 1958, pp. 32–33; Robert Hutch, "Books in Brief," Nation, Oct. 4, 1958, p. 199.

20. Attributed to Columbia Broadcasting Company News in advertisement in New York Times, Jan. 23, 1959, Sec. L, p. 23.

21. New York Times, Jan. 23, 1959, Sec. L, p. 23.

22. Cong. Rec., May 15, 1959, p. 8239.

23. "Address by Chester Bowles—Will Foreign Policy Be Decisive in 1960?", Cong. Rec., April 21, 1959, p. 6422.

24. Cong. Rec., Sept. 7, 1959, pp. 18332, 18334, 18335.

25. "Vice President Nixon Stresses Need for Study of Communism," Cong. Rec., July 2, 1960, p. 15588.

26. William Lederer and Eugene Burdick, The Ugly American (1958; rpt. New York: Fawcett, 1961), p. 1.

27. These examples are taken from Eric F. Goldman, The Crucial Decade and After: America, 1945–1960 (New York: Random House, 1960). Goldman offers one of the fullest discussions of American anxieties in the aftermath of World War II.

28. Sacvan Bercovitch, The American Jeremiad, (Madison: University of Wisconsin Press, 1978).

29. William Lederer and Eugene Burdick, "Salute to Deeds of Non-Ugly Americans," Life, Dec. 7, 1959, pp. 148–63.

30. For this we mainly must take the word of the authors, but Colonel Edwin B. Hillandale (like Greene's Alden Pyle) is clearly based on Edward G. Lansdale, as is evident by the similarity of the names and in their both serving as advisers to the actual Philippine leader Ramon Magsaysay.

31. Leo Marx, *The Machine in the Garden: Technology and the Pastoral Ideal in America* (New York: Oxford University Press, 1964), p. 23.

32. For discussion of the economic policies of the United States in regard to "underdeveloped nations," see Emily S. Rosenburg, *Spreading the American Dream: American Economic and Cultural Expansion 1890–1945* (New York: Hill and Wang, 1982); and Ronald Steel, *Pax Americana: The Cold War Empire and the Politics of Counterrevolution*, rev. ed. (New York, 1970; rpt. New York: Penguin, 1977).

33. Turner, *Significance of the Frontier*, p. 27.

34. Quoted from De Gaulle's memoirs in Marianna P. Sullivan, *France's Vietnam Policy: A Study in French-American Relations* (Westport, Conn.: Greenwood, 1978), p. 88. Sullivan reports that De Gaulle's recollection is confirmed by two of Kennedy's assistants who were present.

2. The Return of the Frontier Hero

1. "Jungle Faculty," *Newsweek*, March 6, 1961, pp. 33–34; "The American Guerrillas," *Time*, March 10, 1961, p. 19; Everett H. Ortner, "U.S. Special Forces: The Faceless Army," *Popular Science*, Aug. 1961, pp. 56–59, 172–73; George J. W. Goodman, "The Unconventional Warriors," *Esquire*, Nov. 1961, pp. 128–32; "The Men in the Green Berets," *Time*, March 2, 1962, pp. 19–20; Joseph Kraft, "Hot Weapon in the Cold War," *Saturday Evening Post*, April 28, 1962, pp. 87–91; Will Sparks, "Guerrillas in Vietnam," *Commonweal*, (1962) 76:343–46.

2. Goodman, p. 130; "The Men in the Green Berets," pp. 19–20; Sparks, "Guerrillas," p. 344.

3. Lippmann quoted in John W. Jeffries, "The 'Quest for the National Purpose' of 1960," *American Quarterly* (1978) 30:451–70; Kennan quoted in Goldman, *The Crucial Decade*, pp. 342–43. My discussion of the "quest for the national purpose" draws on both Jeffries and Goldman.

4. John F. Kennedy, *Public Papers of the Presidents 1962* (Washington: U.S. Government Printing Office, 1963), p. 609.

5. John F. Kennedy, "The Vigor We Need," *Sports Illustrated*, July 16, 1962, pp. 12–15. For an analysis of the "cult of toughness" in America during the Cold War see Donald J. Mrozek, "The Cult and Ritual of Toughness in Cold War America," in *Rituals and Ceremonies in Popular Culture*, Ray B. Browne, ed. (Bowling Green, Ohio: Bowling Green University Popular Press, 1980), pp. 178–91.

6. "Jungle Faculty," p. 33; "The Unconventional Warriors," pp. 128–32.

7. "Hot Weapon in the Cold War," pp. 87–91.

8. Kennedy, *Public Papers 1962*, pp. 265–66.

9. Quoted in Richard J. Walton, *Cold War and Counterrevolution: The Foreign Policy of John F. Kennedy* (1972; rpt. Baltimore: Penguin, 1973), p. 81; Charles Bohlen, *Witness to History, 1929–1969* (New York: Norton, 1973), p. 481; quoted in General William C. Westmoreland, *A Soldier Reports* (New York: Dell, 1980), p. 541.

10. Michael Charlton and Anthony Moncrief, *Many Reasons Why: The American Involvement in Vietnam* (New York: Hill and Wang, 1978), pp. 60–61.

11. See Walton, *Cold War and Counterrevolution*, pp. 162–201; Garry Wills, *The Kennedy Imprisonment: A Meditation on Power* (Boston: Little, Brown, 1981), p. 279; Leslie H. Gelb and Richard K. Betts, *The Irony of Vietnam: The System Worked* (Washington, D.C.: Brookings Institution, 1979), pp. 69–95; Norman Podhoretz, *Why We Were in Vietnam* (New York: Simon and Schuster, 1982), pp. 44–63.

12. For a succinct discussion of the results of Kennedy's Vietnam policy and his private sentiments during 1963, see Terrence Maitland, Stephen Weiss, and the editors of Boston Publishing Company, *The Vietnam Experience: Raising the Stakes* (Boston Publishing Company, 1982), pp. 90–91.

13. Quoted in Herbert S. Parmet, *JFK: The Presidency of John F. Kennedy* (New York: Dial, 1983), p. 336.

14. Hackett and Burke, *80 Years of Best Sellers*, p. 196.

15. Interview with Robin Moore, *Mid Day Magazine*, hosted by Warren Pierce, WJR Detroit radio, Sept. 17, 1982.

16. "Glory," *New Yorker*, p. 26.

17. "One Man's War," *Time*, June 25, 1965, p. 109.

18. Robin Moore, *The Green Berets* (New York: Crown, 1965), p. 1. All subsequent references are within the text and to this edition.

19. "One Man's War," p. 110.

20. Gordon Harrison, "Dilemmas in Vietnam," *New York Times Book Review*, July 11, 1965, p. 12; Emil Capouya, rev. of *The Green Berets*, *Commonweal* (1965), 82:568; Daniel Ford, "The Trojan Men," *Nation*, Aug. 2, 1965, p. 64.

21. Daniel Bryan, *The Mountain Muse: Comprising The Adventures of Daniel Boone and The Power of Virtuous and Refined Beauty* (Harrisonburg, Virginia, 1813), p. 44; pp. 45–46; pp. 42–43.

22. My discussion of the "two" Boones draws its essential points from the chapter in Smith, *Virgin Land*, "Daniel Boone: Empire Builder or Philosopher of Primitivism?", pp. 51–58.

23. "Don Juan," Canto 8. 46. 761 in Lord Byron, *Poetical Works* (London: Oxford University Press, 1945).

24. Moore interview, Sept. 17, 1982.

25. Capouya, review of *Green Berets*, p. 568.

26. Kennedy, *Public Papers 1962*, p. 652.

27. See Stanley Karnow, *Vietnam: A History* (New York: Viking, 1983), p. 268, and Maitland, *The Vietnam Experience*, p. 91.

28. Arthur M. Schlesinger, Jr., *A Thousand Days: John F. Kennedy in the White House* (Boston: Houghton Mifflin, 1965), p. 547.

29. Many studies have discussed Johnson's Vietnam policies and their negative impact upon the American public. See, for instance, Doris Kearns, *Lyndon Johnson and the American Dream* (1976; rpt. New York: New American Library, 1977), p. 294; Larry Berman, *Planning a Tragedy: The Americanization of the War in Vietnam* (New York: Norton, 1982), pp. 121–29; Podhoretz, *Why We Were in Vietnam*, pp. 64–132; Harry G. Summers, Jr. *On Strategy: A Critical Analysis of the Vietnam War* (Novato, California: Presidio, 1982), p. 37.

3. The Antiwar Movement and the Frontier

1. "SDS: Port Huron Statement," in Massimo Teodori, ed., *The New Left: A Documentary History*, (Indianapolis: Bobbs-Merrill, 1969), p. 176.

2. Jack Newfield, *A Prophetic Minority* (New York: New American Library, 1966), p. 15.

3. For excellent, succinct interpretive accounts of the antiwar movement, see Godfrey Hodgson, *America in Our Time* (1976; rpt. New York: Vintage, 1978), pp. 288–352; and Allen J. Matusow, *The Unraveling of America: A History of Liberalism in the 1960s* (New York: Harper and Row, 1984), pp. 275–344.

4. Paul Potter, "The Incredible War," in Teodori, ed., *The New Left*, p. 248.

5. Charles A. Reich, *The Greening of America* (New York: Random House, 1970), pp. 215–16.

6. Norman Mailer, *Why Are We in Vietnam?* (1967; rpt. New York: Putnam's, 1968), p. 104.

7. John W. Aldridge, "From Vietnam to Obscenity," *Harper's*, Feb. 1968, pp. 91–97.

8. Richard Pearce, "Norman Mailer's *Why Are We in Vietnam?* A Radical Critique of Frontier Values," *Modern Fiction Studies* (1971) 17:409–14.

9. Podhoretz, *Why We Were in Vietnam*, p. 99.

10. Susan Sontag, *Trip to Hanoi* (New York: Farrar, Straus and Giroux, 1968), p. 3. All subsequent references are within the text and to this edition.

11. Mary McCarthy, *Hanoi* (New York: Harcourt, 1968), p. 129. All subsequent references are within the text and to this edition.

12. See Peter Braestrup, *Big Story: How the American Press and Television Reported and Interpreted the Crisis of Tet 1968 in Vietnam and Washington*, abridged ed. (1977; rpt. New Haven, Conn.: Yale University Press, 1983), pp. 20–47; and Edward J. Epstein, *Between Fact and Fiction: The Problem of Journalism* (New York: Vintage, 1975), pp. 216–20.

13. Herbert Y. Schandler, *The Unmaking of a President: Lyndon Johnson and Vietnam* (Princeton: Princeton University Press, 1977), pp. 80–81.

14. See Hodgson, *America in Our Time*, pp. 384–98.

15. Podhoretz, *Why We Were in Vietnam*, p. 127.

16. For an extensive account of the making and reception of Wayne's film, on which I draw for background, see Lawrence H. Suid, *Guts and Glory: Great American War Movies* (Reading: Mass: Addison-Wesley, 1978), pp. 221–35.

17. "Far from Vietnam and Green Berets," *Time*, June 21, 1968, p. 84; Richard Schickel, "Duke Talks Through His Green Beret," *Life*, July 19, 1968, p. 8; Joseph Morgenstern, "Affirmative? Negative!" *Newsweek*, July 1, 1968, p. 94.

4. Good Sons

1. Lance Morrow, "Vietnam Comes Home," *Time*, April 23, 1979, pp. 22–28. See also David Gelman, "Vietnam Marches Home," *Newsweek*, February 13, 1978, pp. 85–86, and Peter Marin, "Coming to Terms with Vietnam," *Harper's*, Dec. 1980, pp. 41–56.

2. Lance Morrow, "The Forgotten Warriors," *Time*, July 13, 1981, p. 23.

3. James Webb, *Fields of Fire* (1978; rpt. New York: Bantam, 1979), pp. 23–33. All subsequent references are within the text and to this edition.

4. William Turner Huggett, *Body Count* (New York: Putnam, 1973), p. 69. All subsequent references are within the text and to this edition.

5. Philip Caputo, *A Rumor of War* (1977; rpt. New York: Ballantine, 1978), p. 7. All subsequent references are within the text and to this edition.

6. Ron Kovic, *Born on the Fourth of July* (1976; rpt. New York: Pocket Books, 1977), p. 73. All subsequent references are within the text and are to this edition.

7. Caputo, *Rumor*, p. 6; Kovic, *Fourth*, p. 54; Webb, *Fields*, p. 34.

8. Tim O'Brien, *If I Die in a Combat Zone* (1978; rpt. New York: Dell, 1979), p. 20. All subsequent references are within the text and are to this edition.

9. For analyses of the rationale and effects of Westmoreland's strategy see Guenter Lewy, *America in Vietnam* (Oxford: Oxford University Press, 1978), pp. 77–126, and Summers' *On Strategy*.

10. See Roy Harvey Pearce, *Savagism and Civilization: A Study of the Indian and the American Mind* (1953; rpt. Baltimore: Johns Hopkins University Press, 1977), pp. 199–212, and Louise K. Barnett, *The Ignoble Savage: American Literary Racism, 1790–1890* (Westport, Conn.: Greenwood, 1975), pp. 71–99.

11. Robert Roth, *Sand in the Wind* (Boston: Little, Brown, 1973), p. 452. All subsequent references are within the text and to this edition.

12. John M. Del Vecchio, *The 13th Valley* (Toronto: Bantam, 1982), p. 68. All subsequent references are within the text and to this edition.

13. William P. Mahedy, "'It Don't Mean Nothin': The Vietnam Experience," *Christian Century*, Jan. 26, 1983, p. 67.

14. Quoted in Tom Wicker, "Whatever Became of Jimmy Carter?" *Esquire*, July 1984, p. 84.

5. The Hero Seeks a Way Out

1. Eric James Schroeder, "Two Interviews: Talks with Tim O'Brien and Robert Stone," *Modern Fiction Studies* (1984) 30:151.

2. Thomas Powers, "Rev. of *Dog Soldiers*," *Commonweal* (1974) 101:241.

3. Robert Stone, *Dog Soldiers* (1974; rpt. New York: Ballantine, 1975), p. 181. All subsequent references are within the text and to this edition.

4. Schroeder, "Two Interviews," p. 159.

5. David Madden, "Introduction," in Madden, ed. *Tough Guy Writers of the Thirties* (1968; rpt. Carbondale, Illinois: Southern Illinois University Press, 1979), p. xviii.

6. Michael Malone, "Rev. of *Dispatches*," *Harper's*, Dec. 1977, p. 109; William Plummer, "Ecstasy and Death," *Saturday Review*, Jan. 7, 1978, p. 36; Peter Prescott, "In the Quagmire: Rev. of *Better Times Than These*," *Newsweek*, June 19, 1978, p. 82; Roger Sale, "Hurled into Vietnam," *New York Review of Books*, Dec. 8, 1977, p. 35; Paul Gray, "Secret History," *Time*, Nov. 7, 1977, p. 120.

7. Thomas B. Morgan, "Reporters of the Lost War," *Esquire*, July 1984, p. 52.

8. Quoted in Schroeder, "Two Interviews," p. 143.

9. Michael Herr, *Dispatches* (New York: Knopf, 1977), p. 20. All subsequent references are within the text and to this edition.

10. Pearl K. Bell, "Writing about Vietnam," *Commentary*, Oct. 1978, p. 76; John Updike, "Layers of Ambiguity," *New Yorker*, March 27, 1978, p. 130; Richard Freeman, "A Separate Peace," *New York Times Book Review*, Feb. 12, 1978, p. 21.

11. Tim O'Brien, *Going After Cacciato* (1978; rpt. New York: Dell, 1980), p. 313. All subsequent references are within the text and to this edition.

6. Epic Return

1. See Pauline Kael, "The God-Bless-America Symphony," *New Yorker*, Dec. 18, 1978, pp. 66–79; Colin L. Westerbeck, Jr., "Peace with Honor: Cowboys and Viet Cong," *Commonweal*, March 2, 1979, pp. 115–17; Ward Just, "Vietnam: The Camera Lies," *Atlantic*, Dec. 1979, pp. 63–65.

2. For my definitions and discussions of the characteristic elements of the western and hardboiled detective genres, I draw largely on Stanley J. Solomon's *Beyond Formula: American Film Genres* (New York: Harcourt, 1976) and John G. Cawelti's *Adventure, Mystery, and Romance: Formula Stories as Art and Popular Culture* (Chicago: University of Chicago Press, 1976). My discussion of the hardboiled detective genre also draws on George Grella's essay "Murder and the Mean Streets: The Hard-Boiled Detective Novel," in Dick Allen and David Chacko eds., *Detective Fiction: Crime and Compromise*, (New York: Harcourt, 1974), pp. 411–29.

3. Leslie Fiedler, *Love and Death in the American Novel*, rev. ed. (1966; rpt. New York: Stein and Day, 1975), 142–82.

4. Cawelti, *Adventure, Mystery and Romance,* p. 194.

5. Michael Cimino, "Ordeal by Fire and Ice," *American Cinematographer,* Oct. 1978, p. 1031.

6. *Ibid.,* pp. 965, 1006–7.

7. Dialogue has been transcribed from the films.

8. See comments in Morrow, "Vietnam Comes Home," *Time,* April 23, 1979, p. 23.

9. Richard Slotkin, *Regeneration Through Violence: The Mythology of the American Frontier, 1600–1860* (Middletown, Conn.: Wesleyan University Press, 1973), p. 145. An interesting analysis of *The Deer Hunter* that, although it contains some significant differences of emphasis and interpretation, complements my own in its discussion of the film's relation to American cultural myth is David Boyd, "The Deer Hunter: The Hero and the Tradition," *Australasian Journal of American Studies,* (1980) 1(1):41–51.

10. Marx, *The Machine in the Garden,* p. 23.

11. See Michael D. Butler's "Narrative Structure and Historical Process in *The Last of the Mohicans,*" *American Literature,* (1976) 48:117–39.

12. For a discussion of the relation of the hunter myth to the code of the western hero see "Book Two: The Sons of Leatherstocking" in Smith's *Virgin Land,* pp. 49–120, and Slotkin's chapter "Man Without a Cross: The Leatherstocking Myth (1823–1841)" in *Regeneration Through Violence,* pp. 466–516.

13. See Slotkin, pp. 429, 490.

14. Veronica Geng, "Mistuh Kurtz—He Dead," *New Yorker,* Sept. 3, 1979, p. 70.

15. Grella, "Murder and the Mean Streets," p. 414.

16. Joseph Conrad, *Heart of Darkness,* Robert Kimbrough, ed., rev. ed. (1899; rpt. New York: Norton, 1971), p. 17.

17. Conrad, *Heart of Darkness,* p. 63.

18. Kurtz's West Point background and move to the Special Forces, as well as the army's accusation against him of murder in a case of assassinated South Vietnamese citizens, has a possible source in the factual case of Colonel Robert B. Rheault. See Frank McCulloch, "The Fall of a 'Lost Soldier,'" *Life,* Nov. 14, 1969, pp. 35–38.

19. Greil Marcus, "Journey Up the River: An Interview with Francis Coppola," *Rolling Stone,* Nov. 1, 1979, p. 55.

20. Grella, "Murder and the Mean Streets," pp. 422–23.

21. *Ibid.,* p. 423.

22. For a full discussion of psychological imagery in the film, see Garrett Stewart, "Coppola's Conrad: The Repetitions of Complicity," *Critical Inquiry* (1981) 7:455–74.

23. The 35-mm version of the film includes credits accompanied by images of the fiery destruction of Kurtz's compound. The 70-mm version lacks credits (they were originally distributed in the theater lobbies), and Coppola reportedly added the coda to the more widely distributed print to avoid having the long credits run for six minutes against a black

background. Presented in infrared light with only eerie music on the soundtrack, and lying outside the narrative frame, the coda is, according to Coppola, a "fantasy." See Marcus, "Up the River," p. 52. Indeed, with the last shot of Willard, showing him moving down the river away from the compound with Kurtz's "The horror, the horror" echoing in his mind and on the soundtrack, the soundless explosions suggest his mental enactment of "The End" for which Kurtz had come to long, the nihilistic finish to the American apocalyptic view of history from which Willard is withdrawing.

7. Toward New Myth

1. William H. McNeill, "The Care and Repair of Public Myth," *Foreign Affairs* (1981) 61:1–13.

2. Lance Morrow, "Rediscovering America," *Time*, July 7, 1980, p. 29; C. Vann Woodward, "The Fall of the American Adam," *New Republic*, Dec. 2, 1981, p. 15; Charles Burton Marshall, "Lucky No Longer," *National Review*, April 2, 1982, p. 364.

3. Frances FitzGerald, *America Revised: History Schoolbooks in the Twentieth Century* (1979; rpt. New York: Vintage, 1980). See especially pp. 12–16.

4. Joseph Campbell, *The Hero with a Thousand Faces*, 2d ed. (1949; rpt. Princeton: Princeton University Press, 1972), p. 12.

5. "'Our Mythology Has Been Wiped Out' by Rapid Change," interview with Joseph Campbell, *U.S. News and World Report*, April 16, 1984, p. 72.

6. George Lucas, *Star Wars: From the Adventures of Luke Skywalker* (New York: Ballantine, 1976). The quote appears on an unnumbered page among inserted stills from the film.

7. Jack Kroll, "Fun in Space," *Newsweek*, May 30, 1977, p. 60; David Brudnoy, "The Perfect Movie," *National Review*, July 22, 1977, p. 839; Stanley Kauffmann, "Innocences," *New Republic*, June 18, 1977, p. 22; Pauline Kael, "Contrasts," *New Yorker*, Sept. 26, 1977, p. 123.

8. See for instance "The Force Is with It," *Time*, June 13, 1983, p. 70.

9. Richard Grenier, "Celebrating Defeat," *Commentary*, Aug. 1980, p. 62; Robert Hatch, Rev. of *Return of the Jedi*, *Nation*, June 18, 1983, p. 777; Gerald E. Forshey, "Heroism's Dark Side," *Christian Century* (1980) 98:771; Harry Cheney, Rev. of *Return of the Jedi*, *Christianity Today*, July 15, 1983, p. 54.

10. Dialogue has been transcribed from the film.

Index

Academy Award, 94, 100, 172
Adventures of Daniel Boone, The (Bryan), 55
Affluent Society, The (Galbraith), 19
Afghanistan, 100
Alamo, 79, 81, 91, 158
Aldridge, John, 80
Allegory, 23, 102, 119, 139
Alliance for Progress, 36
American Adam, 123, 165, 183, 201, 206, 214, 215, 216, 217, 223
American Graffiti, 209
American Jeremiad, The (Bercovitch), 20
America Revised (FitzGerald), 207
American Revolution, 3, 17, 46, 110, 218
Antonio, Emile de, 94
Apocalypse Now, 169, 171–73, 188–202, 209, 217, 223
Armies of the Night, The (Mailer), 79
Asia Firsters, *see* Asian Lobby
Asian Lobby, 11
Atlantic, 172
Attrition, strategy of, 67, 110, 118

Babyboom generation, 71
Ballads of the Green Berets (Sadler), 69
Bay of Pigs, 50, 67
Bell, Pearl K., 160
Benton, Thomas Hart, 8–10, 32, 35
Bercovitch, Sacvan, 20
Better Times Than These (Groom), 160
Betts, Richard, 52
Body Count (Huggett), 102–3, 109, 115–16, 118–19, 121
Bonanza, 148
Boone, Daniel, 7, 55–56, 64, 113

Born on the Fourth of July (Kovic), 102, 104, 109, 111, 119, 121
Bowles, Chester, 17
Bradbury, Ray, 144
Brando, Marlon, 190
Brudnoy, David, 210
Bryan, Daniel, 55–56
Buck, Pearl, 11
Burdick, Eugene, 3, 15–35, 87
Bureaucracy, 3, 25–26, 36, 45, 51, 74–75, 77, 157, 209, 214
Byron, Lord, 56

Cain, James M., 144
Campbell, Joseph, 208
Cannes Film Festival, 172
Capouya, Emil, 54
Caputo, Philip, 102, 104, 106, 108, 110, 112–15, 118, 136, 161
Carter, Jimmy, 90, 100–101, 135–36, 205
Catholic World, 16
Cawelti, John, 174
Cazale, John, 176
Chandler, Raymond, 146, 188–89, 191, 194
Cheney, Harry, 211
Chiang Kai-shek, 11
Chiang, Madame, 11–12
Chicago Sunday Tribune, 16
China, 7–8, 10–15, 22, 64, 94
China Girl, 12
Chomsky, Noam, 77
Christian Century, 15, 211
Christianity Today, 211
Cimino, Michael, 171, 174–88
Civil War, xi, 4, 8, 10, 43, 46
Cleveland Press, 20
Cold War, 3, 13, 16–17, 23, 37, 43–44,

Cold War (*Continued*)
   49, 65, 100
Cold War and Counterrevolution
   (Walton), 52
Colonialism, 13–14, 22, 25, 38, 49–52,
   62, 85, 188
Columbus, Christopher, 7
Coming Home, 100, 172
Commentary, 160, 211
Commonweal, 41, 54, 140, 172
Communism, 12, 14, 19, 30, 41–43,
   54, 60, 64–65, 99, 114, 221
Conrad, Joseph, 114, 141, 171, 173,
   188–202
Conservatives, 19, 43, 53, 68, 94, 99,
   214
Cooper, James Fenimore, 8, 36, 48,
   57, 81, 107, 111, 115, 118, 173, 176,
   184, 203
Coppola, Francis Ford, 171–72,
   188–202, 209, 232–33n23
Counterculture, 75–78, 146, 155, 198,
   211
Counterinsurgency, 4, 52, 65–66, 112,
   153–54
Crèvecoeur, Hector St. Jean de, 3, 5,
   25
Crockett, Davy, 28, 131
Cronkite, Walter, 89

Davis, Peter, 94
Dean, James, 73, 191
Declaration of Independence, 6
Deer Hunter, The 39, 100, 169, 171–88,
   202–04, 217–223
Deerslayer, The (Cooper), 111, 173
De Gaulle, Charles, 38, 50, 61,
   227n34
Deliver Us from Evil (Dooley), 13–15,
   92
Del Vecchio, John M., 119, 128–34,
   161
De Niro, Robert, 175
Détente, 94, 99
Didion, Joan, 151
Diem, Ngo Dinh, 13, 66
Dien Bien Phu, 13
Dillon, Douglas, 17
Dispatches (Herr), 139, 150–60,
   167–68, 168, 222
Dog Soldiers (Stone), 139–50, 167–68,

   172
Dominican Republic, 68
Don Juan (Byron), 56
Dooley, Tom, 13–15
Doors, 192
Dos Passos, John, 120, 129
Dwight, Timothy, 6

Eastwood, Clint, 171
Edwards, Jonathan, 6
Eisenhower, Dwight, 17, 43, 52, 72,
   108, 136, 166
Electric Kool-Aid Acid Test, The
   (Wolfe), 140
Emerson, Gloria, 180
Emerson, Ralph Waldo, 10, 165
Empire Strikes Back, The, 170,
   210–12, 215–17
Esquire, 44, 45, 82, 151
Europe, 44, 106, 114, 212; America as
   distinct from, 5–9, 14, 22–26,
   28–30, 32, 34, 38, 45, 49–51, 57,
   59–60, 85, 89, 135, 161–62, 166, 170,
   174, 176, 213–14, 218, 219; imperi-
   alism of, 11, 62, 188, 200, 211;
   America as similar to, 76, 81, 83,
   88, 94, 110

Faulkner, William, 174
Fiedler, Leslie, 23, 31, 174
Fields of Fire (Webb), 102–3, 106, 109,
   115–16, 119, 135
Filson, John, 55–56, 113
Fire in the Lake (FitzGerald), 150
FitzGerald, Frances, 150, 207
Flying Tigers, 12
Fonda, Jane, 100, 180
Ford, Daniel, 54
Ford, Gerald, 99, 136
Ford, Harrison, 214
Ford, John, 174
Foreign Affairs, 205
Forshey, Gerald E., 211
France, 13, 22, 25–26, 28–29, 38, 52,
   60–62, 92, 103, 110, 162, 165
Franklin, Benjamin, 28, 34
Freeman, Richard, 160
French and Indian Wars, 46
From Ritual to Romance (Weston),
   199
Frontier, 12, 14, 23, 26, 29, 34, 78, 81,

105–6, 110, 113, 115, 120, 136, 150, 159, 161–63, 165, 170, 173–74, 214, 221–22, 224; definition, 8; virtues, 9, 24, 45, 57, 59, 61, 108, 131, 135, 157; Vietnam as, 15, 35, 46, 51, 66, 112, 116, 128, 160, 166; myth, 38, 49, 55, 80, 93, 118; heritage, 44, 114
Fulbright, J. William, 17

Galbraith, John Kenneth, 19
Gelb, Leslie, 52
Geng, Veronica, 188
"God Bless America," 187
Godfather films, 171
Going After Cacciato (O'Brien), 139, 160–68
Good Earth, The (Buck), 11
Goodman, George J. W., 41, 45
Goodman, Paul, 77
Go Tell the Spartans, 172
Gray, Paul, 150
Great Britain, 7, 15, 22, 25, 110, 114, 213, 218
Great Depression, xi, 144, 149
Great Society, 68
Green Berets, The (film), 69, 90–93, 101, 174
Green Berets, The (Moore), 53–66, 86, 90, 92, 174
Greene, Graham, 14–16, 141
Greenfield Hill (Dwight), 6
Greening of America, The (Reich), 76
Grenier, Richard, 211
Groom, Winston, 160
Guevara, Che, 46
Guinness, Alec, 215
Gulf of Tonkin, 68

Hamill, Mark, 214
Hammett, Dashiell, 189
Hanoi (McCarthy), 82–88, 135
Hardboiled detective hero, 144, 146, 188–202, 214
Harper's, 80, 150
Harrington, Michael, 73
Harrison, Gordon, 54
Hatch, Robert, 211
Hawks, Howard, 189
Hawthorne, Nathaniel, 120, 172, 174
Hayden, Tom, 73
Heart of Darkness (Conrad), 114, 171,

173, 188–202
Hearts and Minds, 94
Heaven's Gate, 174
Hemingway, Ernest, 110, 141, 174
Hero With a Thousand Faces, The (Campbell), 208
Herr, Michael, 139, 150–60, 191
Hitler, Adolf, 13
Hitler Youth, 60
Hoffman, Dustin, 95
Hopper, Dennis, 198
Horn Book, 16
Huggett, William Turner, 102–3, 108–9, 115–16, 118, 138, 161
Hunters of Kentucky, 45
Huston, John, 189
Hutch, Robert, 16

If I Die in a Combat Zone (O'Brien), 102, 105, 109, 111, 119, 160
Iliad, 130
Imperialism, 11, 82, 88, 98, 171, 200, 221; *see also* Colonialism; Europe
Indiana Jones films, 211
Indians (American), 81, 106, 162–63; as American Other, 6, 10, 39, 50, 111, 125; Indo-Chinese as, 14, 22, 28, 33, 48, 63, 86, 88, 92, 112, 118, 127, 159, 172, 177–83, 195; savage virtue of, 76, 95, 117, 145
Iranian revolution, 100
I, the Jury (Spillane), 144
In the Year of the Pig, 94
Irony of Vietnam, The (Gelb and Betts), 52

Jackson, Andrew, 45, 72
Japan, 7–8, 11–12, 31–32, 104, 145
Jefferson Airplane, 76
Jefferson, Thomas, 17, 26, 34, 72
Jeremiad, 21–26
Johnson, Lyndon, 53, 66–68, 71, 74–75, 77, 85, 88–90, 92, 136, 196, 206
Jones, James, 160
Jungle, The (Sinclair), 15
Just, Ward, 172

Kael, Pauline, 172, 188, 210
Kauffmann, Stanley, 210
Kennan, George, 42

Kennedy Imprisonment, The (Wills), 52

Kennedy, John F., 4, 36, 38, 44, 50, 57, 68, 71, 77, 79–81, 94–95, 101, 106, 109, 137, 182, 209; and *Ugly American,* 17–18, 35, 41; and counterinsurgency, 37, 51, 153; campaign, 43, 66; and Special Forces, 45, 58, 69, 112, 115, 197; Vietnam policy, 52, 67, 206; and youth, 72–74, 85; in veterans' narratives, 108, 115, 121, 136, 166; and American myth, 120, 221–23

Kennedy, Robert, 53, 57, 89–90

Kerouac, Jack, 73

Kesey, Ken, 140

Khe Sanh, 151

Khrushchev, Nikita, 37, 42, 50

Kissinger, Henry, 94, 99

Korean War, 12–13, 27, 72

Kovic, Ron, 102, 104, 108, 111, 115, 118, 136, 161

Kraft, Joseph, 46–50

Kroll, Jack, 210

Kuhn, Delia W., 16

Lansdale, Edward G., 14, 227*n*30

Last of the Mohicans, The (Cooper), 184

Lawrence, D. H., 23

Leary, Timothy, 76

Leatherstocking Tales (Cooper), 7, 36, 48, 57; hero of, 80–81, 107, 111, 114–15, 133, 144–45, 152, 165–66, 173, 176, 179, 184, 203, 214

Lederer, William, 3, 15–35, 87

Letters from an American Farmer (Crèvecoeur), 3

Lewis and Clark expedition, 7

Liberals, 16, 19, 43, 53–54, 66, 68, 94, 146, 214

Liebling, A. J., 15

Life, 22, 43, 89, 91–92

Lincoln, Abraham, 10, 43, 72, 137, 194, 223

Lippmann, Walter, 42

Little Big Man, 95

Lonely Crowd, The (Riesman), 19

Long, Russell, 17

Love and Death in the American Novel (Fiedler), 31

Lowell, Robert, 77

Lucas, George, 208–20, 223

Luce, Henry, 11–12, 16

McCarthy, Eugene, 89–90

McCarthy, Mary, 77, 82–88, 94, 101

McCarthy period, 12, 18

Macdonald, Dwight, 77

McGovern, George, 94

Machine in the Garden, The (Marx), 30

McNamara, Robert S., 41

McNeill, William H., 205

McPherson, Harry, 89

Madden, David, 149

Magnificent Seven, The, 184

Magsaysay, Ramon, 28, 277*n*30

Mailer, Norman, 77–82, 94, 120, 129, 151, 157

Malone, Michael, 150

Manifest Destiny, 6, 50, 55, 113

Mansfield, Michael, 67

Manson, Charles, 198

Mao Tse-tung, 12, 29, 46

Marcuse, Herbert, 76

Marion, Francis, 46

Marshall, Charles Burton, 206

Martian Chronicles, The (Bradbury), 144

Marx, Leo, 30, 183

Media, 89, 94, 154

Melville, Herman, 120, 128, 174

Meos, *see* Montagnards

Merrill's Marauders, 46

Metternich, Klemens, 94

Middle landscape, 30, 32, 34–36, 87, 110, 131, 183, 200

Milius, John, 209

Millennium, 6, 9–10, 30, 34, 48, 127, 200, 205, 219

Missionaries, 6, 10, 14, 132, 149

Mission civilisatrice, 13

Moby-Dick (Melville), 128

Modern Fiction Studies, 80

Montagnards, 49, 62–65, 85–86, 91, 193, 201, 221

Moore, Robin, 53–66, 86, 90, 92

Moral geography, 7, 23–24
Morgenstern, Joseph, 91
Morrow, Lance, 100–101, 205
Mosby's Rangers, 46
Munich, 13
"My Country, 'Tis of Thee," 187
My Lai, 94

Naked and the Dead, The (Mailer), 78, 120
Narrative, ix-x, 137, 222
Nation, 16, 54, 211
National Book Award, 140, 150, 160
National Review, 206, 210
Nation-building, 13
Nazi, 76, 92, 110, 170, 213–14
Nelson, Ralph, 95
Newfield, Jack, 73
New Frontier, 35–38, 41, 44, 47–49, 52, 59, 69, 73–75, 79, 88, 95, 106, 108, 154, 182, 218, 222, 223
New Left, 73–74, 76–78
New Republic, 43, 206, 210
New York Film Critics Circle, 172
New York Herald Tribune Book Review, 15
New York Review of Books, 82, 150
New York Times, 17, 43
New York Times Book Review, 16, 54, 160
New Yorker, 160, 172, 188, 210
Newsweek, 45, 91–93, 150, 210
Nietzsche, Friedrich, 144
Nixon, Richard, 4, 18, 93–94, 130, 136, 206
Northern Lights (O'Brien), 160

Objective Burma, 13
O'Brien, Tim, 102, 105–6, 109–11, 115, 118, 139, 160–67
O'Donnell, Kenneth, 67
Open Door note, 11
Organization Man, The (Whyte), 19

Pacification, 110
"Passage to India" (Whitman), 9–10
Peace Corps, 4, 36, 44, 47, 73, 81
Pearce, Richard, 80
Penn, Arthur, 95
Physical-fitness program, 4, 36, 44
"Pioneers! O Pioneers!" (Whitman), 9

Plummer, William, 150
Podhoretz, Norman, 52, 82, 90, 206
Poe, Edgar Allan, 120
"Port Huron Statement," 73
Potter, Paul, 75
Powers, Thomas, 140
Prescott, Peter, 150
Presley, Elvis, 73
Prairie, The (Cooper), 107
Progressive Era, 6, 10, 132
Prophetic Minority, A (Newfield), 73
Pulitzer Prize, 43
Puritans (New England), 6, 20–22, 43, 114, 181, 183, 187–88, 205, 221
Pynchon, Thomas, 141

Quiet American, The (Greene), 14, 16, 20

Racism, 51, 57, 74, 88, 116–17, 175, 180
Reagan, Ronald, 99–101, 206, 222
Redeemer nation, 6, 28
Reich, Charles, 76
Reston, James, 50
Return of the Jedi, 210–12, 217–19
Revolution, American, *see* American Revolution
Rheault, Robert B., 232*n*18
Riesman, David, 19
Rockwell, Norman, 34
Roger's Rangers, 46
Roosevelt, Franklin, 72, 137, 223
Roosevelt, Theodore, 45, 72, 137
Roth, Robert, 119–28, 136, 161
Rough Riders, 45
Rumor of War, A (Caputo), 102, 104, 109, 112, 119, 121, 135, 222

Sadler, Barry, 68
Sale, Roger, 150
Sand in the Wind (Roth), 119–28, 121, 222
Sands of Iwo Jima, 105
San Francisco Chronicle, 16
Santa Anna, 79
Saturday Evening Post, 15, 34, 46–50, 55, 63
Saturday Review, 16, 150
Savio, Mario, 74
Schickel, Richard, 91

Schlesinger, Arthur, Jr., 67
Scoggin, Margaret C., 16
Scott, Nathan A., 15
Searchers, The, 184
Seltzer, Louis B., 20
Shaw, Irwin, 160
Sheen, Martin, 171, 188, 191
Silent majority, 93–94
Slotkin, Richard, 183
Soldier Blue, 95
Sontag, Susan, 77, 82–88, 94, 101
South, American, 10
Soviet Union, 12, 15, 19, 21–22, 24, 30, 37, 42, 50, 63, 94, 100, 221
Sparks, Will, 41
Special Forces, 4, 37, 41–69, 68, 73–75, 81, 86, 88, 92, 95, 114–15, 134, 152–54, 159, 173, 175, 178–79, 182, 196–97, 200–01, 223, 232n18
Spielberg, Steven, 210
Spillane, Mickey, 144
Sports Illustrated, 44
Sputnik, 15
"Star-Spangled Banner, The," 187
Star Wars (film), 210, 212, 15
Star Wars (trilogy), 208–20
Steinbeck, John, 20
Stevenson, Adlai, 20
Stone, Robert, 139–50
Streep, Meryl, 177
Students for a Democratic Society, 73, 75
Styles of Radical Will (Sontag), 82
Symbolic landscape, 7, 23, 30, 38, 49, 75, 99, 120, 137, 139, 141, 162, 169, 172–73, 204, 213

Tate, Sharon, 198
Technology, 34–35, 37, 44, 47, 67, 74, 75, 81, 88, 92, 99, 107, 113–14, 134–35, 148, 194, 196, 208, 213
Tet offensive, 89–90, 92, 120, 126, 127, 151, 158
13th Valley, The (Del Vecchio), 119, 128–34
Thompson, Hunter, 151
Thoreau, Henry David, 81
Three Soldiers (Dos Passos), 120
Thunderbolt and Lightfoot, 171
THX 1138, 209
Tillich, Paul, 93

Time, 16, 41, 43, 54, 58, 91–93, 100–101, 150, 205
Trip to Hanoi (Sontag), 82–88, 135
Truman, Harry S., 52, 72
Turner, Frederick Jackson, 8, 36
Twain, Mark, 174

Ugly American, The (Lederer and Burdick), 3–4, 15–38, 41, 43, 48, 59, 66, 75, 83, 86–88, 92, 134, 173, 175, 178, 221
Ullman, James Ramsey, 15
Uncle Tom's Cabin (Stowe), 15
Unconscious, 23, 175, 181, 183, 185, 207, 213
Updike, John, 160
U.S. News and World Report, 208

Valenti, Jack, 90
Veterans, 100–37, 207
Viet Cong, 54, 60, 89, 91, 126–27, 148–49, 175, 180, 183, 199–200
Viet Minh, 13–14, 22, 24, 28
Virginian, The (Wister), 48
Vonnegut, Kurt, 141

Walken, Christopher, 176
Wallace, George, 90
Walton, Richard, 52
Washington, George, 23, 223
Washington Post, 160
Wayne, John, 69, 90–93, 100, 101, 105, 131, 152
Webb, James, 102–4, 106, 109, 115–16, 118, 161
Weems, Mason Locke, 23
West, American, 7, 10, 23, 71, 85, 90, 94–95, 109, 135, 212; see also Frontier; Western films; Western hero
Westerbeck, Colin, 172
Western films, 31, 91, 95, 101, 148, 172–88, 202, 209, 215
Western hero, 28, 39, 56–57, 59, 109, 112, 115, 144, 146, 148, 170, 173–89, 196, 201, 214; Green Beret as, 45–47, 58, 64
Westmoreland, William C., 113
Weston, Jessie, 199
Whitman, Walt, 9–10, 32, 35, 127
Whitney, Asa, 7

Who'll Stop the Rain?, 172
Why Are We in Vietnam? (Mailer),
   78–82, 157
Whyte, William H., Jr., 19
Why We Were in Vietnam (Podhoretz),
   52, 82, 206
Williams, Roger, 28
Wills, Garry, 52
Wilson, Woodrow, 50
Wister, Owen, 48, 174
Wolfe, Tom, 140

Woodward, C. Vann, 206
World War I, 110, 120, 129
World War II, 11, 27, 46, 71, 78,
   90–91, 101, 103–5, 109, 116, 120,
   129, 160, 162, 164, 212–13, 221;
   films, 101, 215, 219

Yarmolinsky, Adam, 51
Yellow peril, 11
Young, Andrew, 135